Curating Worlds

Curating Worlds

Museum Practices in Contemporary Literature

✦

Emma Bond

NORTHWESTERN UNIVERSITY PRESS
EVANSTON, ILLINOIS

Northwestern University Press
www.nupress.northwestern.edu

Copyright © 2025 by Northwestern University. Published 2025 by
Northwestern University Press. All rights reserved.

Printed in the United States of America

10   9   8   7   6   5   4   3   2   1

Library of Congress Cataloging-in-Publication Data

Names: Bond, Emma, 1979– author.
Title: Curating worlds : museum practices in contemporary literature / Emma
    Bond.
Description: Evanston, Illinois : Northwestern University Press, 2025. |
    Includes bibliographical references and index.
Identifiers: LCCN 2024028487 | ISBN 9780810147959 (paperback) |
    ISBN 9780810147966 (cloth) | ISBN 9780810147973 (ebook)
Subjects: LCSH: Museums. | Collective memory in literature. | Museum
    techniques.
Classification: LCC AM7 .B634 2025 | DDC 069—dc23/eng20240927
LC record available at https://lccn.loc.gov/2024028487

CONTENTS

List of Illustrations	*vii*
Acknowledgments	*ix*
Introduction Orientation	*3*
Chapter 1 Collecting	*19*
Chapter 2 Curating	*37*
Chapter 3 Display	*55*
Chapter 4 Storage	*75*
Chapter 5 Conservation	*103*
Chapter 6 Restitution	*123*
Conclusion Deaccession	*145*
Notes	*165*
Bibliography	*195*
Index	*211*

ILLUSTRATIONS

Fig. 1. Screenshot of "APES**T" (YouTube) — *4*

Fig. 2. The entrance to the Risiera di San Sabba — *20*

Fig. 3. Example page of Daša Drndić's *Trieste* — *25*

Fig. 4. View of via Aprica, Gorizia — *34*

Fig. 5. Internal view of the ground floor, Museo Henriquez della Guerra per la Pace, Trieste — *51*

Fig. 6. A selection of Henriquez's notebooks on display in the Museo Henriquez della Guerra per la Pace, Trieste — *51*

Fig. 7. The Museum of Innocence, Istanbul — *57*

Fig. 8. Photographs — *58*

Fig. 9. Calligraphy by Mir Ali — *73*

Fig. 10. Depot Boijmans Van Beuningen, Rotterdam — *76*

Fig. 11. Photograph from *Lost Children Archive: A Novel* — *79*

Fig. 12. The *Kill Your Darlings* exhibition, Perth Museum and Art Gallery — *101*

Fig. 13. The Viennese Elephant — *104*

Fig. 14. The Josephinum, Vienna — *108*

Fig. 15. The Medici Venus — *109*

Fig. 16. View of wax models in Room 5, the Josephinum — *114*

Fig. 17. The *Depositi aperti* exhibition, Museo delle Civiltà, Rome — *134*

Fig. 18. Konso statue on display in the *Depositi Aperti* exhibition, Museo delle Civiltà, Rome — *136*

Fig. 19. *Norme e consigli per chi va in A. O. Italiana 1*, 1936 — *139*

Fig. 20. Newspaper clipping from *Campioni del Mondo*, 1934 — *140*

Fig. 21. Mended Roman bust on display in the *Depositi Aperti* exhibition, Museo delle Civiltà, Rome — *143*

viii   Illustrations

Fig. 22. Front cover of Leanne Shapton, *Important Artifacts and Personal Property from the Collection of Lenore Doolan and Harold Morris, Including Books, Street Fashion and Jewelry*   *146*

Fig. 23. The Museum of Broken Relationships, Zagreb   *153*

Fig. 24. Objects on display at the Museum of Broken Relationships, Zagreb   *154*

ACKNOWLEDGMENTS

This book was designed and drafted in a period of research leave funded by the Leverhulme Trust. I will be eternally grateful to the trust for awarding me a Philip Leverhulme Prize in 2019 and giving me the opportunity to think and write about museums and literature for the following two years. I would also like to thank two institutions that hosted me for fellowships that inspired and facilitated my research into this area in equal measure: The Wolfsonian–FIU in Miami Beach in 2017, and the British School at Rome in 2021–2022.

I learned a huge amount about how museums work through various collaborative projects with heritage institutions in Scotland between 2016 and 2022, and I would like to thank the staff at the Watt Institution in Greenock, V&A Dundee, and the Museums of the University of St Andrews, in particular, for allowing me such valuable behind-the-scenes insight. Thanks are also due to individuals who supported my field trips to the museums discussed in this book: Felix Clam-Martinic for his tour of the Josephinum in Vienna, Riccardo Cepach for his help in Trieste, and Hania Elkington for coming with me to Zagreb in November 2022. Special thanks to David and Nia for their patience as I dragged them through countless museum exhibitions, displays, and guided tours in the UK and abroad. I promise to stop now.

I'm grateful to the people who read and commented on early drafts of some of the material included in this book (David Evans, Ramsey McGlazer, and Saskia Ziolkowski), and to colleagues who invited me to share my work in progress at events, seminars, and lectures: Joseph Ford (on behalf of LINKS and the ICLS in London), the postgraduate community at University College Cork, Diana Garvin at the University of Oregon, and the postgraduate convenors of the Research Seminars at the University of Oxford. The conversations we had and the feedback you gave all provided me with valuable opportunities to reflect on and improve my work.

Heartfelt thanks go to all the team at Northwestern University Press, and especially to my brilliant editor Faith Wilson Stein. Faith instantly understood what I wanted to achieve with this project and championed it throughout the editorial process. I'm also grateful to Maia Rigas for steering the book through production, to Madeline Schultz for help with marketing, and to Elizabeth Yellen for her meticulous copyedits. Thanks go to Courtney Smotherman for helping me through the odyssey of rights and permissions, and to all those who granted me the right to reproduce their work or the work of

ix

others here. I acknowledge the generous funding of the New College Ludwig Fund for the Humanities from Gene Ludwig, which helped meet the costs of image permissions in this work.

During the final drafting process I lost my beloved uncle, Ian Dudley Brawn, and I miss him hugely. He would have been so proud to see this book out in the world, and I am honored to dedicate it to his memory.

Curating Worlds

Introduction

Orientation

Introduction

In the darkness of night, a man wearing sleek white feathered wings crouches outside a museum (fig. 1). Church bells chime as the camera pans outward, taking in the illuminated facade of the imposing building behind him. The man cracks his fingers and then rubs his palms together, readying himself for action, before the camera shot switches to reveal the neon-lit interior of the museum, and the music to the Carters' 2018 song "APES**T" starts. The museum is the Louvre, and its instantly recognizable gallery spaces and artworks merge to inform a powerful statement of positionality by two of the world's most successful contemporary cultural figures. Although we see the crouching figure outside the museum walls, his costume aligns him with the exhibits featured on the inside, particularly the Winged Victory of Samothrace, which overlooks many of the complex choreographed segments in the video. Dense with allusions, the winged Black figure at the Louvre in "APES**T" weaves in and out of a network of references to Carrie Mae Weems's *Museums* series, Nicolas Philibert's film *La ville Louvre*, Isaac Julien's *Looking for Langston*, and Essex Hemphill's poem "Visiting Hours," to name but a few. He is a story within a story that activates the museum as a site of power that can be deconstructed through the use of narrative. Occupying a parallel semantic space to Weems's muse, he acts as a guide, an "engaged persona pointing toward the history of power," and an "unintended consequence of the Western imagination."[1] And as the camera follows Beyoncé and Jay-Z around the masterpieces of the Louvre, the museum itself maps out a story illustrated by the song's lyrics, one that offers us "a different angle" on its own contents and function.[2] "APES**T" has been viewed over two hundred million times on YouTube, and the Louvre itself reported a record 25 percent increase in visitor numbers in the year following the video's release.[3] The way that the Louvre is deployed in the making of the "APES**T" video clearly

Fig. 1. Screenshot of "APES**T" (YouTube). © The Carters.

illustrates Philip Fisher's claim that "the museum is more than a location. It is a script that makes certain acts possible and others unthinkable."[4] What else can the visual narrative of this video signal to us about how and why museums have entered into the mainstream of contemporary cultural discourse? Can the angle it develops help us to trace an evolution in the relationship between museums and other cultural forms? Does it reveal a trend toward a sophisticated new understanding of the museum as a storytelling engine, and of the myriad ways in which people can more actively intervene to engage with the stories museums have to tell?

As W. Stanley Jevons states in his 1882 piece, "The Use and Abuse of Museums," "The best Museum is that which a person forms for himself."[5] Indeed, every museum uses the objects or artworks in its collection in tandem with the spaces in which they are displayed in order to offer up a story to its visitors. That story might relate to the history of a local place, a craft or industry, or an individual biography. It might, like the Louvre, operate on a much more monumental, or even national scale. Whatever the story it is telling, the museum will utilize a series of carefully constructed modes of directing and engaging with its visitors so as to function as a narrative space. These are known as "orientation devices." Museums typically implement these devices in order to help visitors physically navigate their layout, in ways that can easily be aligned with similar techniques enacted by and in works of fiction. This book will investigate the intimate relationship between museums and literature by exploring a range of practical devices and techniques that they both deploy when telling stories about objects. The first point of convergence between the two has to do with plot and the spatialization of narrative:

Orientation

as Allan Hepburn points out, narratives about objects "function as spatial entities," which are analogous to boxes, trunks, or vitrines.[6] In museums and literature alike, objects not only generate stories but also trigger plot moves and character development, and introduce an idea of sequencing through their arrangement and juxtaposition with other objects. The second analogy is located in the similar ways in which both spaces work to salvage and restore objects for posterity, thus providing new mediated contexts between past and present, history and memory.[7] These two similarities will lead us to explore how museum techniques can meaningfully intervene in debates around representational strategies and display in literature, thus feeding into what Matthew Mullins has identified as the principal preoccupation of contemporary fiction: "the work of assembling, gathering, and constructing" material arrangements in order to shed light on evolving social categories.[8]

Despite these points of similarity, it is important to note that unlike most literary fiction, the narrative design of the museum is not necessarily explicit. Visitors are not always aware upon entering the museum that they are being told a particular story. We have to look closely at what is on display (and especially at what is *not*) in order to identify all the practices that contribute to the formation of a museum narrative. This book will show how key museum practices work together to build a three-dimensional narrative that can, in turn, offer us new ways of assessing, interpreting, and understanding literary texts. The texts that I have chosen to focus on all operate as spaces of salvage for the objects, memories, and events of the past that they proceed to gather up, arrange, rearrange, and narrativize. Through identifying similarities in the ways in which they deploy, care for, and manipulate objects, I want to blur the lines of distinction that have traditionally defined how we think about museums and novels as separate narrative spaces. For if the museum makes use of literary techniques in order to tell stories through its object collections, then surely it makes sense to explore the potential of using theoretical works from museum studies to interpret fiction? As a field, museum studies has traditionally been concerned with tracing the history and development of museums, but it has more recently seen a turn toward scholarship that is engaged in exploring the museum's power structures and relations to communities, and in theorizing professional training. The shift to what is known as "new museology" from the 1990s onward has drawn attention to changes in expectations and assumptions around the function and practices of museums. The museum is no longer theorized as an elitist, collections-based institution whose aim is to educate the public, but one that is visitor oriented and focused on providing a wide range of accessible interpretation to support the objects and stories it holds.[9] One of the guiding questions that informs the analysis of this book is, therefore, how these new theoretical and critical models of museum studies can help us to decode contemporary object-based literary texts.

A Genealogy of Museum Texts

Curating Worlds draws together an array of contemporary works of world literature into a composite corpus of texts that are particularly preoccupied with the question of how to tell stories through the arrangement of material things.[10] My corpus is primarily composed of novels but includes some works that straddle fiction and nonfiction, and others that do not fit neatly into any one genre. The works are transnational in scope, and their narrative action spans most of the continents around the world. They are contemporary publications but build on longer-term traditions of representing diverse forms of collecting, display, and exhibition in literature. Indeed, one of the first literary representations of a museum that strikes me as particularly relevant to the claims this book advances is the one formed by Bouvard and Pécuchet in Flaubert's eponymous novel of 1881. As one episode in a series of failed experiments to achieve mastery of the known world, the two protagonists decide to use their recent interest in archaeology to form a varied collection of objects in their home, which they refer to as a museum. Yet their "museum" is characterized by its "irreducible heterogeneity," and the set of objects it contains "is sustained only by the *fiction* that they somehow constitute a coherent representational universe."[11] In fact, they soon abandon the idea of a museum and turn from seeking truth in material objects to writing historical fiction. "They concluded that external facts are not the whole story. You also need to factor in psychology. Without imagination, history is flawed. 'Let's send for some historical novels!'"[12] Flaubert uses Bouvard and Pécuchet's aborted museum-making ambitions not only as a way of satirizing the nineteenth-century drive to classify knowledge through detail but also as a comment on the representational limits of reality itself: limits that are repeated in the various failures of the protagonists to engage with theories and disciplinary fields, and which are epitomized in the novel's own unfinished status. Narrative is revealed as a necessary method to orient oneself, however imperfectly, within understandings of the material world.

Twentieth-century fictional works that employ museum techniques such as collecting and display in order to narrativize history often operate in response to the traumas of the modern age, reacting in particular to the aftershocks of transatlantic slavery, the legacies of racism and inequality left in the wake of global empires, the two world wars of the twentieth century, and various waves of displacement across national borders. Affective modes of engaging with memory, and even postmemory, are privileged over positivist classifications of historical fact that can more often be seen to preoccupy nineteenth-century texts. Silke Arnold-de Simine's analysis of the intertextual relationship between W. G. Sebald's novel *Austerlitz* and Daniel Libeskind's Jewish Museum in Berlin is typical of this twentieth-century preoccupation with trauma. Arnold-de Simine highlights the emergence of "memory museums," which perform a different function to previously dominant "history

Orientation

museums" in their emphasis on multimedia narratives. These are museums that resemble stories in the emotional impact they provoke, in which objects are "considered to be the material hinges of a potential recovery of shared meanings, by means of narrativization and performativity."[13] The museal strategies that Arnold-de Simine identifies in contemporary works of fiction such as *Austerlitz* also inform the methodology of this book, which gathers together a much broader corpus of texts that seek, as *Austerlitz* does, to "transgress the medial boundaries of traditional fiction towards a hypertextual network, a non-sequential collage and bricolage which denies the linear and clear-cut progression from the event and its remembering to the mediation of memory."[14]

One consequence of the recent emphasis on memory over history in both museums and literature has been what Madhu Dubey terms the contemporary "storm of commemoration," which leads to the project of "museumizing" historical traumas such as both transatlantic slavery and the Holocaust. This practice of externalizing uncomfortable histories into "elaborate narrative worlds" of museum dioramas, immersive experiences, and abstract architectural features demands that we ask questions about the purpose and logic of such memorial mobilizations.[15] These are questions that Dubey probes through an analysis of Colson Whitehead's 2016 novel *The Underground Railroad*, a text that she reads as functioning in "museum mode." Pointing out that the novel's publication coincided with the opening of the Smithsonian National Museum of African American History and Culture, Dubey sees similarities in the novel's and the museum's self-aware employment of representational techniques such as historical framing and spatial design. But it is also notable that the novel's protagonist, Cora, works actively to disrupt her own "representation" on the museum stage as a formerly enslaved person. As part of a living history display, Cora reverses the preordained order of her own exhibition, moving "backward" from Plantation to Slave Ship and then to Darkest Africa as each day progresses. She also fixes the museum visitors who come to stare at—and often to taunt—her, with an evil-eye stare. "It was a fine lesson, Cora thought, to learn that the slave, the African in your midst, is looking at you, too."[16] In this way, Cora evades what Bill Brown has famously termed the "grid of museal exhibition" and its tactics of display that aim toward intelligibility.[17] The mediated nature of museum representation in Brown's grid leads, in Peter Schwenger's analysis, to feelings of melancholy because systems of art and perception mean that the object is "simultaneously apprehended and lost." Schwenger traces this melancholy in various art forms that do not seek to reassemble this loss, but which instead question "what it means to assemble in the first place."[18] Museum displays can also work to upset received literary notions of temporality and reality through assembling ad hoc compositions, revealing further analogies with narrative techniques employed in fragmentary, defamilarizing texts such as Bruce Chatwin's 1988 novella *Utz*. The collecting mania of

Chatwin's eponymous protagonist "disorders readerly expectations" through practices of overaccumulation, and the book suggests, in turn, the possibility that "the museum can *remake itself* through less orderly displays."[19]

The point that Allan Hepburn makes here about *Utz* takes us one step further in sketching out an analogy between museums and narrative strategies. Hepburn perceives that the design of literary texts can actually influence museum practices. He identifies the high number of broken objects on display in a range of postmodern texts as a sign of an anti-modernist desire to "unmake the museum," and can thus be seen to inform Mullins's theory of a post-postmodernism "in pieces."[20] As contemporary texts work to make and unmake the museum through their engagement and appropriation of museal techniques, they collide with a sector that itself is always already in a crisis of identity.[21] Indeed, ideas about what museums are and do differ enormously and are subject to frequent revisions: the ICOM (International Council of Museums) definition of 2019 was not ratified at the annual meeting in Paris in 2020, and the proposed version remained in draft form until its eventual approval in August 2022.[22] What most working definitions seem to agree on, however, is that a museum is first and foremost a *collection of objects*. The purpose of the formation of that collection at the time of its entry into the museum space, and the shifts in meaning that occur through its preservation, curation, interpretation, and display since, all vary enormously from institution to institution. But what remains at the core of any definition is the objects in the collection themselves, without which the museum would not exist.

Most museum professionals and theorists would also agree that the objects that make up the museum collection are invested with a greater scale of significance or value than is represented by their monetary worth alone. A lot of this value is bound up with the relationship of these objects to the past: to memories and values (both individual and collectively held), and with their metonymic status as markers of history and evidence of continuity or change in human life and society over time. And of course, most people working in the museum sector would now agree that none of the information that objects store and transmit is neutral—collections have usually been amassed from a particular perspective that deemed what was valuable, what deserved to be preserved, and what instead should be discarded or destroyed. The violence of colonial-era collecting meant that vast swaths of objects were routinely decontextualized and estranged from their communities of belonging for display in Western museum spaces. How things have been stored, catalogued, and interpreted is also inflected with huge variations on a scale of personal and institutional bias, something that has come under intense scrutiny over the past few years thanks to community activism, calls for the decolonization of institutional museum and gallery spaces, and the increase in public debate over monuments and memorialization triggered by the contemporary Rhodes Must Fall and Black Lives Matter movements. In the museum sector,

Orientation

this work has been spearheaded by La Tanya S. Autry and Mike Murawski, who established the Museums Are Not Neutral global advocacy initiative in the summer of 2017 through online fundraising and social media awareness campaigns.[23]

But perhaps the most persistently mistaken conception of the museum is that it represents a sort of storehouse—a static, passive repository for the ongoing preservation of linear history. In fact, the opposite is true. The museum is a constantly active and dynamic agent in creating the narrative of its own collection, and in so doing, in scripting its own narrative of history. This narrative can shift or stay the same, but either way, it requires a huge and collective effort to bolster, maintain, develop, or overhaul. The dynamism involved in this museum work is evident in the language of the 2022 ICOM definition, which abounds with verbs of action: "A museum is a not-for-profit, permanent institution in the service of society that *researches, collects, conserves, interprets and exhibits* tangible and intangible heritage." These verbs tell us a lot about what goes on in museums in general, and it is exciting to think through how these different actions are enacted on various levels and scales. Each object in the museum collection is narrativized not only in its accompanying text label but also through its position vis-à-vis other objects (whether it is alone or with others), its physical display (in a case, on a shelf, in a drawer), its relationship to the wider narratives written for panels, rooms, or exhibitions, and to the overarching narrative constructed by the space of the building itself. This all combines into an enormous labor of storytelling. In the chapters that follow, I will show how we can read objects, displays, museum rooms, and whole exhibitions in much the same way as we can read literary fiction and vice versa, and how these parallel processes of reading, writing, and interpretation can shed light on how history is written in both of these storied spaces: the museum and the novel.[24] Specifically, I will suggest that we can identify a new class of contemporary world literature novels that enact the very same set of museum practices suggested by ICOM above (researching, collecting, conserving, interpreting, exhibiting) that allow them to function as mobile object collections on display. As we read through a series of displays, collections, and texts in tandem with one another in the chapters to follow, new strategies of encounter and engagement with both will allow us to enact a shift in what we think of as a museum, and what we think of as a text, and to identify where the overlap between the two lies.

What I find particularly generative about reading contemporary museum practices alongside narrative techniques in world literature is the importance both place on participatory action, and the active involvement of museum visitors and readers in interpreting the objects they hold in store or on display. This is, in both cases, a question of giving your visitor-readers the tools or the instruments to explore, discover, and play for themselves with the materials, objects, and collections that have been archived, curated, or put on display. It involves no longer considering the visitor-reader as a passive recipient of a predetermined narrative. The reason why this is exciting is that it allows in both cases for much more dynamic and multiple rereadings of history to emerge. We are no longer confined to reading books or material displays as if they are capable of presenting us with one authoritative and authorized version of "History." Rather, we are invited into past narratives in museums or in novels as a way of intervening in history, of offering new perspectives, making our own connections, and creating our own rewritings through the primary material on offer. The work of the imagination in altering or supplementing the narratives displayed either by the museum collection or the contemporary work of fiction is a critical element in the interpretation of the material on display, and it characterizes the new visitor-reader experience.

I thus read my chosen corpus of texts for the orientation devices that allow for this co-creative work to happen. In museum language, orientation devices might include things like signage, aural and tactile landmarks, surface colors to guide visitors, displays, interactives, and text.[25] In the books explored here, I identify orientation devices in the archival insertion of primary material (photographs, songs, newspaper clippings, and so on); in the segmented nature of their structures (thinking about their use of epigraphs, headings, and subdivisions), in their addenda and supplementary materials, and in the research and intertexts that underpin their stories. I interrogate these books as narrative containers, looking at the formation of their structure in tandem with the boxes, baskets, ledgers, display jars, and glass cases that house their primary material. I delve into the collecting impulse and acquisition practices that guide their narratives forward through the accumulation of emblematic objects. I pay special attention to the ethics of care and repair that determines the curation or conservation of broken, absent, or obsolete narrative things. And I think through strategies that encourage active reader participation as parallel to museum objectives toward greater access, orientation, and community engagement. In this way, the book aims to offer a heuristic model of how to read contemporary object-oriented works of narrative fiction in museum mode.

Theorizing the Museum

To my knowledge, no literary study has yet used the rich theoretical field of museum studies to define practices such as collecting, curating, accessioning, cataloguing, archiving, storing, labeling, exhibiting, conserving, and deaccessioning as a complete set, series, or system of narrative tools. In so doing, and in proposing museum practices as a new lens of critical interpretation, this book aims to provide a new theoretical framework for scholars looking to engage with object collections in literature. My argument is that museums are narrative spaces that we can use to shed light on literary form: on how stories are created, shaped, and communicated. The continuous labor of

Orientation

arranging and rearranging objects that takes place in museums in order to tell stories about cultures and histories seems to me to have inherent similarities to the work of a number of contemporary authors whose narratives depart from a loss (a death, perhaps, or the break-up of a relationship, a disappearance, or displacement through war, persecution, or migration) and then work to salvage what has been lost; to reinstate it by sorting through objects: collecting, curating, conserving, and displaying them, cataloguing their presence and producing a two-dimensional archive that reads like the textual description of a museum space. As Gaynor Kavanagh has written, "Societies gather together the dross and detritus of human activity and experience. These become primary tools in re-casting the events of the past into a pattern that makes some sense today." Individuals, too, "deeply need to find self-definition and explanation through the cognition of a past in which their part is duly recorded."[26] Museums become a primary means of gathering up this "detritus" human activity of "codifying the past," and of sorting the events of our collective history into a story that makes sense.

The books that I analyze here have all been published (in English or in English translation) over the past decade or so. And indeed, the high number of contemporary literary texts that enact museum practices might reflect the fact that we are living in something of a museum moment. Ambrose and Paine note the modern "boom" in museums (prior to the COVID-19 pandemic), stating that in Europe for each museum that existed in 1950 there are some four today; that in China, 3,500 museums have been built since the late 1970s; and that there are around 36,000 museums in the United States of America alone.[27] Attention to museum methods and practices has also recently intensified through both the growing impetus toward decolonization and, I would argue, thanks to the pandemic itself: new digital modes of audience engagement have flourished, while the absence of the possibility to visit physical museum spaces and collections has thrown their societal and cultural value into sharp relief. But is there something more about the contemporary moment that makes the museum *as method* particularly relevant as a mode of cultural inquiry? "Curating" has certainly shifted in the general public understanding from a specific form of museum expertise to a universal label for a wide range of "aesthetically conscious" activities, from curating life experiences to playlists, and from closet space to social media feeds.[28] Does our growing interest in curation, and self-curation, also mean that we are becoming more aware of the narrative building structures in museums, of how museums curate not only the objects in their collections but also our experience as visitors?

Museums tell layered and constantly shifting stories about our global, national, and local identities. They act as dynamic storehouses and interpreters for our memories. They chart both change and continuity in our societies. But they also play an important role in providing evidence through material proof of historical events, which is why we invest them with high levels of authority. There is a certain pact of trust between the museum and the public: we believe that the artifacts on display really are what they are labeled as being, that they can reliably function as "witnesses" to historical moments, people, and places.[29] And yet, they are not displayed without bias: Michael Ames reminds us that the traditional privilege of the museum is that of controlling history, through modes of both inclusion and exclusion.[30] Collections are arranged into what Carol Duncan terms a "programmed narrative," in which art history replaces history through the aestheticization of displaying material culture.[31] Curation, in the form of the acts of selecting and then organizing objects into relationships with materials (other objects, display cases, labels, and so on), has what Svetlana Alpers calls a "museum effect," that of "turning all objects into works of art."[32]

We must therefore be mindful of the fact that museums do not just give us an account of history, but they themselves manufacture the historical.[33] We also need to acknowledge that the histories manufactured and reproduced in museums are patchy, fragmented, and incomplete. Igor Kopytoff's notion of object biographies has taught scholars and readers of material culture that objects live varied lives, and that different stages in their biographies are often triggered through moments of cultural redefinition.[34] The passage of an object as it travels outside a context of "use" into a museum context of aestheticization is one such moment. But not every scrap of information on who created the object, who bought, used, and repaired it, and how it came into the collection (whether through sale, donation, or even theft), can possibly be included in the interpretation provided by the museum. The museum curator must decide which elements or events in an object's past to highlight or foreground when it is presented to the public. Also, no one museum has complete, representative collections of the histories it is trying to tell, so it must deal with gaps in those stories, which it will sometimes try to do in creative narrative ways. Yet on the other hand, reviewers of the books I am working with here have often discussed their authors' engagements with objects as if the presence of so much stuff was somehow artless. Writing in *The New Yorker*, James Wood speaks of the interconnecting stories in *Flights* "as if they were found objects and Tokarczuk merely an itinerant gatherer."[35] In the *Spectator*, Peter Pomerantsev describes the experience of reading *In Memory of Memory* as "closer to exploring an abandoned palace than following a story."[36] There is something about the material engagements in these texts that makes them appear as lesser forms of fiction somehow. Yet, as I will demonstrate, understanding them within a framework of museum practices allows us to appreciate their material methods as a series of complex and sophisticated *narrative* techniques: techniques that allow them to negotiate absences and presences within a framework of salvage constellations.

My project to recast museum practices as a series of literary devices takes us back to the unsteady nature of the notion of the museum, and how its meaning has shifted across historical time and space. If it is true that

Orientation

a museum is first and foremost a collection of objects, then it is also true that different types of object collecting predated the concept of the museum by some centuries. While we know little about historical collecting habits among non-elite groups, it was encounters with new, distant, and unfamiliar stuff that primarily sparked the formation of collections in the Middle Ages. Wonders, which had to be rare, mysterious, and real, both "marked the outermost limits of the natural" and "registered the line between the known and the unknown."[37] In the medieval world, such encounters with marvels were initially not visual but *narrative*, as those who had traveled shared their experience by means of storytelling. These textual reports were akin to a symbolic mastery of the world. And when accounts were accompanied by material things, these marvelous objects became symbols of high levels of wealth or of knowledge, or both. Access to such modes of exploration and discovery was very much limited to society's elite groups, however, so the vast majority of the population still relied on verbal reports of the speaker who had seen objects of wonder, rather than experiencing those objects for themselves.[38]

Collecting habits diversified and increased in the fifteenth and sixteenth centuries as networks of commerce, trade, and banking became globalized. Private collections expanded from princely or religious hoards to the *studioli* of the Italian Renaissance and the cabinets of curiosities that were becoming common across much of Europe. Such cabinets became so fashionable in the Netherlands that "even dolls' houses were not complete without their own miniaturized collectors' cabinets complete with tiny sea shells and carvings in drawers no larger than a thumb."[39] The desire to collect objects that would provoke wonder slowly shifted to the urge to form collections that represented values of good taste and connoisseurship, and as the Enlightenment approached, methods of organizing and classifying objects—such as the Linnaean system—became of primary importance. Scientific approaches that had additional educational purposes became paramount in the postrevolutionary world. As European nation-states were formed and re-formed through the late eighteenth and early nineteenth centuries, large national museums that could function as a "revolutionary device" were born: the Louvre opened in 1793, the Prado in 1820, London's National Gallery in 1824 and British Museum in 1852, and the Altes Museum Berlin in 1830.[40] More recently in the twentieth and twenty-first centuries, a new shift has seen museums direct more energy and resources toward questions of community access, social change, visitor engagement, and active learning as they embrace what Sarah Longair has called the model of the "relational museum," where the primary focus of the museum is nurturing and building relations between people, objects, and the museum space.[41]

These new models of the museum as an experience-driven, relational, and active space lead me to identify literary fiction as one of the latest generations of alternative sites where museum-making practices abound. Indeed, the complex dynamics of viewership within this model of the relational museum require active participation on the part of the visitor-reader in order to complete the meaning of the object: a meaning that will necessarily change in every single encounter.[42] Jeanne Canizzo highlights the "transformational power" of their context, stating that museums are "fictional" in nature because meaning is generated through encounters between multiple parties: in other words, "they function as negotiated realities."[43] Questions of authenticity and aura (including the "fetishization" of museum objects through their positionality as stuff on display) collide with notions of value, measure, and control to make the museum a tricky—yet endlessly dynamic—semantic space. Reading contemporary works of fiction as new museum spaces demands that we ask questions about the representation and the nature of evidence through material "facts," when they can be radically reassigned meaning in different moments and places. It also suggests we can learn new ways of experiencing and engaging with history and memory through aligning contemporary works of world literature with museums, enacting a shift in how we understand and apprehend the material world around us.

Conclusion: Reworlding World Literature

One of the running threads through *Curating Worlds* is the interrogation of the notion of museum curation as care, and the identification of alternative modes of conservation and salvage that characterize the management of the object collections I analyze. Indeed, many of the objects that we will encounter are in varying states of repair: although some have been carefully preserved, others might be broken, lost, or missing, or form part of an incomplete set. They might require unconventional tactics of care in order to restore their full range of significance to the reader—something I will argue that the texts in question work hard to achieve. Nonetheless, their partial ruination is significant in itself. It figures as part of a broader operation of *incomplete* recuperation, in which objects are elements in an aesthetic system of salvage that Angela Naimou sees as directed toward their eventual repurposing, redirection, and reevaluation: "Salvage aesthetics both calls into question and refashions the objects and subjects of history, creating literary and visual assemblages of historical fragments figuratively pulled from the wreck of the present."[44] Accepting the loss or partial decay of objects from the past means accepting the violence implicit in the passing of time, and cherishing the imperfections that things accumulate through modes of narrative recuperation and recycling. Use transforms objects and can alter their value: wear and tear may decrease the value of an everyday object, but use by a famous historical figure, for example, can render it priceless. Broken objects can also be generative since, as Sara Ahmed reminds us, "a break can be how something is revealed."[45] And, similarly, Stephen Greenblatt has spoken of how the precariousness of objects is a rich source of "resonance,"[46] a celebration

Orientation

of both their resilience and their vulnerability through their persistence to survive. One body of artistic work that has inspired me throughout the writing and researching of this book has been Kader Attia's *Museum of Emotion*, and in particular his work reassessing Eurocentric ideas about "the values of wholeness and injury, authenticity and repair, belonging and otherness."[47] Attia's creative rehabilitation of repaired objects and his reassessment of the worth of broken or decaying matter chimes with key critical works by Caitlin DeSilvey, Crystal B. Lake, and Sarah Wasserman that I am in dialogue with in several of the chapters that follow.[48] Paying attention to what is broken thus asks us to rethink the notion of care, especially when we are exploring that notion in relation to curating as a literary practice.[49]

Each text I work with here curates its own "world," and together I think of them as a "constellation" that draws them together under a world literature label. This in part references Tokarczuk's own use of the word to describe *Flights* as a "constellation novel," since, as she states, "Constellation, not sequencing, carries truth."[50] The constellation structure of *Flights* is equally emblematic of the other texts I analyze and shows why I have chosen to explore the place of these works within a system of world literature. Each text I analyze adapts a "co-locational or translocational approach" to history, and when looked at together they interlace "localities and nationalities with one another in a globally imagined space."[51] They are arguably more interested in motivations and responses to action than in past events in and of themselves, and they remain attuned to tracing moments of collusion and resistance, or structures of force, pressure, and emotion that affect the pace and sequence of their unfolding narratives. But they all deal with their own narrative moments within a wide-lens continuum of history that is in constant dialogue with other spaces and times, and which allows us to identify constant processes of repetition and reenactment. They all perform, to use the Warwick Research Collective's term, a "spatial bridging of unlike times."[52] They thus show how acts of contemporary association and interpretation provide stories with afterlives and posthistories to form constellations in which "precisely this fragment of the past is found with precisely this present."[53]

My belief is that aligning world literature and museum heritage practices will allow us to rethink both elements in the world literature label: by emphasizing the commonalities in narrative building between museum collections and literature, and by thinking of worlds as personally constructed (acquired, collected, curated, preserved, and displayed) constellations rather than emblems of the now well-worked-through global systems of capital, cultural exchange, or even ecology. In this sense, I find Pheng Cheah's work theorizing the "world" in world literature to be particularly helpful. As Cheah says, if we think of the world in world literature as temporal rather than spatial, we can enact a "radical rethinking of world literature as literature that is an active power in the making of worlds—both a site of processes of worlding and an agent that participates and intervenes in these processes."[54] Setting aside the spatial ordering of global capitalism and reassigning a normative force to world literature lets literary texts acquire an agency that allows them to open up worlds, and which exceeds and disrupts existing categories and categorizations through their formation of alternative realities in each retelling and interpretative act they engender.

Another element of Cheah's thought on this worlding potential of literature also aligns with the narrative force of museum histories and futures. Museums were first established in Europe as part of imperial projects and were designed with firm nationalist agendas in mind. Many still function either implicitly or explicitly as three-dimensional imperial archives. Likewise, the museum practices I follow in my literary analysis here—of collecting, curating, preserving, and displaying—can all be read as imperialist in their original (and some would argue, ongoing) intent. They are locations for the accumulation of what Stoler has called "imperial debris."[55] This elemental grounding in empire is not meant to narrow down the focus of this study to direct histories or material legacies of colonialism, but rather to recognize that imperial formations persist in contemporary life to inform myriad "processes of decimation, displacement and reclamation,"[56] including migration patterns across the Mediterranean or the US-Mexico border, police brutality toward members of Black communities in particular, and health and access inequalities endured by diverse minority groups. Stoler's point about the all-pervasive persistence of imperial formations is echoed by Azoulay's argument that empire is the zero-sum point of world injustice today.[57] Both scholars ask what kinds of shift in perspective are necessary for us to be able to rewind back to the point of departure—for example, when an object is removed from its original community context to be put in a museum, or a colonial photograph is taken of a disenfranchised subject—and start again from there.

The aim with this process of "unlearning" is not to fill in the gaps that exist in archives and museums, nor is it to offer a counternarrative that still refers back to empire as a given point of reference in time. Rather, it asks us to wind back to right before the camera shutter clicked to create an image, or to the moment preceding the exchange (or surrender) of an object, and to create a new fabulative version of what could or what should have been possible without the original imperial intervention. I believe that the creative, fictional narratives I explore through the following chapters offer one way of doing this. They highlight what Stoler calls the "creative, critical and sometimes costly measures people take to become less entangled (in imperial formations)—or to *make something new of those entanglements*."[58] In a similar vein, in discussing world literature, Cheah states that we "cannot undo the history of Western imperialism and colonialism by nostalgically recuperating romanticized precapitalist pasts. We must instead patiently search for extant resources for reworlding the world."[59] This process will consist in first *unworlding* (mapping the calculations of ruin brought about

Orientation 17

by global capital—colonial slavery, border formations, the displacement of peoples, communities, and objects, etc.)—and then starting anew from the original point of fracture. I would venture that someday, theories of world literature might even be usefully employed within museums in order to enact new ways of telling the narratives around dispossession and dislocation that are inherent in their collections.

Both museums and literary fiction represent impossible scales of travel in time and space that allow for an exhilarating sense of potential to emerge. As John MacKenzie writes, the museum serves "to collapse both chronological and spatial considerations, opening up a number of dimensions within its portals."[60] It is this active approach to undoing and redoing time and space that places the works examined here into dialogue with each other, and in fact I would argue that a sort of impulse toward cross-border and cross-temporal mobility drives and guides them all in different ways. Borders and other expressions of nationalism (including imperial time and colonial drives) act as antagonists within their plots, but antagonists that lead to new creative, adaptive acts. In fact, both museums and creative writing allow for objects to exist in a kind of four-dimensional space, which includes the experience of the past in the present, a kind of "crossing of the barrier of change in time."[61] Museums hold the raw content that allows us such experiences within their object collections. As Lake explains, it is the dynamic materiality of objects themselves that "allows them to be plotted simultaneously in various temporal moments."[62] But objects can exceed the interpretative capacities of their interlocutors and act as unreliable narrators of their own histories, "compelling representations that swerve between facts and fictions."[63] The incompleteness of their own self-narration means we are always drawn to generate our own narratives about them, yet in doing so we are simultaneously placed within an impossible space of doubting that our inventions and fabulations are correct. Their "invitations to indulge in thought experiments about the past" are thus never completed or completable,[64] and can lead to endless inventions and reinventions on the part of the museum visitor, or indeed, of the reader.

Curating Worlds assembles this particular collection of texts as a constellation of world literature because I agree, following the routes of queer curation theorized by Gayatri Gopinath, that we ourselves—as critics and readers—make worlds through our choices and selections, as individual, affect-driven and idiosyncratic as they may be.[65] As Chris Andrews writes, "We construct literary worlds by discerning relations at a range of scales."[66] I chose to work with these particular texts because the relations I saw emerge between them helped me to form the argument of this book. These are works of fiction that function as, and which can thus shed light on the workings of, conceptually portable spaces such as archives, libraries, display cabinets, and museum stores. They do so through specifically enacting strategic museum practices that allow them to deploy narrative objects as devices to better orient their readers. I align my own methodology of selection and analysis with DeSilvey's call to "take up the proposals offered by things," thereby bringing objects into legibility through placing them within a wider network of connections. This mode of practice is also, necessarily, "in relation to my own imagination, to my intellectual aims, and to my haptic experience of textures and forms."[67] *Curating Worlds* is my own object collection of contemporary texts, texts that I present here to show how they deploy particular museological strategies in order to tell new stories about the material world around us.

Chapter 1

Collecting

Introduction

The Risiera di San Sabba is located in the far southeast of the city of Trieste, before the Adriatic coastline curves around the bay to the town of Muggia and then winds farther on toward the Slovenian border. I decide to walk to the Risiera from the center of town one hot August morning, somewhat to the surprise and consternation of local friends. Due to its complex topography, the backstreets of Trieste crisscross a maze of tunnels and steep hills that are hard to navigate as a pedestrian, but after an hour or so I reach the huge cemetery at Valmaura, with its Catholic, Greek Orthodox, ex-military, and Jewish sections, and then go past the city's sports stadium, which is still adorned with large painted murals dedicated to the memory of Stefano Furlan.[1] After passing a large supermarket I turn left down a smaller road, and walk past a closed gym, some car parks, and garages. On my right, partially hidden by trees, is an old red-brick industrial building. It doesn't seem out of place here, a relic of a different time amid so many others. What strikes me more as a visitor are the stark pale-gray concrete walls built next to it, which appear to both support the buildings and to frame them (fig. 2). The contrast between the sleekness of the new brutalist structures and the decay of the old brick buildings is jarring. As I turn the corner to go in, the concrete walls form a high, narrow walkway down to the entrance, producing an intense claustrophobic effect as the blinding sun beats down from above.[2] The sensation is one of walking into an inescapable void.

The Risiera started life as a rice-husking factory at the end of the nineteenth century and was expanded into its now recognizable form in 1913. San Sabba was even more disconnected from central Trieste back then, but it still formed part of a lively industrial suburb. Rice production ceased in 1927, and the factory was effectively taken over by local police for use as barracks.[3] After the Italian surrender to the Allied forces in September 1943 and the subsequent Nazi occupation of central and northern Italy, the Risiera was transformed into a temporary prison facility for Italian servicemen known as *Stalag* 339, and subsequently functioned as an internment camp, or

19

Fig. 2. The entrance to the Risiera di San Sabba. Photograph by Emma Bond.

Polizeihaftlager for the transit of deportees bound for concentration camps in Germany and Poland. It was also used as a storage facility for confiscated goods and property, and for the internment and execution of political prisoners, partisans, and Italian Jews. It is notorious for being Italy's only territorial concentration camp that was equipped with an incinerator for murdering prisoners. Partially destroyed by Nazi troops when it was abandoned in April 1945, it then served as a refugee camp for Italians leaving Yugoslavia after the territorial exchanges between the two countries,[4] and it fell into a state of dereliction before being declared a national monument and renovated as a museum in 1975.

The architect tasked with restructuring the ruined site, Romano Boico, used the squalor of the decaying, partial remains as his guiding principle: "I thought that this total squalor could rise as a symbol and itself become a monument. I decided to remove and restore rather than add."[5] In accordance with this principle, Boico entirely emptied the six-story building where most of the prisoners were kept, retaining only the load-bearing beams. The

Collecting 21

outline of the crematorium, in the open-air courtyard, is marked by faded lines and traces on the wall and floor. A suggestive steel installation marks the point where plumes of smoke from the incinerator were calculated to have risen up to meet the sky. Yet, as Dasa Drndić herself comments, "It remains questionable to what degree fundamental rot can be fully salvaged."[6] Indeed, other things have been added in subsequent moments to supplement the presentation of the ruins: scraps of testimony by a former inmate of the camp, Haimi Wachsberger, and some confiscated objects that once belonged to former inmates of the Risiera. Wachsberger's words are printed on laminated cards and taped onto the pillars in the *Sala delle croci*; the objects are a selection of those retrieved from storage in a Roman ministry after the war, and are now embedded into recesses in the walls of the Lager. A green fountain pen, an opal ring, a pocket watch, and some hairpins and ornate combs, all carefully labeled with numbered tags, are displayed in backlit boxes in the otherwise empty room. It is this partial collection of personal memories and things that adds a supplement of meaning to the space, gesturing toward the stories behind the names and numbers of those who were held here, and who—more often than not—lost their lives within it.[7]

This attention to acknowledging the individuality of the Risiera victims through the collection of storied objects takes a central role in Drndić's 2012 novel *Trieste*. The novel features a distinct middle section entitled "Behind Every Name There Is a Story." Numbering nearly fifty pages, the section lists the names of the approximately nine thousand Jews who were deported from Italy, or killed in Italy, or in the countries that Italy occupied between 1943 and 1945.[8] In the original Croatian edition, published five years earlier than the English translation, the pages in this section had perforated edges so that they could be torn out, kept elsewhere, or perhaps given to someone else. At an event as part of Jewish Book Week in London, Drndić asked for a copy of the book to be passed around the audience. People were invited to rip out any pages containing names they recognized, "until the book lost its form, as a society does when an element is removed. The centre does not hold."[9] The world that *Trieste* inhabits and attempts to describe has lost its center, a void that replicates and is replicated in the emptied space of the Risiera. No matter of accumulation, of gathering evidence, of collecting material and stories, will fill the material void of lives lost. Yet the novel itself, in its temporal and spatial framing of an individual loss, provides a beginning and an end to this story, and perhaps suggests a purpose to the material accumulation of story in response to lived trauma. As Peter Brooks notes, "Narrative demarcates, encloses, establishes limits, orders," and plot is the "organizing line . . . that makes narrative possible."[10] In a way, the novel's structure acts as a mirror to Boico's brutalist concrete walls: encircling and giving shape to an interior vacuum that has been decorated with addenda of detail.

In the rest of this chapter, I will perform a close reading of selected object interventions in *Trieste* in order to show how the way in which things are amassed and manipulated within the narrative functions as a deliberate plot device. My reading of *Trieste* will provide a model for how practices of object collecting align with the notion of assembling (and perhaps even dismantling) a narrative plot. More specifically, in the case of *Trieste*, it will see collecting as a way of reframing objects or other material elements within a world where historical context and official records have been manipulated and warped to fit an ideology of belief; where what remains has been diminished by the atrocity of past events. Collecting here does not represent a solution, nor a corrective resolution to that diminishing. More often than not, it is a painful, dangerous or even degenerate act. But the practice of collecting helps to "story matter" and to "surface meaning":[11] to plot a narrative that provides some sense of order and coherence to memory, and to offer an alternative to a partial History generated and recorded by others. Processes of collecting are intimately related to those of recollecting, as Caitlin DeSilvey reminds us throughout her wide-ranging work on heritage and decay. The acts of connection and assembly common to both memory and collection can thus be seen to work "by a logic not of sequential reconstruction, but of association."[12]

In *Trieste*, several scales of collecting and *re*-collecting collide. This chapter will aim to circle through each of these scales in order to posit the collecting of stuff as a key element of contemporary narrative design. The primary set of objects collected by the protagonist, for example, unfolds against a backdrop of obsessive Nazi collecting and classifying that irrevocably alter the demography, cultures, and landscapes of Europe. The protagonist of the novel seeks to track down the only missing, "stubborn" element of her collection (her son), whose recuperation will signal the collection's completion and thus also the closure of the novel. As the narrative shifts to tell his perspective in the closing sections, we understand that while mother and son are both searching for reunion, she collects in order to achieve resolution, but his is a collecting impulse that "reaches only 'behind,' spiraling in a continually inward movement rather than outward toward the future."[13] Before delving deeper into these interlinking spheres of material object collections in *Trieste*, I will first examine key preliminary issues that affect them all: the temporality of collecting, the psychological elements involved in its practice, and notions of value and coherence, order, and control, in order to show where and how they can shed light on the formation of narrative plot.

Collection Histories

As stated in the introduction to this book, collections and collecting practices predate the more modern concept of the museum by some centuries. But collections are also the literal stuff of museums. Most museums display collections of objects that were bequeathed or donated to them, or that they

Collecting

themselves have acquired through various means (some more ethical than others). Many contemporary museums are still actively involved in collecting activity, where the impetus is to look forward rather than back, thus "recording the present for the future."[14] As they enter the museum, objects become part of a wider material assemblage, forming new network relations with the existing objects in the collection and acquiring new meaning—both individual and collective—through the process.[15] The act of collecting also exceeds the museum, of course, and is practiced on various scales by individuals and other nonmuseum organizations and groups worldwide. But the guiding principles of forming a collection are fundamentally the same, whether they apply to a museum or an individual. Russell Belk has defined collecting as "the process of actively, selectively, and passionately acquiring and possessing things removed from ordinary use and perceived as part of a set of non-identical objects or experiences."[16] Issues of order and control loom large in any analysis of collecting as a practice: Belk comments elsewhere that collecting, whether carried out by individuals or organizations, is "essentially a modernist project of assembling, organizing, and controlling a part of the world."[17] Value becomes a malleable, personalized concept: the monetary worth of any one component is not as significant to its owner as its value as part of a collection. The value of objects is thereby enhanced by what Benjamin would call their "fateful" entry into the collection: the most important fate of an object is its encounter with the collector as it is the collector who sets the stage of their existence and recasts it as a story of his own making.[18] The narrative of the collection, and thus also the narrative of the individual collector, eventually succeeds in replacing the narrative of history.[19]

Control inflects the relationship between the collection and its own temporality: as Susan Stewart has described, the collection becomes an autonomous world in which history is replaced by a form of ahistorical classification proper only to the collection itself.[20] The issue of temporality is also bound up with the fraught question of when a collection might ever be considered to be complete. Collecting has been theorized as signifying the "urge to erect a permanent and complete system against the destructiveness of time,"[21] which renders it not only an impossible task but also one propelled forward by a desire for it not to end. One will always yearn to acquire the final, missing element in a collection, but the incompleteness of the collection allows its owner to avoid closure, prolonging the pleasure of desire in the meantime. What parallels can we draw between this conflicted desire to complete (and yet to *not* complete) a collection and the reader's pleasure in reading while simultaneously desiring to reach the conclusion of a story? Working with the idea of a Freudian masterplot, Peter Brooks would say that our desire in narrative (and in life) is the desire for an end that does not come before its time: an end achieved without falling foul of short circuit. There has to be space in the middle of the life plot for transformation, for what Roland

Barthes terms "retard, postponement, error, and partial revelation," before we reach the satisfaction of the ending. In this way, our desire for the end is a desire "reached only through the *at least minimally complicated* detour."[22] We require the circuitous mechanics of plot in order to satisfy our desire for narrative. In the same way, the long, patient process of forming a collection "simply involves waiting, creating the pauses that articulate the biography of the collector."[23]

In much the same way as the time of the novel exists in a distinct and self-referential construction, "the setting up of a collection itself displaces real time," since the fundamental project of all collecting is "to translate real time into the dimension of a *system*."[24] In temporal terms, the narrative of *Trieste* begins where it ends.[25] The opening description is of the protagonist of the novel in the contemporary moment, a now elderly Jewish lady called Haya Tedeschi, who sits in her apartment in the Italian border town of Gorizia and awaits news of her long-lost son Antonio. Antonio was conceived during a love affair between Haya and a high-ranking SS officer named Kurt Franz, who was stationed in Gorizia, and then Trieste, as part of Operation Reinhard (1943–1945).[26] Antonio was stolen from his mother at the age of six months as part of the Nazi "Lebensborn" program, which aimed to ensure the future racial purity of the German nation. Haya spends the rest of her life assembling the evidence to prove the theft of her child and attempting to relocate him. Everything that she collects she keeps in a big red basket at her feet, a receptacle that is so tall it reaches up as far as her knees. This is a dynamic collection that Haya physically manipulates in acts of constant movement as she waits:

> From the basket she takes out her life and hangs it on the imaginary clothes line of reality. She takes out letters, photographs, postcards, clippings, magazines, and leafs through them, she thumbs through the pile of lifeless paper and then sorts it yet again, this time on the floor, or on the desk by the window. She arranges her existence.[27]

The fragments of re-collected autobiography contained in the objects in Haya's basket tell a story that is repeated in the plot system of *Trieste:* the narrative follows Haya's gestures of sorting and rearranging and as she picks up a paper or a photograph, the story follows the thread contained in her memories of that object. The basket itself, as container, is key to the system organizing the collection since, as always, "the space of the collection is a complex interplay of exposure and hiding, organization and the chaos of infinity."[28] In the same way, the book itself also acts as the container of an accumulation of intertextual fragments: the list of the names of Italian Jewish victims mentioned above, transcripts from the Nuremberg trials, song lyrics, music, photographs, biographies of SS troops, maps, poems, and footnotes. The novel itself is an active assemblage of assorted material (fig. 3).

Collecting

The outlines of the demolished crematorium

The prison building from which camp inmates were taken who were targeted for transfer to Dachau, Auschwitz and Mauthausen

> *We were afraid of spies. We didn't ask questions, we didn't talk. A certain Kabiglio, a Jewish shopkeeper who was from Mostar, said, Look, that is an oven. They are burning people. Then I looked and I saw people disappearing beyond the door. Everything was happening at around ten or eleven at night. I heard the footsteps of the prisoners dragging on the stone paving, I heard women's sandals, they made the loudest noise. The S.S. would turn on the engines of their lorries or the music way up, as if they were partying. Sometimes I heard cries for help. Sometimes I didn't. I began to scribble down notes on the goings. There were no comings. One night I counted the footsteps of fifty-six people who went from the courtyard to the entrance of the crematorium; another night, seventy-three. Then I stopped counting, I stopped keeping track. My fourteen-year-old daughter was with me in the cell. They were killing children. I heard children calling*

Fig. 3. Example page of Daša Drndić's *Trieste* (p. 195), showing captioned photographs and reported testimony. Photograph by Emma Bond. Courtesy of Quercus Publishing Limited.

But the bricolage that Drndić assembled during the archival research she carried out in preparation for writing the novel shifts from being underpinning material to constituting the very fabric of the plot, and—crucially—forms the basis of a new relationship between reader and text. The novel provides a space of mediation for the visitor-reader to encounter and understand the material collected within it as a series of plot markers. As Drndić rather drily replied to an interviewer's question about how the archival materials in her fiction helped her to articulate or complicate the trauma of history, "They do not help me, they are supposed to help the reader. The reader who has lost the capacity to imagine, to rely on the word, on language, and its immense possibilities that are less and less recognized and abused."[29] The inserted intertextual details are props for readers to manipulate and rearrange at will. In the repetition of these actions, readers take ownership of the material narrative, achieving mastery over the "grammar of the plot,"[30] ultimately becoming akin to a collector in their own right.

Collecting items involves the physical handling of objects, their storage, positioning, cataloguing, and sometimes (though not always) their display. In addition, individual collectors have rights of tactile access granted by their ownership of objects—access that the museum visitor usually does not have. And yet both museum visitors and readers can become active participants in meaning-making operations during their encounters with object collections, due to their subjective acts of interpretation. As Susan Pearce points out, "The message of the meaning which the object offers is always incomplete and each viewer fills in the gaps in his own way, thereby excluding other possibilities: as he looks he makes his own decisions about how the story is to be told."[31] So the meaning that the object holds changes from person to person, and changes further still over time. Objects are folded into individual experiences of time and place, and hold the power to actually change the viewer through the new relationship of meaning that is formed as and when they meet. Encounters with written objects function in the same way, since "the meaning of the past does not reside in the past, but belongs in the present. Writing signs into the present and the process of writing is transformative in itself."[32]

Narrative Collecting

Reading and experiencing objects thus brings past collecting activity into the here and now of the material encounter in the text or the museum display. But, as Mieke Bal asks, how do you start a collection? "Where does it all begin?"[33] What can we learn about the mechanics of shaping a story from watching how someone like Haya puts together and then pulls apart a set of things? *Trieste* is a book which brims full of collections of objects. We start in the time of the Austro-Hungarian Empire, which incorporated both Trieste and Gorizia, and where the stories of the modern history of the region begin. We hear of the visit of Archduke Franz Ferdinand and his wife Sophie to Gorizia, and of his collections of hunting trophies, "bison, thousands stuffed and arranged in glass cases," his armor collections, thousands of sculptures of St. George, "antiques, paintings by 'naïve masters,' village furniture, all sorts of big and little utilitarian and useless objects of ceramics, stone and minerals, stained glass, watches and medals," all kept at his castle at Konopište.[34] We hear of the "collectibles" of the battles of the First World War, medals and mementos now sold in online auctions: a war that was triggered by Franz Ferdinand's assassination in Sarajevo and fought along the river of the Soča, the Isonzo, that runs through Gorizia.[35] We hear how during the Second

Collecting

World War, as the Tedeschi family moves from Gorizia to Trieste, to Naples, Albania, and back to Gorizia, Haya's younger brother Orestes would collect shrapnel around the town, "the exemplars of which he trades and hoards on a shelf in the kitchen in the large apothecary jar."[36] This is the same jar his Slovenian-speaking grandmother Marisa used to keep flour in, flour that she would use to bake walnut crescents for the Austro-Hungarian armies stationed in the town during the First World War.[37]

Within this layered context of historical and re-collected accumulations, it is the sudden appearance of Triestine author Claudio Magris's book *Un altro mare* in Haya's mailbox that heralds the start of her own collecting. Haya is a retired mathematics teacher, and the book is sent to her in 1991 by a former student, Roberto Piazza, with an accompanying letter asking a question that reads more like an accusation: why did she never mention the war during her classes at school? And since she taught Roberto between 1971 and 1976, why did she never take them to the new museum of the Risiera di San Sabba when it opened in 1975? The arrival of the book, alongside the previously mentioned list of the names of about nine thousand Jewish people deported from or killed in Italy between 1943 and 1945 and an account of Roberto's own investigations into the disappearance and murder of Jewish inhabitants in Gorizia, triggers a physical reaction in her.

> Haya senses that a little cemetery is sprouting in her breast with a jumble of tilting tombstones . . . she feels as if the already rotten, damp and blackened crosses and faded stars are knocking against her ribs; *they are crowded*, the crosses, the stones, the stars seem to be growing in her breast, reaching her throat and choking her, so she says, *I'm having trouble breathing.*[38]

Roberto uses the writings of Magris and Carlo Michelstaedter[39] to insert Haya in a hypothetical, imagined justification of her own association—*collaboration* even—with the SS troops she frequented in Gorizia and Trieste during the war. He speaks of how Michelstaedter believed man to be a "passive being" who "re-works, revises and appends his own biography and the biographies of those around him" throughout his life.[40] The suggestion is that Haya succumbed to the twin illusions of rhetoric and persuasion, embodying a passivity that allowed her to assume a lingering blindness to the atrocities being committed all around her. It is no accident that Haya did not herself acquire Magris's book, but that it was an unexpected gift. "In relation to the plot of collecting, the initial event is arbitrary, contingent, accidental. Only retrospectively, through a narrative manipulation of the sequence of events, can the accidental acquisition of the first object become the beginning of a collection."[41] Haya had other elements of the collection in her possession already (personal mementos and souvenirs of the Second World War, some given to her by Kurt Franz), but it is the act of gathering it all together into a sequence and consciously manipulating it into meaning that transforms it into an actual collection.[42]

Roberto's envelope, bulging with the names of the dead, is the first item that Haya places into the red basket that will house her collection: she lays it at the bottom of the tall basket "as if lowering it into a grave."[43] When she reencounters it fifteen years later in her endless sifting through the accumulated material in the basket, "she puts it in her lap and rocks it as if it is a stillborn child."[44] This reference to maternity triggers the reader's first encounter with the story of Haya's own loss: the theft of her son Antonio. And only then do we understand that the narrative of Haya's collection will not be complete without the repossession of the missing element: Antonio himself. It is Antonio's *lack* within the plot that makes us read on, and that makes Haya pursue her collecting impulse.[45] Her narrative motivation is driven by the desire to acquire the missing element in the story, yet paradoxically, it is the incompleteness of the collection ("the fact that it lacks something") that makes it a collection rather than "mere accumulation."[46] Antonio, as the missing item, is "an indispensable and positive part of the whole."[47] When he reappears at her apartment in Gorizia as Hans (the name he was given by his adoptive parents in Austria), the collection is complete and the novel concludes: the acquisition of the final object denotes the termination of the narrative. The final chapter, which recounts their meeting, is narrated in the future tense, as if, much as the start of the collection is a "false start,"[48] so too is the ending a matter of subjective determination. Indeed, Stewart describes the direction of force in the desiring narrative as taking place in the "future-past," since the deferment of experience travels backward toward the time of origin.[49] Absence allows for simulation to take place through processes of envisaging,[50] so conversely, presence denotes a violence that forecloses the possibility for imagination. The time of writing thus also precludes a false ending, a projection that takes us back to the start.[51]

Partway through gathering her collection, Haya learns the truth about how Antonio came to be stolen from her, and how the betrayal committed by the Catholic priest who had baptized Antonio in secret was part of a much more widespread involvement of the church in the mass kidnapping of Jewish children during the Second World War. She notes that in this moment "the red basket is empty. I have cleared out the years. I see the bottom. . . . Space has turned into time."[52] As James Clifford remarks, collecting presupposes a story, and that story occurs in a "chronotope."[53] The chronotope also characterizes the space of the museum, in which "time, as it were, thickens, takes on flesh, becomes artistically visible"; likewise, in both the museum and the novel, "space becomes charged and responsive to the movements of time, plot and history."[54] Within the fragmented temporality of Haya's collecting, History is—in plot terms—an active character in the novel. History possesses the ability to bend, stop, or sidestep time, creating an alternative discourse and temporal register to the events taking place concomitantly.

Collecting   29

> History decides to hide, to go underground for a spell. I need a break, says History, turns its back on the here and now, sweeps up all its rattles, leaving a huge mess behind, a hill of rubbish, vomit everywhere, and with a satanic cackle, witch-like, it soars heavenward.[55]

It is as if History is aligned with the time of the collection, and thus also with the time of the narrative, rather than tracking a coherent series of successive events in the past. History, here, is on the side of the reader, and creates a new version of chronological time that follows the line of the "syuzhet" rather than the "fabula." In an analogous way, time is subordinated to stuff in the system of the collector: time is displaced into a *pastime*.[56]

The reason why this is significant is that the collection and the narrative now compose the history that remains to us. As Didier Maleuvre points out, museums claim as historical that which survives history,[57] and they package that history into a neatened narrative. "History is served on a platter in a tidy fashion, sifted, polished, compressed into the grains that roll around noiselessly on the stone floors of San Sabba."[58] The history of the twentieth century in this northeastern corner of Italy is somehow disrupted by the lingering presence of incomplete personal stories and now ownerless object collections—objects such as the three paper sacks of ash and human bone left behind by the fugitive Nazis in the Risiera that evidenced the serial murder there, and the collections of items that were confiscated from their victims.

> The Allies find trunks and jute sacks full of stolen goods which they had spent two years eagerly collecting—sent off to Rome to languish for fifty years. Oh, there are all sorts of things in these sacks and trunks: watches, spectacles, combs, jewellery—rings, brooches, chains; there are powder compacts, pipes, beautiful pipes; there is money and bonds, furniture, bank books, insurance policies, silver, there are paintings, carpets, clothing, a lot of clothing, bedding, bicycles, typewriters, cameras; there are large wheels of Parmesan cheese, toothbrushes, tableware, fine porcelain—all of it nothing more than patches, debris, shreds of lives no longer living, of lives of those deported to Auschwitz, Buchenwald, Dachau, Mauthausen, Ravensbrück and San Sabba.[59]

Material evidence such as this acts as an uncomfortable foil to the records of history, which, in Thomas Bernhard's words, are "all falsified, and always transmitted in falsified form."[60] The International Red Cross sends Haya a Christmas card every year, but is unable to reunite her with her lost son.[61] Haya initially begins forming her basket archive in 1976, at the time of the Risiera trials. Yet by then, only two "big fish" remain to be accused, of whom one dies the year before the trials start, and the other is sentenced in absentia

30   Chapter 1

since he cannot legally be extradited from his comfortable home in Austria. In both Haya's and Hans-Antonio's experience, parsing the evidence contained in lists and biographies of victims and perpetrators is as pointless as "grabbing at dry dandelion fluff," or "catching eiderdown in a warm wind. . . . Forgotten dossiers, sealed archives open slowly, slowly, and what emerges is no more than water dripping from cracked sewer pipes."[62]

History records this same agonized impulse to collect in different stages through the narrative. Perhaps the first sign could be seen in the early Nazi obsession with object collecting through systematic art theft, which was inspired—as Monika Ginzkey Puloy states—by the historical example of Napoleon.[63] Through highly organized actions of confiscating and looting, the vision of the Nazi elite was to rearrange the contents of the museums, art galleries, and private collections of Europe and beyond.

> The mad grandeur of the whole thing, which envisaged nothing less than a complete redistribution and reorganization of Europe's peoples and their patrimonies, is impressive. In the purified New Order all would be perfect and homogenous. Undesirable thoughts, sounds, images, and beings would be eliminated. Then everything would be magnificently organized, efficient, and clean, classified and arranged in the gleaming new cities, to the Glory of Germanism.[64]

As well as eliminating degenerate art and creating new "supermuseums" filled with Aryan collections in Hitler's chosen cities of the new Germany, other modes of collecting (by force) and classifying objects saw the mass transit of confiscated goods across Europe, some transiting in warehouses at the Trieste harbor.[65] As the war closed in around Hitler's dream of a Nazi supermuseum in Linz, Allied advances "resulted in the ruthless rampage and shunting around Europe of art collections, first to repositories, to safe underground mines, snatched from incorporation into the Russian Zone," until they reached Central Collecting Points where restitution processes could begin.[66] This mania of degenerate collecting left an overwhelming material legacy not only in the infamous stores of Altausee and Neuschwanstein but also in the obsessive, excessive documentation of atrocities committed. The archives of the International Tracing Service in the central German town of Bad Arolsen are described as a "vast collection of documented horror" which "preserves the patches, the fragments, the detritus of 17 million lives on 47 million pieces of paper"; a "baroque palace" that "preserves, cleans, cleanses, fine-tunes in its belly a city of paper, a paper city, a papier-mâché model of Europe, of life, of compacted tragedies, gigantic tragedies squashed into yellowed slips of paper."[67]

The Nazi obsession with amassing and classifying collections is pushed to its conceptual limits by Elsner and Cardinal, who propose that the Holocaust itself functions as a collection of victims:

Differentiated by a specious scientific classification that was then cor-
roborated by a zealous bureaucracy. In its ambition to achieve its
own perfect "set," to install the absolute of the master race, the Third
Reich, in a monstrous parody of connoisseurship, exerted god-like
mastery (over what didn't fit) and through parallel processes of labelling and denigration made a negative definition synonymous with a
decree of extinction. The Holocaust is collecting's limit case.[68]

The aftereffects of this zealous ideological overclassification have negated the
initial desire for totalitarian elimination. Too much has been carefully preserved.[69] Alongside Bad Arolsen, other archives across Germany and Austria
hold the devastating evidence of planned genocide. The Office in Ludwigs-
burg is described as the "brain, a paper memory, a bureaucratic memory of
the Nazi past," where "lost lives huddle in steel cabinets."[70] The Berlin Fed-
eral Archive is the largest Nazi archive in existence, with over fifty million
pages of evidence registered. Hans-Antonio visits Gmunden with Thomas
Bernhard to see Schloss Oberweis, once known as Alpenland, where stolen
Lebensborn children such as he were housed, processed, and redistributed.[71]
Hans's own collection is testament to the uncanny persistence of stuff: "Old
photographs, unfinished manuscripts, hidden diaries surface; archives open,
movies are made, books are written, the pebbles of history roll underfoot and
in time our step grows less steady."[72]

But despite careful preservation, practices of overaccumulation will inevitably lead to rot and decay, something that will be explored in more detail in
chapter 5 in relation to Olga Tokarczuk's novel *Flights*. Within the narrative
of *Trieste*, Hans-Antonio variously describes History as muck or fecal matter
that endlessly reappears despite attempts to flush it away, and as a disease
endemic to the blood and brains of the second generations.[73] The vocabu-
lary of decay is repeated through imagery of overripe fruit—"rotten cherries
from which worms inch"—and the past is envisioned as a "fat, dead cat."[74]
This is an important signal that Hans-Antonio's collecting functions differently to Haya's: he is not looking for her (as she is for him), but for himself.
Hans risks converting his collecting into the pathology of hoarding: in calling
pieces of evidence his "treasures," he reveals that the objects are no longer
assigning added value to him as their collector, but that the value he places
on them himself has become overdetermined.[75] This type of disordered collecting signals a regression to the anal stage of psychic development, where
behavioral patterns of accumulation, ordering, and aggressive retention seek
to allow the collector-hoarder to "exercise control over the outer world."[76]
Every object accumulated adds to the extension of the self, since, as Baudrillard remarks, "it is invariably oneself that one collects."[77] The self becomes
fetishized as Hans-Antonio's story diverges and he assigns the things in his
collection "the power to fixate or disconcert rather than simply to edify or
inform."[78] In order to recuperate the materiality of a lost past that belongs

32 Chapter 1

only to him, Hans-Antonio seeks to convert evidence into souvenirs, thereby moving history into private time and enveloping the present within the past.[79] As Susan Pearce has demonstrated, souvenirs

> make public events private, and move history into the personal sphere. . . . They are an important part of our attempt to make sense of our personal histories, happy or unhappy, to create an essential personal and social self centred in its own unique life story, and to impose this vision on an alien world.[80]

Hans-Antonio's desire to achieve coherence of his life narrative through the accumulation of stuff mirrors the collecting impulse of the museum. Gaynor Kavanagh remarks that "the museum form has given rise to various means of codifying the past, of organizing the physical evidence of human existence and experience."[81] This is the creation of a symbolic world that can be arranged and rearranged according to principles of play. In this way, history is replaced with classification, "with order beyond the realms of temporality."[82] As Hans-Antonio's and Haya's narrative collections merge in the concluding pages of *Trieste*, they have achieved their aim of transforming temporality into a spatial, material phenomenon. It is the novel itself that affords the necessary framing, that marks the narrative with a beginning and end. Narrative plotting, much like the stages of procedural collecting, reframes objects and materials "within a world of attention and manipulation of context."[83] The book itself is a miniature world, a microcosm, which can finalize and bring closure to this painful history. Within *Trieste*, this framing is symbolized by the object container of Haya's basket, and the reach of the story folded into its collection is determined by its demarcating boundaries.

But although the novel brings its own sense of closure to a story, the finalizing motions of organizing and classifying things carry risks, as we have seen. In the museum, "the ordering and labelling of exhibits risks tidying away the past: the knick-knacks of memory settled into a convenient space."[84] And in personalized, museum-making practices, we replicate categorization in our own histories in order to try and sort and make sense of our own histories.[85] We need to pay close attention to the sophisticated methods employed by museums in order not to "present the 'facts,' but rather to find ways to educate visitors about the very nature of facts."[86] We have the responsibility to use material culture in both narrative fiction and museums not as evidence but in order to ask questions about the nature of evidence and to identify new questions about the past. Museums have enacted adjustments in their telling of the past that can help us achieve this: "the event giving way to action, story to episode, the diachronic to synchronic, sequence to structure and relationships."[87] Alongside this, we must also acknowledge the agency of objects, their sometime resistance to collection, and any stubbornness at being narrativized. As Marilyn Strathern reminds us, "There is no master narrative.

Collecting 33

We must learn to perceive others and their artefacts as non-collectible. The reason is that nothing is discrete: no single label will do. On the contrary, everything seems hybrid, subversive, partial."[88]

Conclusion: Collecting Clues

Trieste has often been described as "documentary fiction," an "unnecessary classification" that Drndić herself chafed against. "As I see it, literature is a mélange of experienced events, proven facts, and 'invented' detail which exploits language that is supposed to give it flavour, depth, spice it up, mold it, Botoxize it."[89] And indeed, there are clues in the narrative that ask the reader not to place too much authority in accumulated facts, in material evidence, or in detail, as I myself discovered when I took the train from Trieste to Gorizia to walk through the narrative spaces of the novel. The train ride is beautiful. You pass along the Adriatic coast to the Hapsburg castle of Miramare, and if you are lucky you will spot the raised ramparts of the fortress at Monfalcone before the train line travels up through the Karst. The earth is shrubby, flat, and rocky. The train snakes close to and then away from the Slovenian border. Low, white houses, each with well-tended vines growing in their small gardens, flank either side of the tracks. Freight trucks go in and out of sight, moving goods from country to country. You can see war monuments, cypress trees, and Italian flags flying proudly as you approach the Isonzo river. There are old agricultural buildings, cemeteries, and high, gray clouds. The land is thickly forested.

Gorizia itself is eerily quiet when I arrive. It smells strongly of pine, and the vibrating chorusing of cicadas is the only sound I hear when I disembark at the station. There is a memorial to the Jewish deportees from the town that is written in Italian, Slovenian, and Hebrew, and which lists the concentration camps of Dachau-Buchenwald-Auschwitz-Mauthausen-Flossenburg-Ravensbrück-Risiera di San Sabba as if they were sinister stops on a forgotten train line. It is hot and breezy; chestnut trees line the Corso d'Italia. The Parco di Rimembranza is empty, graveled, and now looks a little unloved. I notice elegant older ladies walking along the shade of the sidewalks: one is lithe and sinuous with her hair teased up into a high bouffant and wears oversized sunglasses. Another, dressed all in black, walks slowly, arm in arm with a man who may or may not be her son. She has very clear eyes. I imagine them as Haya and Hans-Antonio.

Gorizia disorients me and I forget what I have come here to do. I sit with an iced Campari and soda at the Caffé del Teatro and try to regain my bearings. Distracted, I ask the waitress where to have lunch, and she directs me to a cool courtyard where they serve local dishes of goulash, mlinci, and gnocchi, with ice-cold Tokaj wine and Kaiser-Wasser ("l'acqua minerale dell'Imperatore"). The Hapsburg Empire lives on in Gorizia. Another elderly

Fig. 4. View of Via Aprica, Gorizia. Photograph by Emma Bond.

couple take their seats at the table next to me: the lady is dressed all in white with an elaborate, decorative necklace; her companion is louche in an unbuttoned military khaki shirt and aviator glasses. A trolley comes around with a whole grilled fish waiting to be filleted in front of them. I leave the restaurant, somewhat reluctantly, looking for map points that will ground the story of *Trieste* in this place. I look for the site where Haya's shop stood. I may or may not have found it. I take a picture and move on. It is so hot in the early-afternoon sun that I am the only person walking around the town. There is no view, no sight of the horizon or the castle that I know is there but never appears. I fail to reach the Isonzo. From Piazza Transalpina I walk down again through the main square and past the twin domes of Sant'Ignazio, looking for via Aprica. I want to see where Haya waited for Antonio all those years, at her apartment at number 47.

To my surprise, via Aprica is a modern-looking road in a southern suburb of the town (fig. 4). Its houses are mainly square, two-story, all with gardens. It is quiet. A black cat walks slowly down the street while children play nearby. The street numbers stop at 35. Haya's apartment is described in *Trieste* as being "on the third floor of an Austro-Hungarian building in the old part of Old Gorizia."[90] This description has no place here. It is missing, a false referent. I sit down on the sidewalk in the shade and smile. Collections

Collecting   35

of objects found in museums and novels alike are revealed to be narrative constructions, and the fictions they generate can work to supplement history when the rotten remains of the past cannot be salvaged otherwise. And yet as often as these objects can help us to assemble a desirable plot of events, they can equally work to destabilize any understanding of History as a set of objective facts. It is more accurate to say that object collections allow us to rediscover a sense of order and coherence on a personal, individual level through permitting us mastery in our manipulations of stuff. In this way, narrative replaces history as the collection assumes its own autonomy in a process of salvage association. Time is dislodged from a strict linearity and freed up to follow the logic of these narrative collections, both in museums and examples of literary fiction such as *Trieste*.

Chapter 2

Curating

Introduction

In spring 2021, the Victoria and Albert Museum in London announced a series of proposed changes to its operational running in order to make up for the crippling loss of revenue it had suffered during the COVID-19 pandemic. Although substantial job cuts were involved, what caused much more dismay in the media and in international art circles was the radical reconfiguration of its curatorial departments being put forward.[1] The V&A had previously organized its collections (and curatorial teams) on the basis of material specialism: for example, in furniture, ceramics, or textiles. What the current director now planned was the replacement of these departments by "cross disciplinary teams" focusing on time period or geography. There would be three departments for European and American collections (organized into "Medieval to Revolution," "The Long Nineteenth Century," and "Modern and Contemporary"), one merged "Asia and Africa" department, and a new department of born digital material, design, and performance. The resulting media and sector-wide uproar was so great that the idea of a curatorial reshuffle was quietly shelved little more than a month after the proposals had been made public. But the suggested changes reveal a great deal about how the museum functions as a meaning-making space, and what we can learn about the mechanics of literary scaffolding from how museum structures are organized. Material histories, in the museum, can be arranged and rearranged according to shifting criteria and interventions that come from either inside or outside the institution. In the case of the V&A, the organization of the histories on display was slated to change from a material categorization to a mix of temporal periodization and geographical mapping. A seventeenth-century perfume sprinkler from Murano, Venice, would no longer be curatorially understood within the context of the other objects in the Glass Room, which shows the development of glassblowing techniques from the earliest specimens to the present day. It would now fall into the temporal remit of the "Medieval to Revolution" team and be conceptually separated from any earlier glass pieces and from colorful contemporary designs.

37

I do not mean to discount the possibility that exciting cross-media comparisons between pieces in the V&A collections would have emerged from the curatorial reshuffle. I am simply more interested here in the way the proposed changes reveal the museum's ability to arrange and rearrange objects into different groupings through curatorial activity, thereby changing the stories we tell and receive about human history. Thinking spatially about how museums tell stories about the past, and their dynamic ability to change the organization of those stories even when using the same primary materials, also gives us curatorial insight into how stories themselves work. In so doing, it aligns with some of the mapping techniques and spatialization theories that have galvanized and distinguished the field of contemporary world literature theory. As Hans Ulrich Obrist has written, using spatial terms that would not seem out of place in a critical text on world literature, curating is about connecting cultures, making junctions, and creating zones that allow for contact. "You might describe it as the attempted pollination of a culture, or a form of map-making that opens new routes through a city, a people, or a world."[2] This chapter will use Claudio Magris's 2015 novel *Non luogo a procedere*, which was translated as *Blameless* by Anne Milano Appel and appeared in Yale's prestigious Margellos World Republic of Letters book series in 2017, as a primary lens of interpretation through which to examine the narrative activity of curating. Reading *Blameless* as a work of world literature allows me to expand on the concept of "curating worlds" that gives this book its title, and to contextualize my own theoretical work within the critical world-making practices elaborated by critics such as Pheng Cheah, Wai Chee Dimock, Debjani Ganguly, Franco Moretti, and Rebecca L. Walkowitz.[3] I will begin this chapter by situating curatorial activity within this world literature framework and alongside the attention paid by critics to the varied spatial arrangement of stories. I will then turn my attention to literary aspects of the figure of the curator: to descriptions of the curator as an author, editor, or even a translator of object meaning. This will necessitate giving a brief history of how our understanding of curating has shifted and changed over the centuries, and what this history can tell us about curating as a contemporary world-making activity. One of the curator's chief tasks is to be an exhibition maker, and I will pay special attention throughout to museum studies texts that allow us insight into spatial considerations of storytelling through, for example, the mapping of different routes through rooms and displays, and the options available to the curator for the use of various interpretation aids.

Paul O'Neill, for example, explains how exhibitions bring "temporary forms of order" to a chosen moment in history, thus functioning as "'time capsules' in which the particular choices of the curator are fixed as a group."[4] This curatorial work of construction is laid bare for the reader in *Blameless*. The novel tells the story of an unnamed individual whose character is based on the true-life story of Professor Diego de Henriquez, a brilliant, eccentric Triestine who dedicated his whole life to collecting weapons and military

Curating

material of all types in order to build an original, overflowing War Museum for Peace (which actually exists in Trieste today, the Museo Henriquez della Guerra per la Pace).[5] The novel, however, is told from the perspective of the woman who has been brought in to plan and curate the museum, Luisa Brooks. The accumulation of objects means that the chapters open with Luisa struggling with the potential layout of particular rooms, where to place different objects, and how she can use those objects to tell a story of war that will lead to peace. She tries to envision "the sequence of the pieces, the use of icons on the monitors, the guiding theme through the program, the objects and the stories that spring from them like genies from Aladdin's lamp."[6] But Luisa's curatorial work in the museum is also interwoven with her attempts to construct and to reconstruct her own fractured family history. Her mother was a Triestine Jew who met her African American father during his military service at the local aeronautical base after the end of the Second World War. Her grandmother Deborah had died during the war in the Risiera di San Sabba, Italy's only territorial concentration camp, the same former rice mill in Trieste that forms the backdrop of Daša Drndić's eponymous novel, analyzed in chapter 1. But Deborah was accused of having denounced people she knew were protecting Jews to the authorities, and was therefore potentially guilty of multiple deaths, as well as being a victim of the same fate herself. Deborah's daughter, Sara (Luisa's mother), is left traumatized by the unanswered questions in her family history and disappears from Luisa's recollections as she slides further into depression following the accidental death of her husband on the runway of the base at Aviano.

Just as Luisa will never know for sure whether her grandmother did in fact betray the hiding places of other Jewish family and friends, Henriquez does not live to see the dream of his museum take flesh. He dies in 1974, in a fire in the storerooms where he has taken to sleeping in a coffin, a fire that also destroys the notebooks he claims to have filled with the names he copied down from graffiti on the walls of the Risiera. These are names that would have implicated people in the horrors of Nazi-Fascist violence and mass murder, people who are still circulating freely in Trieste at the time of his death, since the first trials only took place there in 1976. Luisa agonizes over how to represent these missing materials.

> To begin with, they could erect a wall in the Museum . . . , a wall entirely plastered with blank sheets of paper, at least to show that there was something missing . . . and then, right after that, to accentuate the contrast and emphasize the disturbing absence of those notebooks even more, display all the papers and countless objects, even the insignificant ones, that he had begun to collect and save at the age of eight.[7]

Salvage and destruction are the two poles that arrange and rearrange the history Magris assembles through his museum rooms in the novel, around the absence of Henriquez's missing notebooks: "Their absence will in any case have to be the nucleus, the core of the Museum, Luisa thought with angry determination; their disappearance is the key, the strong point of the entire thing."[8] The walls of the Risiera are whitewashed over in time, and the camp's structure itself transformed into today's historic monument and museum. But something remains precisely through the obliteration of human life, and through the destruction of evidence, that implicates future generations in acts of fragmented postmemory of absence, and that is nurtured by acts of "imaginative investment, projection, and creation."[9]

The "non luogo" [non-place] of the book's title may originally refer in Italian legal terminology to a lack of grounds for pursuing criminal charges, but it too draws attention to the fact that absences count, and that whole stories can be constructed around what absence indicates.[10] The Risiera names are missing, but Luisa finds a page from one of Henriquez's notebooks that has not been completely torn out, "where part of a drawing remains, copied—the note says—from the wall opposite cell number 8."[11] It shows half a face in profile, an "unremarkable" face, "urbane and generic."[12] Henriquez is convinced that the half portrait is drawn by an inmate prisoner of the camp and that it conceals the identity of a murderer, a spy, or an informer. He tries in vain to complete it in various ways. In the museum-novel, Luisa engages technology to continue his work:

> Room no. 31 – On the upper part of the large white wall facing those who enter, an enlarged projection of the torn page with the half-face. At the bottom, on the left, a computer screen that attempts to reconstruct the entire face, constantly correcting it.[13]

It doesn't really matter whether the computer momentarily alights on the "right" face (who would know?), just as it isn't important in narrative terms in which room of the museum Luisa Brooks decides to place the various machines and weapons that Henriquez has collected. What matters is the work of elaboration that her curatorial thinking lays bare—work that aligns the world-making activity in this museum-novel with Dan Hicks's notion of object necrographies (as opposed to biographies) as death-histories, histories of loss, "in which the museum will variously dismantle, repurpose, disperse, return, re-imagine, and rebuild itself."[14] Here, the museum ceases to function as a place of memory, and becomes a non-place which is "never totally completed": a palimpsest "on which the scrambled game of identity and relations is ceaselessly rewritten."[15]

Curating World Literature

In essence, both museums and novels are in a constant process of creating and re-creating their own world, if we understand the "world" in world literature

Curating

to be a personally constructed constellation of meaning: a type of world-making activity that allows us to imagine a world. Pheng Cheah has argued that the world itself has a "literary structure," and the structures of literary form "enact the opening of a world."[16] Literary and, I would add, museum space and time are, in Wai Chee Dimock's words, "conditional and elastic: their distances can vary, lengthen or contract, depending on who is reading and what is being read."[17] The operation of narrative building based on interpretation in both spaces is an active, contemporary one, allowing both the museum visitor and the reader of the novel to cross temporal dimensions as well as to span impossible spatial distances within one single microcosm. Where else—other than the museum or the novel—could you travel easily between all the continents of the world in a space the size of a storage box, or a book? Space and time are "operational effects," then, that "derive their lengths and widths from the relative motion of the frames in which measurements are taken."[18] This is why the active role of the reader or the visitor in the interpretation of the material on display becomes such a key factor in the process of making meaning. World literature is also (and not least) a mode of reading, as David Damrosch has emphasized: it involves a human surplus or supplement of world making.[19] This framing of the act of reading as an active process seeks to interrogate the nature of the "worldedness" of the text, its "world-desire." But it also speaks to the ambition of the critic of world literature, where the world "remains in the equation as a marker of scale, a figure for the relationship between the method of discovery and the breadth of its applicability."[20]

Geography shapes world literature, then, and it particularly influences its narrative structure. Franco Moretti has shown how "maps bring to light the internal logic of narrative: the semantic domain around which a plot coalesces and self-organizes."[21] Furthermore, map *captions* (much like museum object labels) "sketch a further array of interpretative paths; towards a text, a critical idea, a historical thesis."[22] Moretti tracks plot action and character movement through, for example, mapping the beginnings and endings of nineteenth-century novels—often revealing quite a limited sphere of activity. More recently, Rebecca Walkowitz has added nuance to many of Moretti's ideas (proposing a shift from distant reading to close reading at a distance, for example), and in so doing, has altered how we understand the geographies of books. Walkowitz is not interested in mapping locations in narrative plots, or even in mapping narrative markets, but uses spatial analysis to show instead how the contemporary world novel builds transnational movement and translingual exchange into its very form, thereby becoming what she terms a "born translated" cultural object. This succeeds in "tipping the balance of literary history from writers to readers, from a language's natives to its users, and from single to multiple chronologies."[23] The born translated book as narrative object becomes understood as a multiple entity: "The way it relates to different objects in the same language, the same object in different languages, or objects of the same colour or size or location," thus becoming part of a network of meaning.[24] This is literature that seems to be "both an object and a collection of objects"—a narrative unit that can function, that is, like a museum collection, whether understood singly or as the sum of its parts.[25]

Walkowitz emphasizes the importance of the active input of the reader or visitor into the process of meaning making, and thus also the role of audiences "in the ongoing production of the work."[26] In multistranded novels such as many of the ones examined in this book, of which *Blameless* is a prime example, this means tracking the way the work "gather(s) materials from disparate geographies," thus developing "new models of accumulation."[27] Indeed, Diego Salvadori counts no fewer than fifty-three different narrative units within Magris's novel.[28] The reader needs a curator to manage this multistranded gathering in order for its overabundant collection to make sense. In Walkowitz's analysis, the author-curator here makes use of three specific devices in order to do so: sampling, collating, and counting. The sampling occurs in the representative nature of the different narrative strands, which use single examples to stand in for larger units. These strands then need to be arranged, or "collated," to use Walkowitz's term.

> I call the arrangement of these strands collating *because the multistranded novel curates as well as collects*. By segmenting and ordering strands, collating adds meaning rather than simply organizing it. In a novel, collating requires decisions about category and order. What are the principles of organization? How will each strand be arranged? And it also requires decisions about duration and interval. How many chapters or sections will each strand occupy? How frequently will each strand appear?[29]

This process of selection turns the object into a humanly defined museum piece through its "detachment from [its] natural context and organization into some kind of relationship with other, or different, material."[30] The curator is figured here as an author or editor of meaning. As curator Barnaby Drabble states, "Curating is a mode, not a simple question of display or production, curating is always authorial in some way."[31] This work is not individual, however, but relies on collaborative networks that put the curator at the "interface between artist, art institution, and audience in the development of critical meaning."[32] The work of curators is distributive, and they represent just one node in a network of creative activity. Gaynor Kavanagh points out that the museum holds a double function—as both the storage provider for a data bank of primary material, and as the interpreter or arranger of that material: "It is continually determining how the past should be seen, as much as by what it chooses to acquire and the depth of information recorded, as by what it chooses to leave out. The museum is an archive; the curator is its

Curating 43

editor."[33] Key here, then, is the curator's role in the selection and arrangement of collected materials. This signals a significant shift in emphasis from *Trieste* to *Blameless*, even when dealing with the same microhistory grounded in the common geographical marker of Trieste's Risiera. It is the curator Luisa who controls the narrative here—not the collector, Henriquez. The collecting has taken place prior to the narrative action, and even the notes he has written to accompany and narrativize each object will need to be rewritten. Henriquez in fact makes a plea for Luisa to rewrite his labels using the first-person singular.

> Moreover—given the revisions, scrawls, and erasures that, I know, make my papers almost illegible—I imagine that you will recopy them, transcribe them, in short, write them, and therefore it will be, it is you who write them, they are yours.[34]

And she does, in one instance copying his handwriting to add in passages he himself had noted but then erased.[35] This proactive work of interpretation looms large across all the strands of the narrative: Henriquez himself works as an interpreter in the later stages of the Second World War and carries messages between the fighting armies in Trieste. Often, he admits, "I would add something of my own or delete passages that might inflame tempers even more."[36] Luisa's mother, Sara, also works as an interpreter for the Allied Military Government, a role she enjoys because "when she translates, she leaves her own head and enters that of someone else."[37] The book's translator, Anne Milano Appel, further remarks on the presence of the theme of translation in *Blameless* in the translator's note, and cites Magris's belief that "the translator is a co-author" of the text.[38]

Magris's own role as author (or coauthor) sees him function as both a collector of stories and as one responsible for their selection, arrangement, and mediation. As indicated above, the novel is notable for the insertion of multiple different stories within the frame of the main narrative that span centuries and continents beyond the world of twentieth-century Trieste: stories of figures such as the ethnologist Albert Vojtěch Frič, Luisa de Navarrete, the Black Pearl of the Caribbean, Emperor Maximilian of Mexico, Cherwuish the Chamacoco visitor to Prague, and Otto Schimek. The accuracy of detail included in these cameo appearances reflects my own experience of encountering Magris's historical research in the preparatory notes and drafts of his preceding novel, *Alla cieca* [*Blindly*], which he has deposited in the archives of the University of Pavia's Centro Manoscritti.[39] During my visits to the center in the autumn of 2021, I was handed huge, bulging folders full of pages scrawled with Magris's terrible handwriting, often on loose sheets headed with the insignia of the Senato della Repubblica. I imagined Magris jotting notes as he sat in endless voting sessions as a senator, or his mind drifting as he sat in meetings and dreamed of his characters. I gave silent thanks

44   Chapter 2

when notes had been typewritten, or articles photocopied and included in the files. Photography is strictly not allowed in the center, so I dutifully copied down all the lists and notes I could decipher: notes and letters from libraries and collaborators in London, Copenhagen, Warsaw, and Hobart, Tasmania, and cuttings in at least seven different languages (German, Danish, English, Portuguese, French, Italian, and Croatian).

As evidenced by this cornucopia of detail and scope, *Blindly* shares *Blameless*'s complex, multistranded structure: zoning both in and outward from the central story of Jørgen Jørgensen's life and travels. Jørgensen (1790–1841) was a Danish naval officer, the first Dane to circumnavigate the globe, self-declared king of Iceland, a prolific writer who spent years in prison in England, and latterly a colonial police officer in Tasmania. The protagonist of *Blindly*, a communist asylum inmate named Cippico, believes himself to be Jørgensen. To this complex, unstable biography, Magris weaves histories of Italian emigration to Australia, population exchanges in Istria, digital texts and cyberpunk, and descriptions of native Brazilian vegetation in the states of Santa Caterina and Recife. In one note present in the archive, Magris writes:

> Jørgen's life is an endless bibliography; incomplete and unreliable. His written works vary in tone, they shift, and rewrite themselves continuously. They are condensed into a title, then expand into an introduction to a work that is never written, or one that is reformulated soon after, reworked into a version that completely alters the original meaning, or reintroduced in a cycle of unfinished or even unstarted works.[40]

Links with the material Magris uses in *Blameless* abound: there are several mentions in both novels of the merchant Willem Bolts (who worked for the British East India Company) and his links with the ill-fated Imperial Asiatic Company of Trieste, which he established with the approval of the Hapsburg empress Maria Theresa in 1776. Even Henriquez is mentioned in a section of notes on collections of ship figureheads. Jorgensen's life bears similarities to Magris's fictional depiction of Henriquez, and both testify to the author's fascination with prolific, baroque accumulators of stories, adventures, and objects. The files spill outward with these stories, they exceed categorization, they cry out for an editor or a curator to help them make sense. Catalogued in the archive, the pages are presented in ways that suggest the author once anticipated the future interest of scholars and readers: sections are cut out, corrected in a different color, crossed out, or removed and then Sellotaped back in. The tape is yellowed and curling, showing how long ago the editorial intervention must have taken place. There is a dynamism in this overabundance, and in the curation of its details. Leaving sources open uncovers how the author has constructed his narrative, and furthermore shows "how those meanings might change in the future" as the book (or the archive folder)

Curating

passes from reader to reader: a nod to Walkowitz's observation that while "monuments fix, narratives unfold."[41]

Narratives of Curating

Today, "curating" is a term one hears everywhere: its meaning is being constantly extended to refer to the creation of playlists, menus, and lifestyle experiences. Terry Smith ruefully points out that nowadays "the title of curator is assumed by anyone who has a more than minimal role in a situation in which something creative might be done."[42] The complexity of the discussion around the definition and role of the contemporary curator demands that we take a step backward in time to examine the development of the current all-encompassing scope of curatorial activity and see where and how it aligns with literary production. Without this understanding of how curating has developed, we run the risk of decontextualisation, of falling prey to "the amnesia of curatorial history."[43] In the age of what David Balzer has termed "curationism," can anyone self-describe as a curator?[44] Beryl Graham and Sarah Cook have posited that given the current popularity of collecting anything, from music to Barbie dolls, and the proliferation of web-based technologies that help collectors to collate and curate their possessions, "then it can be argued that blogging, linking, and bookmarks are the raw starting materials of 'selection'."[45]

But curating is not just a process of selecting: it also requires interpretation that is enacted as a caretaking event, especially when objects recall difficult or traumatic histories. As Erica Lehrer and Cynthia E. Milton say, curating difficult knowledge is "a kind of intimate, intersubjective, interrelational obligation."[46] It is the task of the curator to support museum and gallery visitors through tactics of display, interpretation, and custodial care. Museums should be discouraged from absolving themselves from any interpretative responsibility in favor of the visitor's free choice, as such a stance may lead to "whatever" interpretation.[47] Objects can be used to tell all sorts of different stories, and it is up to the curator to decide which one to tell, and how to do so in a responsible manner. Exhibitions are "constructions," "representations," and "interpretations" of the past: a version of the past, not the past itself. "The stories we tell ourselves about ourselves are institutionalized and materialized in museums."[48] But this still requires input from audiences: indeed, Sarah Longair has explained how increased community engagement in the museum sector has shown "how curators learn from their audiences and use their skills as communicators and wider contextual understanding to bring objects to life."[49]

In order to analyze the curatorial activity in evidence in *Blameless*, we need to wind back briefly to the start of the history of curating. Balzer recalls the original use of "curate" in the times of the Roman Empire as the name used for "bureaucrats responsible for various departments pertaining to public works."[50] In the Middle Ages, the curate (or parish priest) took on a religious function, but his role maintained its previous focus on care, concern, and responsibility. Only in late Middle English did the word take on a related sense of healing, or cure, and thereby also acquired "a more powerful ability to transform."[51] "Curate" became an active term in the precursors to museums, those private collections of art and other curiosities that were fashionable from the sixteenth century onward, and it designated someone who cared for the objects on display in cabinets and chambers. The major shift in its meaning took place over the course of the second half of the twentieth century: from an emphasis on a profession dedicated to scholarship and collections management, it has come to mean creating exhibitions and curating the audience experience. "In the last thirty years, to put it simply, curatorial practice has changed 'from caring to creating.' "[52] This new emphasis on the creative elements of the role adds nuance to the idea of curator as an editor with authorial rights relating only to selection and arrangement. Curating here becomes a "cross-cultural method," where the emphasis is on "practices of translation (as world-making), enactment and performance of culture."[53] This idea of curation as translation is reinforced by James Clifford:

> If you consult "curator" and "curate" in a dictionary, you find that they come from curare, which means to care for something. In the recent work of Donna Haraway on inter-species relations, the idea of caring ceases to be a practice of protecting by enclosing and becomes a profoundly relational activity of crossing and translating.[54]

But how do museums "translate" objects into meaning? What creative methods do they employ? Perhaps the most evident curatorial interventions to the museum visitor are to be seen in object labels and wall text. But, as Alison Grey, Tim Gardom, and Catherine Booth explain, the text on display is a secondary means of interpretation: "The text we see in a museum is not there to tell the story, it is there to support it. You are telling a story in three-dimensional space, with objects and pictures to help you."[55] This spatial arrangement of museum exhibitions as a three-dimensional story gives exciting insight into what narrative structure would look like "off the page," and the kind of interventions you might make in order to produce certain effects in the reader.

> When your display is finished, your visitor will "walk through" your narrative. They will physically start in one place and finish in another. For them, that will be the beginning and the end of your story. As they walk, certain pieces of information will be revealed. Structuring your storyline and the order and pace at which information is released needs to take into account the physical space.[56]

Curating 47

Grey, Gardom, and Booth then outline some "classic" ways of structuring a museum narrative: first, they mention the "intestinal" route, which denotes a prescribed order of walking past displays in a fixed, sequential narrative with strict chronology. The narrative unfolds through the exhibition, but leaves no option for comparative elements, and the visitors cannot go back around to look again. Then comes the "pinball" route, where the choice of the itinerary is left to individual visitors, who are free to explore the displays in whichever direction they please. The "there and back again" route allows visitors to exit the exhibition by going back past the first thing they saw: an object that they will now view differently, having experienced the rest of the displays in the meantime. Finally, the "hero in the middle" is an exhibit where everything refers back to single idea. The questions Grey, Gardom, and Booth pose to the reader who is looking to choose between these spatial storytelling options are revealing, almost mind-boggling for scholars of literature:

> Do visitors need to follow the story in a particular order, or can it be understood in any direction? Do they need to encounter key information at the beginning? Is chronology important? Are themes important and if so, do you want a more open structure that enables comparison? Can you weave stories together, giving visitors a choice on which to follow? Can you layer your stories so that at each stage in the narrative there are elements of fact, opinion, individual stories, and interactive or investigative material? Do you want to leave things open, or reach a conclusion?[57]

In *Blameless*, we enter the text via the museum lobby, with a description of the projected advertisement that Henriquez had placed in a local newspaper toward the end of his life: "Used submarines—bought and sold." The text speaks of his obsessive optimism for his project, the desire to double back on the issues facing him in the present (especially his debt, and a chronic lack of space for his collections), and to continue collecting just as he tries to part with objects. Luisa considers placing the words on a "large black screen, rippled by an indistinct flickering, the sound of water in the background," with his face looming in from the photographic background.[58] His reconstructed voice narrates the text of the advertisement, in front of a real-life Royal Navy U-boat from Henriquez's collection. "Entering the Museum the way you enter night, neon-lit promises; it could be a good idea, Luisa thought."[59] As readers, we then exit the text by following the visitor's route out of the museum at the end of the novel, most closely resembling the "there and back" method described above. "When you come to the last gallery, you turn back to exit, you retrace the route you followed earlier, rediscovering everything you thought you had left behind, and you leave through the same door from which you entered."[60] But this is not aimed at being an operation of discovery, or at triggering a process of realization. Rather, it functions to

48   Chapter 2

show how the museum itself is a construction aimed at reversing the passage of time: one whose aim is "to modify the past"; "to reverse time, reduce it to a one-way street."[61] This recalls Henriquez's own reclassification of death as an "inverter," "a machine that simply reverses life like a glove, but all you have to do is let time flow backward and everything is reclaimed. Time regained, the triumph of love."[62] The vast collections are props in a staging of this inversion of time, just as the museum itself is figured as a "mutable hypertext in which everything streams by or vanishes and is nullified."[63]

The plans Luisa describes in the novel are nothing more than a hypothesis, as the physical museum does not yet exist at the time of her writing. In her preparatory work, she discusses the rooms by number in chapters that interweave with her own family history and the cameos of other characters: she describes twenty-two of the rooms, to be precise, as well as the entrance lobby and the exit route. The order that she introduces them is nonchronological, though, going from—for example—room no. 15, to room no. 7, room no. 23, room no. 22, room no. 2, and room no. 11. Room no. 12 is the only one to be mentioned twice. However, the rooms mentioned span from 2 to 43, meaning that a further twenty-two rooms are not mentioned in the narrative. Half the museum remains silent, unnarrated in the text. The process of selection Luisa enacts here draws further attention to what isn't there and what is not on display, again recalling the missing evidence of the Risiera notebooks, of course, but also more broadly the dead spaces of museum stores where objects gather unwitnessed by visitors.

In Luisa's imagination, the objects of the collections on display are both organized by themes and animated by expensive, often fantastical-sounding special effects. Posters, leaflets, and other items of wartime propaganda are placed under a large glass bell in room no. 19 and animated at regular intervals by gusts of air produced by wind machines.[64] She envisages the museum as a sensory experience, and "was thinking of placing in room no. 17 the sweat of underwear that hasn't been changed for weeks in the trenches."[65] An air raid siren is to be placed just past the entrance in such a way "that those entering do not immediately notice it and are startled, frightened, when they hear the abrupt deafening wail and see a large clock suddenly light up before them."[66] Some displays are so complex that they appear more like art installations than object groupings, with little consideration for either conservation or textual support:

> Room no. 12 – A large panel under glass, mounted vertically on the wall. In the center, a reproduction of a banknote with the highest denomination in the world. A Hungarian banknote from 1946, in pengö. Around it, bills in other currencies. . . . Dollars, liras, florins, crowns, dinars, yen, yuan, dirhams, levas, leus, rubles, assignats issued during the French Revolution, huge sacks of paper spill into relevant trash bins, which quickly fill, the bills overflow, strewn about on the floor like garbage, the wind scatters them here and there.[67]

Curating 49

In these flights of conceptual fancy, Luisa enacts the final stage in the historical journey of the role of the curator that I have sketched out in this chapter. From an authorial position with editing rights of selection and arrangement, the curator shifted to a position akin to a translator who mediates cross-cultural meaning. Finally, as in *Blameless*, the curator-narrator becomes a mostly autonomous generator of content to which she also assigns value. The element of storytelling is present across all these modern iterations of curation, although the person assigned storytelling rights can still change. Contemporary creative "super curators," such as Harald Szeemann and Hans Ulrich Obrist, have enacted a shift in the visitor's experience of exhibitions from "a historical approach of order and stability via static displays, to a place of flux and instability, the unpredictable."[68] This open space brings a new understanding of the role audiences play in interpretation. Robert Storr's series of articles for *Frieze* magazine in 2005 built on Roland Barthes's essay "The Death of the Author" in order to reject the idea of curators having authorial intent and to propose new thinking along the lines of reader-response theory, in which "the unity of the text is not in its origin, it is in its destination."[69] Storr's argument leads us back to Walkowitz's affirmation that the reader's mind is the key site for the generation of plural literary meanings, meanings that are "far in excess of the original source."[70] In analogous ways, Cheryl Meszaros has advocated a turn toward constructivist learning theory in which the power of interpretation shifts to audiences, obliging curators to ask "what (and how) museum visitors may be learning."[71] In this model, curators will learn from visitors, and, as Nicholas Serota says, the museums of the future will be spaces in which "the story line becomes less significant and the personal experience becomes paramount."[72] The museum as conceived here becomes a space for Walkowitz's textual unfoldings, or even a space in which visitors are empowered to write their own scripts. As Paul O'Neill writes, "Rather than texts waiting to be read, exhibitions have the potential to activate discursive processes that enable dialogical spaces of negotiation between curators, artists, and their publics."[73]

Conclusion: Curatorial Narration

There is, of course, a considerable gap between the fictional representation of the museum in *Blameless* and the visitor experience of the real-life Museo Henriquez della Guerra per la Pace in Trieste. The entrance is eerily similar to Magris's vision, however, and features a real-life tank alongside a large-scale photograph of Henriquez wearing a white, hooded coat over a woolen hat, standing proudly in front of the same tank in the field of action. An introductory panel detailing Henriquez's life story and collecting mania leads the visitor into the story of twentieth-century war in the ground-floor gallery: war is figured as a moneymaking exercise, and the question is posed of who exactly profits from mass violence. The meanings and manifestations of war are curated into a picture of, variously: a capitalist venture, a colonial enterprise, and a political game. Propaganda posters stand next to warning signs used in army camps and on roads. Close attention is paid to the everyday life of soldiers, particularly in the trenches of northeastern Italy: their daily routines, operational mechanics, the chance to make craft through the creation of "trench art." Games of scale see enormous weapon carriers and tanks lined up in rows between display cases of smaller, quotidian objects in the vast space of the ex-hangar (fig. 5).

The museum narrative becomes more localized as you move up to the first floor. The focus is on Trieste and the city's experience of the two world wars: its territorial transfer from Austro-Hungary to Italy in 1919, its widespread adherence to fascism, the persecution of its Jewish and Slav populations during the time of the racial laws, and its eventual return to Italy after the period of the Allied Military Government in 1954. The personal story of Henriquez is also explored in more depth upstairs, with large displays dedicated to his role as soldier, collector, and interpreter. Reams of telegrams in different languages assert his right to move between and across enemy lines during the war, and jumbled collections of photos show the growing collections he housed in temporary, ramshackle plots of land. The last element displayed in the gallery is a selection of his notebooks, with mention of the "missing" notebooks that contained evidence of the identities of perpetrators and collaborators with those who ran the Risiera (fig. 6).

A notice at the end of the exhibition announces that the museum "will soon be completed" with the restoration of two additional buildings of the former barracks, in which to house and display more of the extensive collections. These are listed as: more than 100 military and civil vehicles; 2,766 weapons, 11,771 objects, 23,588 photographs, 287 diaries with 38,000 pages written by Henriquez himself, 12,000 inventoried books, 2,600 posters and leaflets, 500 prints, 470 maps, 30 archival holdings, 290 music sheets, 250 newsreels, and 150 paintings. No museum could ever display such holdings in one location, regardless of how extensive the space available is. Selections must be made in order to form a narrative that makes sense. The driving argument of this chapter has been that this eventual museum narrative will change and continue to change through the repeated future selections and arrangements made by its curators, and that the input of its visitors is fundamental in the ongoing cocreation of plot. As the curator character of Luisa in *Blameless* realizes:

> Every story, every text, every life . . . is a palimpsest, a page wiped clean so it can be written on again, always with the same story but superimposed on a previous one, writing that covers other writings with corrections difficult to read but not erased, it too destined to be retouched and rewritten but not completely obliterated.[74]

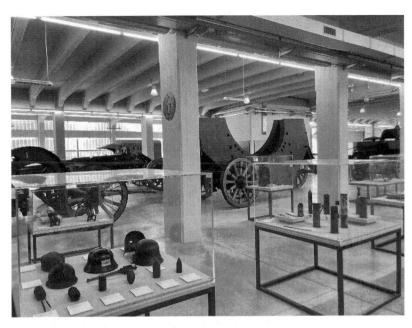

Fig. 5. Internal view of the ground floor, Museo Henriquez della Guerra per la Pace, Trieste. Photograph by Emma Bond. Courtesy of the Comune di Trieste.

Fig. 6. A selection of Henriquez's notebooks on display in the Museo Henriquez della Guerra per la Pace, Trieste. Photograph by Emma Bond. Courtesy of the Comune di Trieste.

Despite the optimism of the notice cited above, I would thus wager that the museum will never be completed, because this work of curation and interpretation must be active and ongoing in order to make its narrative meaningful. It is what stops the museum from becoming a mausoleum.[75] If the museum becomes fixed within one route of interpretation, we deactivate the lessons of trauma contained in material memories of war and violence, and we circumscribe objects, leaving them "well-guarded and isolated inside the armor of osseous cutaneous shields" that make up the "integument" of the display case.[76] When we see objects as static and fixed, but meaning as fluid and multiple, we furthermore run the risk of "deepen[ing] persistent colonial inequalities, repeat[ing] and exacerbat[ing] dehumanizations, reproduc[ing] and extend[ing] dispossessions."[77]

"Death is fitting for Museums," Luisa reflects, because exhibits are fixed as a "still-life" and the people who visit them are preparing for their own death in visiting them.[78] It is through the project of writing the stories of death and loss in the museum, which Hicks terms *necrography*, that signs of life can emerge through the "bringing to attention" of what is missing, of what has been lost. This necrography is a meticulous, archaeological method, which requires starting with the first layer and excavating downward, slowly, to find out what remains: even when what you do find is unstable, incoherent, or no longer there. It is the story of Otto Schimek that perhaps sums this up best within the multistranded universe of *Blameless*. Schimek was a young Austrian soldier globally celebrated for his refusal to shoot a group of Polish civilians in 1944, but his act of heroism collapses into myth under the weight of a lack of witnesses or evidence.

> All we found was a gun that didn't exist, that is, we didn't find anything. But how do you find a piece, even a tiny piece, of a story like Schimek's which doesn't exist yet and therefore cannot be verified or even corrected because you don't yet know what to look for to then be able to tell about it?[79]

Was Schimek really executed for refusing to murder civilians? And does the truth of the story matter to those who have chosen to celebrate his story: either as a pacifist, a rare Austrian war hero, or even as an anti-communist activist? Schimek's story is powerful for what it means to different segments of these communities, and little matters whether it is accurate or not. In *Blameless*, Luisa goes to visit the assistant of Martin Pollack and Christoph Ransmayr, authors of a 2013 article which sought to dismantle the myth of Schimek's heroism. Yet as the assistant tells her, "A story, too, is a world, one of several possible worlds; who knows how many such universes there are besides ours . . . a world, a story, with its chapters, its parts, its settings."[80]

Blameless is a narrative which centers absence, and which curates a multistranded narrative world around that absence. In showing the fallibility of

Curating 53

narrative, it reveals the power of storytelling, and specifically the meaning we invest in stories even as they shift and change. "Stories come and go, you find them in your pocket, who knows how, then they fall out of your pocket and you can't find them anymore."[81] Curators might have oversight of the production of some museum narratives, but this storywork is being more and more readily recognized as a collaborative process—a network of meaning making that involves material objects, curators, visitors, and beyond. In museums and novels alike, it would seem that we are all implicated in the narrative curation of worlds.

Chapter 3

Display

Introduction

The other chapters in this volume deal primarily with books which I have identified as using museum techniques to tell the stories of the object collections they amass within their pages. In my analysis, I myself have aligned these books with a series of museums and museum objects, but this act of critical juxtaposition is not necessarily intrinsic to their original design. The present chapter will inevitably be rather different, since it deals with a storytelling project that brings together a novel and a museum that were both created by the Turkish author Orhan Pamuk. The book and the museum share the same name (*The Museum of Innocence*) and aim to tell the same story. This unique pairing will allow me to unpick the differences between the two narrative modes, and ultimately to show how each mode alone is insufficiently equipped to tell a story that is so consciously composed of material objects. In narrating the story of an obsessive love affair through a collection of things, the novel employs a logic of display that I will term "deictic storytelling." But when the museum itself takes on the mantle of narration, and when the interpretative grid of the story thus plays out in spatial rather than temporal terms, we can use the exhibition narrative to shed light on the true complexity of a project which forms a multifaceted assemblage across multiple scales. In the museum, I identify elements of assemblage in the intricate construction of individual chapter-boxes, the coming together of all seventy-nine chapter-boxes into a spatialized story, the storied elements in the physical building, and its relations with the neighborhood and the city around it. This assemblage is then folded into a network made up of the novel, museum, catalogue, translations, merchandise, locations, and various human actors (including the author, translator, readers of the novel, museum visitors, and the craftspeople involved in the construction of the museum and its objects). My main analysis in this chapter will thus be directed at decoding this web of relationality so as to establish where and how a logic of narrative display is most effective in presenting a story made up of things. In order to do so, I will draw on elements of object-oriented philosophy and

56   Chapter 3

actor-network theory in the work of Graham Harman and Bruno Latour, in particular, but I will also engage with the collage philosophy of the midcentury American artist Joseph Cornell. Aligning Cornell with Pamuk highlights their shared skill in crafting storywork through the juxtaposition and display of gathered objects and offers new insight into the workings of a new narrative carpentry of things.

Pamuk's eighth novel, *Masumiyet Müzesi*, was published in Turkish in 2008, with an English translation by Maureen Freely released the following year. The museum, in the Istanbul neighborhood of Çukurcuma, opened in 2012; a map of its location and a ticket allowing free entry to anyone who comes with the novel in hand are both printed inside the book. The catalogue Pamuk authored for the museum, entitled *The Innocence of Objects*, tells the story of the design and philosophy of the exhibition in a series of photo essays; other angles of the story are covered in Grant Gee's 2015 film *Innocence of Memories*, which is in turn projected within the museum. The displays in the museum are also narrated by an audio guide voiced partly by Pamuk and partly by an actor voicing excerpts of the novel and the catalogue. These elements thus coalesce to form a dizzying intertextual kaleidoscope. I visited the museum one sunny September morning, walking from my guesthouse in nearby Karaköy and getting lost more than once in the maze of steep streets around the museum. The museum building at once reflects and amplifies its setting: painted a striking deep brick-red color, it occupies the corner position on a street that winds its way up toward Istiklal Avenue, facing dozens of junk and craft shops that spill over onto the narrow sidewalks and provide shaded space for street cats to sleep stretched out between baskets of rusty, discarded objects (fig. 7).

If I am honest, I found the experience of visiting the museum somewhat overwhelming. For the first time since starting work on this project, I didn't immediately know how to frame my analysis of this particular museum and book. The way that they were presented as offering two sides to the same narrative seemed to have been comprehensively achieved, and I felt worried about my ability to identify a fresh angle of study into the works of such a popular author. Upon leaving the museum building, I wandered straight into the junk shop opposite, staring at the objects piled high on shelves without really seeing any of them. On a whim, I bought three lots of passport-sized photographs in small plastic packets, on sale for the price of a few lira each (fig. 8). The meaning of these objects evaded me as I looked into the faces of a plump young woman with carefully groomed eyebrows and a sixties hairdo, a lady photographed with a child in beautiful, manicured gardens and then again leaning forward into the camera with a blurred cat in her arms, or a family posing midswim in the sea shallows. Why were they there, for sale, and not preserved in family albums, or half-hidden at the back of drawers or in stored trunks? Who would be interested in buying photographs of people they didn't know? And then, what stories could you construct around people

Display

Fig. 7. The Museum of Innocence, Istanbul. External view. Photograph by Emma Bond.

if you didn't know anything about their lives? In the end, keeping these photos close by as I drafted this chapter helped by providing me with a cast of unnarrated characters that I could use to mimic Pamuk's methodology as I turned back and forth from the "real" photo-objects in front of me to the potential stories of relationships, travels, and the objects that might have made up the lives of those represented in them.

As I work through this chapter, I will focus first and foremost on the novel, identifying instances of deictic storytelling to show how the book assumes the logic of object display to pace out the telling of the story. At intervals, I will turn to the narrative exhibition contained in the museum, noting how the museal space takes on the display of the plotline and how it disrupts its chronology to reveal instances of narrative insufficiency in the novel's handling of objects. I'm particularly interested in exploring the interconnections between

Fig. 8. Photographs. Photograph by Emma Bond.

time and space across the two storytelling modes of novel and museum, and I will return throughout to issues of modernity, memory, originality, and authenticity that motivate the narrative. We saw in chapter 1 of this book, on Daša Drndić's novel *Trieste*, that when objects are pursued and accumulated into a collection, they can function as trophies that signal a desire for possession through control. Here, on the other hand, objects refract the possibility of mastery and instead offer a conduit to memory through association. Yet it is precisely the act of display, which the protagonist encounters on his global tour of small museums toward the end of his life, that allows him to respond to his collected objects with pride rather than shame. Displaying these objects and sharing them with a public audience is, indeed, "the only way [he] could ever hope to make sense of those years," working through loss to reach a sense of partial self-fulfillment.[1] Rounding off this discussion of the logics of display, the final section of the chapter will introduce a new narrative element to Harman's theory of the carpentry of things,[2] which emerges once we place Pamuk's multifaceted artistry into conversation with the surrealist collage boxes created by Joseph Cornell. Elements of arrangement and assemblage come to the fore in my conclusions and will thereby offer insight into the object networks that underpin the logic of display in Pamuk's work.

Deictic Storytelling

Pamuk's fabricated network of stories revolves entirely around the romantic relationship between Kemal, a wealthy man in his thirties from a well-respected Istanbul family, and his distant relative, an eighteen-year-old girl named Füsun whom he meets when she is working in a local clothes

Display 59

boutique. The supposed veracity of this story is maintained across the various narrative modes: the novel, the museum, and its audio guide, and is bolstered by the presence of Pamuk within all three. The novel is narrated by the character Kemal, but Pamuk himself is introduced as a minor character early on, and Kemal's choice to entrust the telling of his story to Pamuk is covered in some detail at the end of the novel, when Pamuk the writer-character switches to a first-person account of the museum's construction and Kemal's death. Tracy Ireland has commented on how this "ambiguous presence" of Pamuk in the text, as well as his "curatorial and creative hand in the museum, interweaves the speculative with the autoethnographic, the fictional with memory, and the personal with the political."[3] This deceit that blurs the boundaries of fiction is repeated in the narrative of the displays, the catalogue, and the audio guide. More importantly, perhaps, the thin line between invention and reality is similarly tested in the shifts in Pamuk's own perspective on the relationship between the museum and the novel. On the one hand, he suggests that he wants the two to function as separate, individual entities (as he says, "The museum is not an illustration of the novel, and the novel is not an explanation of the museum"[4]); on the other, he maintains that they are inextricably linked in telling the same story. The question of which holds interpretative primacy thus triggers a set of discourses on originality which in turn affects the perception of the "authenticity" of the objects on display. In the catalogue, Pamuk states that he "wanted to collect and exhibit the 'real' objects of a fictional story in a museum and to write a novel based on these objects."[5] His initial idea was for the novel to be "an annotated museum catalogue": a book in which "I would describe an object to a reader as if I were presenting it to a museum visitor" and in which he would then go on to detail the memories and emotions that the object evoked for his characters.[6] Yet, as Pamuk started to draft the manuscript (and to collect the associated objects), he decided that the catalogue format did not allow him enough space to narrate the emotional lives of his characters and so resolved to write the story "in the form of a classic novel."[7]

This set of open-ended statements leaves us with a lot of latitude in how we can approach and interpret Pamuk's establishment of the narrative across the museum and novel formats. Since they follow the same loose chronology in their presentation of events, we can look to ascertain any slippages between their display of individual objects, and thus form a comparative analysis of their methods and techniques. My main focus in this section will be to explore how the novel presents the objects that Kemal has gathered in order to tell the story of his love for Füsun to the reader. Their love story is set in motion by a particular object: a designer handbag that Kemal buys for his fiancée Sibel from the boutique where Füsun works. The object is first seen by Kemal and Sibel when it is in the window of the boutique, thus foregrounding and layering up diverse notions of display, perception, and observation.[8] It works as a material conduit between the two main characters—they handle

60   Chapter 3

the bag together at the point of sale, affording them a physical proximity that
is heightened by Kemal's openly erotic interpretation of Füsun's actions.

> Hooking the bag, she returned to the counter and with her long,
> dextrous fingers, she removed the balls of crumpled cream-coloured
> tissue paper, showing me the inside of the zippered pocket, the two
> smaller pockets (both empty) as well as the secret compartment,
> from which she produced a card inscribed JENNY COLON, her whole
> demeanour suggesting mystery and seriousness, as if she were show-
> ing me something very personal.[9]

When Kemal gifts the bag to Sibel that evening, she tells him that the bag is
a counterfeit, her expert eye deconstructing the stitching of the label onto the
leather as a sign of its inauthenticity. She compares the "real" Jenny Colon
bags she has seen in Paris with this one, which she sees as using "cheap
thread."[10] Kemal, though, looks at the bag and sees "genuine thread," and
feels uneasy and troubled by Sibel's verdict that the bag is "fake." Fake is
placed in quotation marks in the narrative, highlighting Kemal's diffidence
toward the judgment. Sibel's verdict here is presented as being related to her
anxieties about class and propriety, which fold into anxieties they both hold
about sexual liberation and the slow Westernization of Turkish societal traditions. Füsun, on the other hand, is presented as a more "modern" woman,
untroubled by the habitual social policing of women's behavior in 1970s
Istanbul: she removes a heeled shoe and hitches up her short skirt in order
to remove the bag from its window display, and handles it with a care and
intimacy that Kemal imbues with sexual suggestion. Kemal's return of the
bag to the boutique after Sibel's negative verdict on its authenticity triggers
the set of encounters that leads to Kemal and Füsun's embarking on a sexual
relationship. The bag thus displays a certain "thing-power" that moves the
narrative forward and is henceforth transferred from object to object, creating an assemblage with "the ability to make something happen."[11] On his
way home after returning the bag, Kemal buys a yellow jug on impulse. His
mother hands him a key tied with red ribbon and asks him to find a vase in a
flat she uses as a depot for old furniture and objects. When Füsun and Kemal
meet in this apartment, they explore the family's object collection together,
finding things that remind them of shared childhood memories: a tricycle, for
example, and a crystal sweet bowl. Füsun places Kemal's refunded money
next to a fez, and he hides her umbrella to ensure that she comes back to
meet him again. These artifacts populate the story with their ability to "animate, act, [and] produce effects dramatic and subtle," and are re-presented
as a "living, throbbing confederation" on display.[12] The narrator of the novel
takes on the role of a guide to this animate collection, using such gestural
phrases as "here I display" or "here I exhibit" as he introduces each new
object that makes up his story (and later on, his museum) to the reader.

Display   61

As we have seen, at the start of this deictic journey Pamuk uses the "fake" Jenny Colon bag to ask a series of wider questions about craftsmanship and authenticity that give it an emblematic role within both the novel and the museum. The separate revelation of how the bag on display was made especially for the museum rather than "donated" (as the narrator states was the case with the boutique sign and entrance bell) gestures toward the constructed nature of the fictional narrative.[13] In an interview, Pamuk stated that since it is an "imaginary brand," "we went to the fake-bag producers of Istanbul, and there are many. We designed this and they helped us with the production of it."[14] The name of this invented brand conceals a layer of intertextuality: Jenny Colon is the name of the muse of the nineteenth-century French poet and writer Gérard de Nerval. Nerval is also referenced within the novel as someone who also experienced the same intense heartbreak as Kemal, which he expressed in the feeling that since the loss of his love, all he had left were "vulgar distractions."[15] Yet some biographers of Nerval have pointed out that the importance Colon had for his life and works has been exaggerated in more recent accounts.[16] Indeed, in most of his works, women function more as symbols, archetypes, or mythologically inspired figures than as representations of real-life figures. Colon is thus perhaps more accurately to be seen as a symbol that Nerval could activate in order to furnish his affect-led imaginings with a concrete feminine presence: something that echoes Füsun's own narrative significance with the *Museum of Innocence* project. The power that this bag manifests as it draws the two protagonists together and allows them to embark on an object-filled plot is thus folded into a wider discourse around the blurred lines between authenticity and fiction that Pamuk pursues across all his writing related to this project,[17] yet it is also imbued with intertextual references that place this ambiguity into a longer cultural and literary history. As I will show, the way in which the bag is displayed within the wider collage of the museum chapter-box allows Pamuk to express all these different layers to the story which ultimately put its own "authenticity" into question.

Given the pivotal role that the bag plays in the formation of the relationship between the two main characters, and thus also in the narrative on display, it is interesting that it doesn't have more of an impactful opening position within the museum. Visitors to the museum will instead first be confronted by the enormous panoramic display of 4,213 cigarette butts that takes up the entire right-hand wall on the ground floor of the building. Although this display is actually numbered as chapter 68, it is the initial "chapter" in the museum plot. Perhaps this decision to disrupt the chronology of the plot was dictated by the confines of the museum space itself, but the combination of this collaged collection, which allows Pamuk to present himself as a craftsman,[18] plus the emblematic spiral design on the floor below it, offers some revealing contextual information to visitors before they climb the stairs to encounter the separate chapter-boxes. The spiral floor design is visible throughout the museum thanks to the central void of the building's staircase, and recalls Aristotle's conception of objective, measurable time as a "straight line containing discrete moments."[19] This infinite multitude of moments is reflected in the excessive collection of objects that Kemal accumulates within the novel, and the story is the through line which connects each thing together into a plot. The cigarettes themselves play a key role in this device. "Of the objects I collected, it was the cigarettes that I found to correspond most truly to Aristotle's moments. . . . one by one, they would recall the particles of experience until I had summoned up the entire reality of sitting at the dinner table with Füsun and her family."[20] Yet, here again, fiction intervenes and the butts on display are revealed to be facsimiles, or "fakes," as real cigarettes would fast decay and rot within their framed context.

The bag itself is in the second chapter-box, on the first floor of the museum, which in both the novel and the museum is named after the Şanzelize boutique where Füsun worked when she first met Kemal in adulthood. It is displayed at the bottom of the box, underneath the sign showing the shop's name, the suspended entrance bell, and one of Füsun's glossy lemon-colored, midheeled pumps, which is elevated on a spike into midair and framed by a black square of paper behind it. Coiled up next to the bag is a flesh-colored, lacquered belt. The display thus at once mimics the sort of shop window display that would have appeared to Kemal and Sibel when they first saw the bag themselves and simultaneously assembles into a composite group the set of objects that struck Kemal as he later entered the shop to meet Füsun. In describing his compositional process in designing the chapter-box, Pamuk reveals how the linear connection between object and story can in fact flow in either direction: "It's not that I first wrote the book and then searched for the yellow shoe. First I found the shoe, and I thought this was appropriate for a person like this. So the objects, in ways, form the characters of the plot."[21] Pamuk also reveals that this box was the first that presented him with cause for concern as he designed the museum displays. The first numerical box, which contains the earring Füsun lost the first time that she and Kemal made love, did not cause him anxiety, but the design of this second one left him with multiple questions.

> What kind of compositional logic should I use to place the objects in the box? What shape should each box take? . . . Should I put the objects in the box according to the order in which they appear in the book or should I make a different tableau out of them?[22]

His conclusion was that the design of the chapter-boxes needed to be object led rather than following the precise logic of the novel's storyline. The emphasis thus needed to be on the spatial aspects of the display rather than on obeying a strict chronological thread. He placed importance on aesthetic beauty and the autonomy of each box, which he felt added a touch of "lyricism" to the museum as each box took on the status of object in its own right.

Display   63

The autonomy of each box is here represented by an original element not present in the novel: the wallpaper used as a backdrop to the box is a design inspired by the border illustration of a Mughal manuscript in the Chester Beatty Library in Dublin.[23] Yet no additional explanation for the connection of this floral design to the narrative or to any of the other objects on display is provided. Is it merely ornamental? Or is there something else that the visitor is expected to be able to parse in its presence?

We have noted how the Jenny Colon handbag is "replaced" in the narrative by the yellow jug Kemal buys on impulse after first meeting Füsun, which he says is never mentioned by his family, despite its presence on their table for decades after its purchase.[24] This jug instead appears in chapter-box 6, "Füsun's Tears," forming part of a suspended chain of objects alongside the red-ribboned key and the vase that are linked together in the retelling of the bag's return to the shop. Objects are threaded through the narrative as signs, but their materiality also holds an emotional import that allows viewers to access the memorial landscape they are attached to. When it comes to designing a box that will tell the story of Kemal and Füsun's first sexual encounter, the narrator explains how it is precisely the emotions associated with that event that he wants to evoke, rather than displaying objects that were present in the room at the time.

> So it is precisely to illustrate the solicitude in the caresses . . . that I have chosen to exhibit this floral batiste handkerchief, which she had folded so carefully and put in her bag that day but never removed. Let this crystal inkwell and pen set . . . be a relic of the refinement and fragile tenderness we felt for each other. Let this belt, whose oversized buckles that I had seized and fastened with a masculine arrogance . . . bear witness to our melancholy.[25]

In the same way, Pamuk maintains that it is more important for museum visitors to remember the emotions they felt when reading the novel, rather than the details of objects described in the narrative. Objects hold an increasingly sentimental, consolatory power for Kemal within the narrative too: during both his protracted courtship of Füsun and after her death he takes to stroking, licking, and rubbing objects he associates with her over his face and body in the hope of transferring some of their "charm" and thus soothing his heartache.[26] And although he begins by collecting specific objects that either belonged to Füsun and her family, or which were present at their meetings, he eventually realizes that any object that recalls her *for him* (or even one that just strikes his fancy) belongs within the poetry of his collection. In the same way, objects can be generic, cheap, or mass produced but still be "authentic" enough to conjure up a specific time and place, or even sentiments, atmospheres, and other intangible states for him.[27] But it is important to note that this object-power is directed outward, too, toward the museum visitor, rather than offering its consolatory respite to Kemal alone. It allows the visitor an active role in interpreting the narrative made up of Kemal's memories "in the affective here and now."[28] "Visitors to my Museum of Innocence must compel themselves, therefore, to view all objects displayed herein—the buttons, the glasses, the old photographs, and Füsun's combs—not as real things in the present moment, but as my memories."[29] In Kemal's object kingdom, the "innocence" or even the "unreality" of the things on display derives from their symbolic objectification of the past and its transformation into memory, which is reflected in the timelessness of museum building (which has been described as being positioned "outside the modern world"[30]). Museum collections, like novels, thus "digress from and displace real time" in their transferal of meaning from a temporal to a spatial framework that involves visitors in its meaning-making exercise, as we will now see.[31]

Narrative Exhibition

If on the one hand, the novel *Museum of Innocence* can be read "as a fictional collection of objects" or as a "textual museum,"[32] then how does the real-life museum take on a parallel narratorial role and make up for what Pamuk himself has termed the "insufficiency of the 'thingness' of the novel"?[33] This next section will focus on specific elements of display in order to decode the storytelling power the exhibit holds. Habitual debates around museum display tend to focus on whether to privilege context or object, and whether to see an exhibition as "either a vehicle for the display of objects or a space for telling a story."[34] Unlike most displays, in the Museum of Innocence there is no sustained interest in object provenance, or interpretative information presented to the visitor about the objects themselves: when they were manufactured, created, or acquired, and by whom. If they are being presented as "evidence," it is not in any factual sense, and if the visitor forgoes purchasing the audio guide, very little context for any of the chapter-boxes can be gleaned. What I thus find more relevant to focus on here is, to borrow the words of Sara Ahmed, what sort of stories "we can learn about objects from the objects they are near, from their traveling companions."[35] The catalogue entry for box 9 describes how Pamuk had become frustrated at his inability to capture the spirit and soul of the chapter, until he confined the objects on display behind the framework of a rusty old bedspring he salvaged from a neighboring balcony. The act of framing and displaying allowed the objects to take on new meanings as they found their place in the museum, gradually beginning to talk among themselves, singing a different tune and moving beyond what was described in the novel. The pleasure Pamuk finds in "supplementing" the contents of the novel through his work in the museum is reiterated and explored further in his description of the display narrating the death of Füsun's father, Tarik Bey.

Display   65

> Was it the opportunity to play around, years later, with familiar
> objects that were used for completely different purposes? Was it per-
> haps the chance to show readers what there hadn't been room for in
> the novel? Or was it that I was making artwork out of election cards,
> old combs, photographs, and the like? Putting these things together in
> a box, measuring every centimetre, and making the slightest change
> in search of a particular harmony made me feel as if I were building
> a world, just as I do when I write a novel.[36]

Pamuk is demonstrating how the spatial configuration of the museum display
deeply affects our understanding of the objects being exhibited: a configuration into which he had primary physical and narratological input. The
mechanics of assembly have particular consequences for the meaning that
we extract from displays, and different modes of "amassment" can affect
our interpretation and experience of single, disparate objects as well as
groupings.[37]

How did Pamuk go about this task of assembly? In his own narrated version of events, he suggests that the process was both lengthy and instinctive,
and very much a group effort (although his collaborators are not generally
named or referenced within the catalogue). "After many years of collecting
objects, of visualizing and sketching cabinet layouts as if I were writing theatrical stage directions, we arranged cups of tea, Kutahya porcelain ashtrays and
Füsun's hairclips inside the boxes through trial and error."[38] Pamuk and his
team deployed several effects in order to achieve the visual impact suggested
by his reference here to a theatrical stage set. As anticipated, the foundational
method is collage, and the combination of often disparate objects to make
surprising, evocative, and even surrealist assemblages. The collage objects at
the forefront of each display are supported by images pasted on to the back
of the box or pinned into the sides of its deep-set frame. Various modes of
displaying individual objects are used, including the suspension of objects at
different heights within the boxes and the use of some objects to prop up or
support others. Pamuk and his team also make use of display effects that go
beyond the visual, such as sound (the music used in the Meltem jingle adver-
tising soda drinks plays in the audio to box 8), or wind effects (the white lace
curtain in box 1 flutters with an automatically generated breeze). Lighting (or
a lack thereof) also alters the effect of various displays, for example in the flash-
ing lights and ambient sounds from fishing boats in the Bosphorus in box 43,
or the sounds of summer rain which accompany boxes 75 to 79. But perhaps
the most significant display technique is that of framing. Many of the boxes
are framed by plush red curtains, recalling Pamuk's reference above to theater.
These curtains are either open, half-drawn, or completely drawn closed to
conceal the box itself, depending on the finished, partially finished, or incomplete status of the box's composition. This technique is first seen in boxes 16
("Jealousy") and 33 ("Vulgar Distractions"), and it increases in frequency

as the museum narrative goes on. Pamuk mentions in the catalogue that the reason for the partially closed curtains in box 33 is that "the corresponding chapter is already filled with detail about its contents," although the same could surely be said for many of the preceding chapters.[39] These "unfinished" boxes are thematically the closest to expressing the key emotions and key events of the story, and it is noteworthy that the final boxes, 78 and 79, are completely closed. The suggestion in the catalogue is that these boxes will, one day, be "completed," although the foreclosure on any sort of definitive interpretation seems to hold an alternative meaning of its own, which we will explore in the conclusions to this section.

It is also worth seeking to understand how the museum displays manage to evoke the spirit or contents of chapters through objects even when there are no material things described in the corresponding pages of the novel. For example, chapter-box 29 ("By Now There Was Hardly a Moment When I Wasn't Thinking about Her") is composed of a black light machine positioned in front of a painting. The machine was allegedly built by Pamuk in order to conjure the sense of radiating darkness that Kemal felt in his heartbreak and "to illustrate fully that Kemal's words are always so precise that they can be represented by objects." Alongside the construction of bespoke objects, states of mind are also represented by means of analogy. Pamuk states: "It is not only objects, views, pictures, and photographs, but also similes and metaphors that have been carefully explored in our museum."[40] Box 34 ("Like a Dog in Outer Space") uses the simile of the Soviet astronaut dog Laika, who was sent into space in 1957, to express the loneliness that Kemal felt as he searched for Füsun in vain. Chapter 57 ("On Being Unable to Stand Up and Leave") represents a long, complex chapter, which is full of political and social context as well as sketching the broad narrative of Kemal's first year of evening visits to Füsun's family home. Yet there are no objects or display notes mentioned in the novel, and the corresponding chapter-box features a display that narrativizes a fictional conversation between Kemal and Pamuk. The conversation explores how Kemal felt like a sinking or grounded ship when he lacked the strength of will to leave Füsun's house and return home. But it also expresses a more general metaphor of failure or defeat, which is visualized in a photo of the slow sinking of the *Izmir* ship in 1957, displayed behind three half-drunk glasses of raki measuring out time, and juxtaposed with the definitive timelessness of a stopped clock. The distillation of narrative into bespoke, constructed objects and the transmutation of meaning from word to thing both show how the museum allows Pamuk to stage a material response to his own expression of dissatisfaction with how "novels put nothing concrete in front of us."[41]

But the sense of the museum as offering supplementary material to the novel through the inclusion of such "concrete" objects is confounded by the presence of displays with no things contained within them. The lyricism of chapter 69 ("Sometimes"), with its repetition of the word "sometimes"

Display 67

to denote the habitual nature of the routine that Kemal settled into during the years of his visits to Füsun's family home, is represented solely by a sound installation in which the visitor hears the hissing of pumps, the cries of beverage vendors in the streets, and the voices of people passing by. The corresponding chapter-box gives an example of how the experience of the museum is folded into the narrative of its display, and it overlaps with the sense of the museum as a tourist destination which aims to preserve elements of the social and cultural history of the city of Istanbul. The museum thus layers different elements of representation in order to shed light on the narrative mechanism of the novel itself. Both are revealed as staging a fiction that draws down its reality only through the emotional experience of the reader or visitor. Yet there is a potential issue of conflict between expectation and imagination when the reader of the novel visits the museum. Pamuk seems to anticipate this when he states that "the art of the novel draws its power from the absence of a perfect consensus between writer and reader on the understanding of fiction."[42] Readers of fiction are expected to be able to suspend disbelief when reading, but when confronted with a material representation of "reality" in the form of objects in a museum, "their dynamic and active imagination is then stilled or frozen." This raises questions about the visitor experience of Pamuk's readers in the museum: as Açalya Allmer asks, "What happens if the reader's imaginative constructs greatly differ from the objects displayed? More importantly, what happens if the museum visitor has not read the novel?"[43]

Allmer's concern brings me back to consider the importance of the closed boxes, and to propose that we envisage the space of display as a space in which the potential latitude in interpretation affords a freedom to both visitor and reader alike. This is an important feature of a narrative characterized by the narrator's impulsive and obsessive compulsion to collect and own objects, experiences, and people. I read the lack of interpretative direction offered by the objects themselves in relation to tropes of resistance against possession and objectification that can be located within the novel. Specifically, Füsun challenges Kemal's narrativization of events on multiple occasions, her behavior striking a deliberate opposition to "the restrictions of gender roles and social expectations for unmarried women in Turkey at that time."[44] Kemal embodies the narrowness of these restrictions even through his physical acts of affection after their reunion: "Her beautiful left hand was like a tired hunted animal that my right hand had turned on its back, roughly mounting it, almost crushing it."[45] In the novel, Füsun pays the price for her sexual liberation as she is forced into agreeing to not one but two marriages instead of pursuing her long-standing dream of becoming an actress. Despite Kemal's interpretation of the shared nature of their love, she mocks his habit of stealing her things, challenges him on his lies, and resents the predatory nature of his desire for possession.[46] Her death—it is unclear whether the car crash she causes was an accident or an act of suicide—means that Füsun ultimately evades Kemal's physical and narrative control, and the closed boxes that represent the final chapters within the museum are indicative of her evasion of a narrative that Kemal subsequently has to remaster and piece together through the collection and display of his associated trinkets.[47]

But more generally, the closed boxes also gesture toward the importance of object autonomy within Pamuk's storytelling project. Jakubowski has commented on how objects in the novel of *The Museum of Innocence* are "not unmotivated, not superfluous" but act as plot elements that are veritable "hinges of the narrative itself."[48] I would argue that the individual objects, and their groupings within the boxes, perform a similar narrative role within the museum. As Pamuk states in the catalogue entry to box 9, "I was trying to make a painting with the objects, but they were trying to tell me something different."[49] In order to privilege the aesthetic, spatial experience of the mounted boxes on the museum walls, the order of the chapters they represent is sometimes altered. I would argue that the disrupted chronology of the chapter-boxes within the museum emphasizes the constructed nature of the narrative, just as the lack of interpretation leaves the objects on display unmoored to float into a fictional realm, a trope which is in turn aligned with the very subjective nature of Kemal's retelling of his and Füsun's story. The final chapters in the novel are "displayed" in the attic of the museum according to what Pamuk terms a "different logic of display"—not through collage-boxes, but through the reconstruction of Kemal's own sleeping quarters, which are "preserved" for the museum visitor to peruse. But it is also where the visitor can observe the final stage in the museumification of novel, in the interpretative panels featuring Pamuk's notes on composition of both forms of the narrative—novel and museum—on the walls. In this way, the museum itself manages to "destabilize the boundary between fiction and fact, language and reality, representation and what is represented," through a new focus on a relational aesthetics that emerges through its display of the "interrelation of things."[50]

Conclusion: Toward a Carpentry of Things

The relationship that Orhan Pamuk shares with his beloved Istanbul recalls that of the American artist Joseph Cornell with his native New York. Between the early 1930s and his death in 1972, Cornell roamed its streets and mined its dime stores for objects that, once assembled into original groupings, would allow him to express his great love for the city that was both his muse and his inspiration. Cornell never really drew, painted, or produced his own "original" images: on the contrary, his collage philosophy was directed at the pursuit of an "art of reassembling fragments of pre-existing images in such a way as to form a new image."[51] Cornell experienced New York City

Display 69

itself as a "pre-existent collage," a "feast of experience," and a stream of "endless revelatory moments of urban juxtaposition."[52] These moments that caught Cornell's attention were rigorously fragmentary, and his selection of certain moments and objects over others presupposes the existence of other material which he discarded or overlooked. The technique of collage, which Cornell developed in particularly luminous, mythological ways in the boxes he prepared as homages or gifts for actresses, dancers, or other women, is significant for Pamuk's work in the Museum of Innocence project. The absence of the figurative in Pamuk's chapter-boxes is closely related to the stories that Cornell chose not to tell through enacting ellipses in his cut-and-paste work with scissors and glue, and it furthermore shows how the contents of both their boxed narratives can be deliberately taken out of context, altered, and sometimes partially or wholly disguised from view—even by their own creators.[53]

For as we have seen, despite professing his commitment to the public display of his object collection, Pamuk's fictional protagonist, Kemal, also works to conceal the meaning of certain displays through the closure or partial closure of boxes. Narrative is thus produced by the interpretative, imaginative work carried out by visitors, where meaning can be located in and through the associations formed between individual objects on display.

> Display techniques can emphasize the aesthetic qualities of material objects, not by elevating them one by one, but by letting them affect each other on material terms. The objects come to function as a material assemblage in which their overlapping shapes and blurred boundaries become more present than their singular object entities.[54]

As Pamuk states in the catalogue entry to box 47, one of the revelations of his museum-making activity was how objects can bring forth unusual emotions when placed side by side. And in some ways, this mode of "unfolding the object itself rather than the context and the stories it might be used to represent"[55] allows us to approach the displays in the Museum of Innocence through an appreciation of the webs of refraction they themselves form. Their grouping into collaged chapter-boxes allows them to form a bond of social communication, or what Bruno Latour calls "a type of connection" between themselves and the objects directly surrounding them. But the object network also spans outward to track and trace associations between things in different boxes, and between shared elements in the novel and the museum.[56] Objects in the museum gain autonomy via their formation of a much wider assemblage of storytelling parts in Pamuk's overarching project, and our understanding that "reality exists exactly and only in the reference," is thus achieved precisely "through the circulation of reference between [objects]."[57]

In Pamuk's project, this circulation takes place across a network composed of the museum, the various books that tell the story (the novel, the catalogue, and other related writings), the translations, the museum building, the merchandise available for purchase in the on-site gift shop, the audio guide, and other actors involved (such as readers, visitors, craftspeople, and attendant staff). The word "actor" has a particular significance in Bruno Latour's formulation of actor-network theory, in which an actor can be anything (human or nonhuman) that *makes a difference*. This difference is a manifestation of acting-as-agency, where agency is understood to be any coordinated action that links human or nonhuman actors. A network can thus be defined as an assembly of actors that share information and coordinate action. While in the object-oriented philosophy of Latour and Harman objects are not necessarily defined by their interactions with humans, they both acknowledge an important element of subject-object engagement that unfolds on different levels. Just as objects can interact through their qualities, so humans can communicate with the world through their physical bodies. Building on the phenomenological work of Merleau-Ponty, Harman describes the human body as "a universal translation tool," "an object that is sensitive to all the other objects, reverberates to all sounds, vibrates to all colours."[58] This is why it is important to note not only the importance that Pamuk confers on emotions in his elaboration of an object-oriented narrative project—speaking often of the innocence of things, the compassion they can engender, and their consolatory powers—but also the emotional experience of the museum visitors and the ways that objects on display can create communicative pathways between individual visitors and the "memories" of events and people in the past that those objects can conjure.

Alongside the emotional experience involved, it is also important to consider the physical bodies of the museum visitors and the impact that their presence has on the objects on display (and vice versa). Pamuk states that museums "are not to be strolled around in but experienced" and that overcrowding should be avoided lest "when the Sunday crowds pour through the museums, the collected objects cry."[59] Indeed, Pilegaard has emphasized how people and objects are both "material objects that share the same space and are part of the same material assemblage."[60] This is especially visible in the museum catalogue, which features various photographs of the hands of the craftspeople at work assembling displays, emphasizing the manual act of assembly. But it is also evident in the museum itself, in the video of a woman's hand smoking which accompanies the initial display of numbered cigarette butts. And just as objects enjoy a level of autonomy from externally imposed interpretative grids which is related to their capacity for relationality with other objects, so the visitor to a museum exhibit is also to be understood as a highly active participant, not "a passive subject for instruction." This has ramifications for the story that emerges from the visitor's interaction with the displays, since when "given information . . . the viewer will construct an intentional description of the object for himself. And deprived of these pieces of information, he will probably make them up."[61]

Display

This potential to grant the visitor interpretative autonomy in the face of gaps in the available information takes us back to how a collage methodology generates partial stories which are always composed of fragments. Both Pamuk and Cornell are drawn to using mass-produced, low-cost, or salvaged items in their collage constructions. And both place particular emphasis on the importance of containing these fragments into boxes. Siofra McSherry sees the process of "reframing," such as we see in the box composition of both creators, as "an exemplary strategy to infuse reality or authenticity into worthless things."[62] Again, the accent here is on questioning the true meaning of "authenticity"—if objects are symbols, then the relations between the objects and the emotional experience of those who come into contact with the objects are where "authenticity" can be located. On a wider scale, Gloria Fisk has considered the question of Pamuk's mediation of Turkish "authenticity" for a globalized readership and concluded that

> Orhan Pamuk's canonization rests on his ability to render Turkish people and places eminently legible to readers who lack the facility to read his words without a translator or to locate his characters and settings with ease on a map. He excels . . . by transmitting the granular details.[63]

This reference to granularity strikes a chord with my understanding of Pamuk's use of individual, small, and often low-value objects to generate authenticity in his visions of the past. In a sense, the museum work he has completed offers an alternative route to access "reality" than the one provided in its representation in fictional narrative which, in the words of Susan Stewart, can offer transcendence but not authenticity.[64] In his "Modern Manifesto for Museums," which is included within the catalogue, Pamuk speaks of the importance of maintaining focus on the human scale, and on individuals rather than nations, in order to conserve and to preserve the memories of particular times, places, and people.[65] This is similar to Cornell's technique of using the "historical, preservationist function of the museum" to express his "romantic longings for the past," and for certain individuals within that past.[66] In order to gain (and to provide) access to the past, both creators place emphasis on the importance of serendipity, of the "accidental beauties" that objects generate when they are gently placed next to one another in arrangement. As Pamuk states:

> What I found most enthralling was the way in which objects removed from the kitchens, bedrooms and dinner tables where they had once been utilised would come together to form a new texture, an unintentionally striking web of relationships. I realized that when arranged with love and care, objects in the museum could attain a much greater significance than they had before.[67]

Cornell perhaps takes Pamuk's accent on the serendipitous nature of arrangement to a new level: Hauptman describes his work as "radicalizing" the notion of the miscellaneous by "transforming collection, combination, and acquisition into a technique." This technique is analogous to the fact of working in the archive, and Cornell used the representation of subjects through the physical act of object arrangement into the museum space as a means of "sending them, together, into the past."[68] Both creators' work is steeped in nostalgia, and it is striking that both also found great inspiration in the work of Gérard de Nerval and his "metaphysique d'ephemera," a term Cornell used to indicate "the supreme importance of the smallest things once the imagination transforms them.[69]

The museum is a medium for object display, and within the museum space, Pamuk's chapter-boxes work as a constellation of display mediums in miniature, in which "each object individually is a talisman; in pairs or trios, though, they join, or collide, two or more realities."[70] As a framing device, they provide the space necessary for object interaction and for the formation of a more complex actor network within Pamuk's multimedia storytelling project. The Museum of Innocence, conceived as both museum and novel within this wider project, thus becomes akin to "an active arena in which events do unfold, in which objects melt or regenerate into each other, transform or fuse into one another."[71] As we have seen, historical time is transformed into a spatial context in the museum building, and is subsequently imprinted and experienced afresh in the memory of visitors. This transformative function enables museums such as the Museum of Innocence "to be used as an apparatus of social memory."[72] But it also has implications for Pamuk's conception of the interaction between the museum and the novel. As Jakubowski comments, "Pamuk turns the original (a real-life museum) into the copy (a collection of real-life objects modelled on verbal objects), thereby questioning the legitimacy of such a representational hierarchy."[73] The representation of reality on display is transformed into relationism—a relationism which is, in turn, the essence of collage. In collage art, "the transposed, juxtaposed fragments do more than just represent displacement and strangeness: they embody it, emphasizing the existence somewhere else of the rest of the fragment, of its original context."[74] What we eventually find is that Pamuk's privileging of a collage or assemblage model offers an interpretative alternative to the "sequential and/or the narrative ordering of things," and this has significant implications both for the museum and the novel.[75] For as Stewart points out, there is a "disjunction between the book as object and the book as idea,"[76] a revelation which allows us to better understand Pamuk's shifting statements on the relationship between the novel and the museum. Pamuk has tried to foreground the materiality of the novel as object by including in it a map and ticket to the museum, as well as by presenting it as a conduit through association to the physical building of the museum itself. But ultimately, the museum that the novel refers to performs a refracted, relational

Display

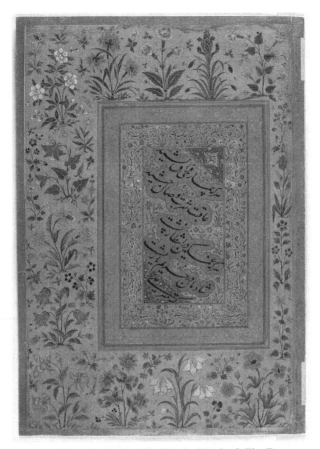

Fig. 9. Calligraphy by Mir Ali. CBL In 07A.8r. © The Trustees of the Chester Beatty Library, Dublin.

repetition of that same insufficient thingness of the novel, replicating it in the uninterpreted state of the object assemblages, and particularly in the closed or partly closed boxes on display. The fractured interplay between the two narrative modes is key to our understanding of Pamuk's modes of display here, since "fiction allows us to see that repetition is a matter of reframing, and that in the repetition, difference is displayed in both directions."[77]

The discourse around framing and display here brings me back in conclusion to consider the reasons behind Pamuk's inclusion of the Mughal border as wallpaper in the second box of the museum narrative (fig. 9). As mentioned, the border is part of one of the *muraqqa'*, the Imperial Mughal albums held in the Chester Beatty Library in Dublin. These albums show details of the lives and worlds of people during the reign of the emperors Jahingir and Shah Jahan during the Mughal dynasty of the first half of the

74   Chapter 3

seventeenth century. What is interesting here is the material formation of the album: as Elaine Wright explains, each page in the albums is made up of different pieces of paper. One side has a painting in the center, the other has a panel of calligraphy, and each is surrounded by wide borders which are cut from separate sheets of paper and joined through a series of narrower strips of borders in between them.[78] This "patchwork construction" lends the albums their name, since the Persian word *muraqqa'* means "album," but also "patched," or "patched garment," and thus clearly recalls the collage work of both Pamuk and Cornell. But even more revealing is the fact that the beautifully decorated piece of paper that Pamuk chose as a backdrop to his box is only the border to the central image, and that the missing status of the centerpiece (be it a painting or a piece of calligraphy) in the museum display denotes a shift in the status of relations between the two. In the *muraqqa'*, the border does not "compete with the central image, but instead functions as a sort of gloss on it, adding a further layer to its unspoken narrative."[79] Placed within the second chapter-box of Pamuk's museum, the border can only direct the viewer's attention to the absence of a central image or portrait, which has been replaced by objects. This recalls the absence of any figurative representations of Füsun within the museum, but also perhaps gestures toward a new concept of the relational reality of fiction that lies at the heart of Pamuk's museum narrative.

The border in question is taken from the so-called Minto Album, and specifically, it would have surrounded the calligraphy folio, or the "A-side," which was produced by the artist Mir Ali in the first half of the sixteenth century in either Iran or Bukhara. The calligraphy that is "missing" in Pamuk's chapter-box display holds a message that would have fit perfectly into Kemal's narrative of heartbreak and loss, and in his desire to re-create a sanctuary with his beloved through the amassment of objects: "Everyone who suffers the illness of separation tastes in the end the nectar of union. Everyone who sits grieving in expectation sits happily in the sanctuary of the beloved."[80] The consolation offered by Mir Ali's work is removed in the museum narrative by a black square of paper which stands mute behind the assembled objects on display. As a replacement to the missing message, these objects must therefore offer their own solace to Kemal, and by extension, also to the museum visitor. My conclusion is therefore that Pamuk offers us an alternative, object-based consolation to loss, one which offers a symbolic pathway toward understanding how and where to locate authenticity in representations of fiction on display.

Chapter 4

Storage

Introduction

As I stood on a crisp, sunny March morning with a crowd of other visitors waiting to enter the new Depot Boijmans Van Beuningen in the heart of Rotterdam's Museumpark, I caught a glimpse of a quiet revolution taking effect across the contemporary museum world. This revolution signals a paradigmatic shift in terms of what we understand the function and appeal of the physical museum space to be. Interestingly, this shift does not concern the public displays and exhibitions that visitors usually see in museums, but rather the parts that have traditionally been kept out of sight from them, in storage facilities located in basements, back rooms, or off-site depots. From New York to Paris, Glasgow to London, and Rotterdam to Cheongju, museums are upending previously held assumptions around visibility, accessibility, and display tactics by opening up their stores to the public—often in custom-built and architecturally bold spaces.[1] And as I looked up at the Depot Boijmans Van Beuningen that morning, marveling at its statuesque, curved structure covered in large mirrored panels, I saw the images of the waiting crowd reflected onto the museum in a way that cleverly succeeded in incorporating me and my fellow visitors into the narrative of the institution on display (fig. 10).

Upon entering, visitors are all asked to put on protective white coats before exploring the vertiginous building. The storage it contains covers six floors and features objects and paintings that are either suspended in glass boxes through open staircases or visible through illuminated windows. In rooms and studios on each floor of the museum, active conservation and research processes were also made available for us to watch and engage with. Storage in the Depot Boijmans Van Beuningen has thus been transformed into a collective project that each visitor intervenes in, perhaps most successfully through the museum's bespoke app. By downloading the app onto a smartphone or other device, you can access information about each of the 151,000 objects held in storage by scanning QR codes placed alongside the cases and vitrines. The app goes beyond providing information in

75

Fig. 10. Depot Boijmans Van Beuningen, Rotterdam. External view. Photograph by Emma Bond.

a passive sense, though, as it asks multiple-choice questions that promote learning through active engagement. And as you click and select things to explore further, the app stores them into your own personal "collection" of viewed objects, which you can then access again unlimited times once you return home. This collection resembles an informal "repository of intentional remembering" that lends it a future-facing feel, and which ties in with Arjun Appadurai's notion of the archive as a site for aspiration rather than recollection.[2] My sense upon leaving the depot was that the team behind the Boijmans Van Beuningen venue had managed to create a holistic new vision of what the contemporary museum is, who it is for, and what functions its visitors can expect from it.

This ongoing storage revolution takes us back closer, in many ways, to the original mission of the museum. In their early iterations, museums would typically display everything they held in their collections to the public. Museums replicated the style of extended cabinets of curiosity, in which object collections would grow to fill, and then overspill, the spaces of the buildings that housed them. As the twentieth century approached, a change took place in how curators thought that their visitors should experience the art or objects on

Storage

display: overcrowding was seen as disadvantageous for the measured contemplation and appreciation of art, and museums made the monumental decision to select their best or most representative pieces to display in a more spaced-out fashion, and to relegate the rest of the collection to storage. This was in part a curatorial decision, pioneered by John Edward Gray, keeper of zoology at the British Museum, as early as 1864. As Steven Lubar puts it, Gray's notion was that "with the mass of the collection stored away, there would be room to arrange the public material to tell stories."[3] But the decision had even more far-reaching implications than this narrative imperative suggests. Holdings were henceforth to be split into two categories: a part of the collections was meant for public appreciation, and the rest was destined for more private, individual, and expert research or investigation. In theory, having the equivalent of multiple "other" collections not on view meant that curators could swap works in and out, changing up their displays and narratives periodically. Deaccessioning, too, would eventually become more common, as we will see in the conclusion to this book. Yet in practice, the shift also meant that museums continued to accumulate objects that they had no way of making public, right up until the contemporary era, in which around 95 percent of most large public collections is held in more or less permanent storage. This leads to the growing sensation that "the most important space in any museum is storage space" and that—because everything in storage still needs to documented through accession registers and catalogues—many museum workers now feel that "our main business is inventory."[4]

Storage, and the management of stored collections, thus places the very idea of the museum into question: for if a maximum of around 5 percent of most collections are on display for visitors, and the rest is in storage (both for safekeeping and for research purposes), then is the museum's primary function really to be a showcase for public-facing display? Or is it in essence closer to that of a storehouse, or a repository of the past for future generations? How does this question affect our understanding of the museum's relationship with other comparable storage facilities, such as the archive, or even the database, and what can we learn through examining their interfaces? Museum stores are full of objects, but they are also vast collections of information, characterized and connected through networks and hierarchies of data and metadata. The recent turn to the digitization of object records, and to the mass creation of digital objects too, compounds these issues around storage, access, and the visitor experience and demands that we ask new questions of museums as cultural institutions. It also challenges our sense of museums as narrative engines, for what is sometimes lacking in the vast realms of digitized collections is any interpretation that allows the visitor to make sense of an object's history, or of its place within a wider collection. Paying attention to the shifting storage trajectories of museums in this way will thus also help us to shed light on the workings and rationale of the contemporary museum novel.

78   Chapter 4

In order to explore how storage and collections management function across both museums and fiction, this chapter will offer a detailed reading of Valeria Luiselli's 2019 work, *Lost Children Archive*. *Lost Children Archive* has been described by the author as being both a novel and the archive of a novel.[5] In this way, it functions a little like a museum with its own interconnected storage facility. The structure of the novel is itself archival: composed as it is through a series of boxes, with short, titled sections that read like index cards to the collection of materials it offers up to the reader for perusal. It pursues the question of how, why, and what to document of the present in order to create a future archive. It records this pursuit as an archivist would, keeping a detailed inventory of its sources and the materials it references and gathers into order. Yet it also offers a coherent narrative story on display. In so doing, it urges us to examine how stores and archives relate to plot and storytelling, and it offers new insight into these practices through its insistence on individual interventions of reenactment. *Lost Children Archive* helps us to tackle the question of how the function of the museum might relate to that of an archive or a database, and thus also how to manage and document stored object collections in literature, by asking: what do we retain of our lives as they shift into the past tense, how do we manage our emotional materials, and why (or indeed how) do we let go of archived memories?

Lost Children Archive is a road trip novel which tells the story of a family caught in a slow process of dissolution. The parents are both researchers: the father is a sound archivist (or documentarian) and the mother a journalist and documentarist. The couple met in New York while working on a project aimed at mapping the eight hundred languages spoken in the city. Each had a child from a previous relationship; they fell in love and were married, and now—as their marriage falls apart—they take a trip toward their future projects: the mother will work on a project documenting the plight of unaccompanied child migrants as they attempt to negotiate the hostile border environment of the United States from various countries in Central America, and the father will record what he calls an "inventory of echoes," which records historical presences of the last free Apache peoples across the southern states from Arkansas to Arizona. As the family head south, these stories interlace: stories of the early frontier wars whose aim was to eventually eliminate Native Americans from their ancestral lands, stories of today's child refugees separated from their families and lost between borders, and stories of the family trip played out against the emotionally tense backdrop of a separation to come. Each family member has his or her own physical box or boxes to fill with materials that help them tell the story of their own experience of the trip. The adults' boxes contain all the research materials needed for them to design and structure their work projects, allowing a complex intertextual trail to intersect with the reading experience throughout. The mother's overarching narrative is eventually replaced by a retelling of the same trip by the son, and then by the daughter (through an account of the

Storage 79

Fig. 11. Photograph from *Lost Children Archive: A Novel*, copyright © Valeria Luiselli. Used by permission of Alfred A. Knopf, an imprint of the Knopf Doubleday Publishing Group, a division of Penguin Random House LLC. All rights reserved.

sounds she has heard along the way). The final box, Box VII, is filled with the Polaroids that the mother and son have taken during the journey, reproductions of which are contained within the last section of the novel itself (fig. 11).

Annotated lists of the contents stored in each of the seven boxes introduce every section of the novel. This is a new, intricately archival type of novel: one that pays close attention to the "materiality of [its] ephemera and documents" but, given its content matter, one that also manages to foreground "the political and aesthetic stakes of research, documentation, artifacts, ephemera, curation and classification practices" within its own pages.[6] The author's prior journeys through other texts and sources are laid bare, allowing the reader to pursue her trails of inspiration and intertextual borrowings from novels by Dasa Drndić, Nathalie Léger, and Dubravka Ugresić, among others, and theoretical works on archives by Jacques Derrida, Arjun Appadurai, Antoinette Burton, and Marisa J. Fuentes. By juxtaposing other fictional and historical accounts of displacement in the same geographical region, the novel also serves an additional archival function: to stand as an "alternative, expanded, or even counterfactual site of historical preservation," thereby drawing attention to the roles that novelists have played as archivists and record creators throughout time.[7] This is evidenced in the fact that the novel's main intertext, Ella Camposanto's *Elegies for Lost Children*, which the mother and son read their own journeys through and against, is a fiction invented by Luiselli, and the photos in the final box are presented not as a visual illustration, but rather as a sign that "the fiction was driving the documentation, like an inverse procedure."[8] Indeed, Valentina Montero Román reads *Lost Children Archive* as signaling a shift in the Big Ambitious Novel genre: aspiring toward the archival rather than the encyclopedic through an exploration of "the fragmented and recursive processes of *constructing* personal and historical memory."[9]

In this way, *Lost Children Archive* uses the fictions and the partiality of the historical archive, and the precarity of our own stored records and memories, both to evidence the challenges of telling the specific story of child migrants arriving in the United States and to draw attention to the fictive mechanics involved in archival-based writing more generally. Luiselli has spoken of how she had to set aside her work on *Lost Children Archive* as she became more and more involved in volunteer work translating the testimonies of child migrants as they seek to find legal representation to help them claim asylum and remain in the United States after traumatic journeys. Luiselli battled with the ethics of finding the "right" story to be able to help others claim legal aid. She fought against the sense that stories become "generalized, distorted, and appear out of focus" the more familiar we are to them, and acknowledged that documents can be translated and interpreted in different ways that lead to multiple, divergent outcomes.[10] Her personal response was to try to tell the stories she encountered in as many different ways as she could, leading to the publication of the nonfiction work *Tell Me How It Ends: An Essay in Forty Questions* in 2017, before she could resume work on the manuscript that would become *Lost Children Archive*. As she says in the earlier work, the "only way to grant justice is by hearing and recording stories over and over again so that they come back, always, to haunt and shame us."[11] In the novel, the story is repeated and reenacted by multiple characters, highlighting the partiality of their own documentation, and thus echoes Antoinette Burton's call for us to "commit ourselves to acknowledging that *all* archives are provisional, interested, and calcified in both deliberate and unintentional ways;

Storage

that *all* archives are, in the end, fundamentally unreliable."[12] This is not an indictment of archival work, nor does it signal the end of history as an archival discipline, but is instead, in Burton's view, "the very condition from which history . . . must proceed."[13] Likewise, the cataloguing of records and documents within archives and museum stores is acknowledged not to be neutral: processes of selection and classification operate here too to create multiple, partial accounts of holdings and histories alike. As Eric Ketelaar says:

> The technologies of records creation, maintenance and use colour the contents of the record, and also affect its form and structure. This is true even for the seemingly innocent technologies of filing and storage. Numerous tacit narratives are hidden in categorization, codification and labelling.[14]

In this chapter, the strategies that govern archival storage and collections management will be examined alongside the aforementioned issues that emerge from the mass digitization of collection objects and their records. Open storage can respond to, yet simultaneously exacerbate, these issues, since any sense of "openness" is still managed and manipulated, while a lack of narrative interpretation means that, as Kimberly Orcutt puts it, "The institutional goal of enhanced access often collides with visitors' desire for further information."[15] This chapter will thus aim to examine the museological elements contained within representations of storage and documentation in *Lost Children Archive* in relation to the narrative possibilities and limitations of both the historical archive and the database, drawing on theories of the networked novel, and writings on the re-coded or digital museum. It begins with an analysis of the explicit structural composition of the text as an archive with its own catalogue or index: the narrator says as she surveys her family's baggage near the start of the trip, "I stand in front of our portable mess, studying the contents of the trunk as if reading an index, trying to decide which page to go to."[16] The structuring of the novel as a series of index cards that relate to these archived objects in the trunk will then guide the rest of my analysis, which is divided into short subsections that share the titles of these cards: (i) archive, (ii) document, (iii) inventory, and (iv) family plot. These index card titles are repeated across the different boxed sections of the novel by the multiple narrators and will allow us to draw together overarching narrative threads that link object, location, and object record in order to tell the multiple potential stories that coexist in the text. Storage, memory, narrative potential, and networked meaning are themes that will appear across all the sections, as I follow the structure and methodology of this archival museum novel, pursue its intertextual links, working with its multimedia elements, and engaging directly with the theoretical works that are referenced within the text.

82   Chapter 4

Archive

What differentiates a museum from an archive? And how can reading a novel like *Lost Children Archive* help us to identify where the points of commonality between the two lie? *Lost Children Archive* opens with an epigraph from Arlette Farge's classic text, *The Allure of the Archives* (*Le goût de l'archive*), which intimately describes the tactile, aesthetic, and intellectual experience of doing work in historical archives. Farge offers a vision of the archive as a mechanism that re-attaches the past to the present, allowing the contemporary user "an unplanned glimpse into an unexpected event."[17] The materiality of the documents stored in the archive provides the illusion of a verified reality that appears more "real" than any contemporary encounter, offering a sense of proof or authority that is separate from, yet runs parallel to, our interpretation of them. As Ray Batchelor has put it, "Objects *are our primary archives*."[18] Interpretation alone can assign meaning to archival objects and documents, since their reality lies "in the sequences of different representations of reality" they can conjure, into which inevitably slip both "fable and fabulation."[19] The citation that Luiselli uses to open her novel references this embodied process of intervening into archival material, stating that "an archive presupposes an archivist, a hand that collects and classifies."[20] Much of Farge's text is concerned with the interface of narration and fiction in the stories we tell from and about the archive, the way that its users "isolate pieces from the archive," making selections that "shape the object of study through the accumulation of detail," "sifting, gathering and classifying" in order to create a specific viewpoint, and a new narrative.[21] The archivist nominated in this epigraph could be easily replaced by a curator, or indeed a novelist, since all three figures are tasked with making sense of raw material, and creating stories out of them. As Burton remarks:

> History is not merely a project of fact-retrieval . . . but also a set of complex processes of selection, interpretation, and even creative invention—processes set in motion by, among other things, one's personal encounter with the archive, the history of the archive itself, and the pressure of the contemporary moment on one's reading of what is to be found there.[22]

Luiselli's reference to Farge lays bare from the outset her own hesitancy and anxieties about the legitimacy of telling any singular story of the experience of child migrants en route to the United States, her admission of the fault lines between narrative, fact, and fiction, and the gaps that any storytelling exercise necessarily involves. One section, entitled "Narrative Arc," details the narrator's political concerns, aesthetic problems, professional hesitance, ethical concerns, pragmatic concerns, and realistic concerns, and ends up listing her "constant concerns":

Storage

Cultural appropriation, pissing all over someone else's toilet seat, who am I to tell this story, micromanaging identity politics, heavy-handedness, am I too angry, am I mentally colonized by Western-Saxon-white categories, what's the correct use of personal pronouns, go light on the adjectives, and oh, who gives a fuck how very whimsical phrasal verbs are?[23]

But the novel also opens up to the creative and ethical possibilities of storying the archive. As Jean-Christophe Cloutier reminds us, archival "documents have an afterlife . . . and can be put to new, unpredictable uses and form the basis for new interpretative and narrative acts."[24] It is not so much that the archive itself functions as a visualization of the work of human memory, but rather that the work of elaborating stories out of archival materials recalls the Freudian processes of retrieval and elaboration of psychic material in order to form a temporarily situated story that functions in therapeutic terms.[25]

Through archived documents, we are presented with pieces of time to be assembled, fragments of life to be placed in order, one after the other, in an attempt to formulate a story that acquires its coherence through the ability to craft links between the beginning and the end. . . . The time woven together by the archive is the product of a composition.[26]

In *Lost Children Archive*, the two adults are initially lulled into the belief that they are creating a solid foundation for their family archive through the accumulation of material stuff. As they put together their new household, they also gather things, "plants, plates, books, chairs, . . . objects from curbsides in affluent neighborhoods."[27] Their attention to recording the sounds and images of their family life also mean that "all of it, us and them, here and there, inside and outside, was registered, collected, and archived."[28] Everything is stored, but nothing is storied, and a difference emerges between the activities of gathering and building, or interpreting that feed into these two states. The narrator poses the question, "When, in the future, we dig into our intimate archive, replay our family tape, will it amount to a story? A soundscape? Or will it all be sound rubble, noise, and debris?"[29] As they prepare to leave New York on their road trip south, it seems as if the future of the archive is compromised because each family member is individually preoccupied with "collecting pieces of the world the way we each know how to gather it best."[30] In practice this means that the husband gathers his own materials as a solitary practice:

He bought some bankers boxes and filled them with stuff: books, index cards full of notes and quotes, cutouts, scraps, and maps, field

84   Chapter 4

recordings and sound surveys he found in public libraries and private
archives, as well as a series of little brown notebooks where he wrote
daily, almost obsessively.[31]

He occupies four of the seven boxes, one of which contains a set of materials
described by the narrator as an "all-male compendium of 'going on a journey,' conquering and colonizing."[32] In contrast, the narrator refuses to limit
herself to an activity of gathering that risks bordering on the extractive. She
collects materials, then she discusses her concerns about what to do with the
results with a friend, "a Columbia University professor specializing in archival studies," and acquires the theoretical texts the friend suggests that she
read.[33] She too gathers all her archival scraps together into one of the bankers boxes (just one), but then she thinks how to distance herself from them
through intertextual narrativization, how to story them, in a practical sense.

> At the very top of the box, I placed a few books I'd read and thought
> could help me think about the whole project from a certain narrative
> distance: *The Gates of Paradise*, by Jerzy Andrzejewski; *The Chil-
> dren's Crusade*, by Marcel Schwob; *Belladonna*, by Dasa Drndić; *Le
> goût de l'archive*, by Arlette Farge; and a little red book I hadn't yet
> read, called *Elegies for Lost Children*, by Ella Camposanto.[34]

The children go a step further than the mother: they leave their boxes empty,
"so that they can collect stuff on the way."[35] In so doing, they pursue a
creative mode of future archiving that goes beyond mere documentation.
Luiselli describes something akin to her own research methodology to the
reader in the mother's archiving technique, but she also points to the only
possible way of creating a satisfactory narrative from the archived material
and experience, which is closer to the children's method. The children see
archiving as a dynamic and active process: one that "combines heterogenous
timescales, scrambles origins and mashes up elements from different horizons . . . opening up vertiginous, imaginary perspectives."[36] The children's
creative responses to archiving are evident in the packing of their suitcases
for the trip, narrated in a section entitled "Future":

> They'd chosen the most unlikely combinations of things. Their suit-
> cases were portable Duchampian disasters: miniature clothes tailored
> for a family of miniature bears, a broken light saber, a lone Roller-
> blade wheel, ziplock bags full of tiny plastic everything. I replaced it
> all with real pants, real skirts, real underwear, real everything.[37]

This short paragraph is constructed in implicit dialogue with Enrique
Vila-Matas's 1985 novella *A Brief History of Portable Literature*. Vila-Matas
discusses how Walter Benjamin and Marcel Duchamp, who were always on

Storage   85

the move, dealt with their mania for collecting by making things miniature: "To miniaturize is to make portable, and for a vagrant and an exile, that is the best way of owning things."[38] But, Vila-Matas continues, "To miniaturize is also to conceal," since tiny things require more careful decoding, and—more importantly for Luiselli's purposes—to miniaturize also means "to make useless," since what is small is "liberated from meaning." "Its smallness is, at one and the same time, a totality and a fragment. The love of small things is a childish emotion."[39] This recalls the collection of objects that are "miniaturized" into thumbnail images through the Depot Boijmans Van Beuningen app (as indeed on any museum website or digital catalogue). Antonio M. Battro suggests that when "the scale of a work of art is 'falsified,' niches of new meaning may be discovered," allowing us all to create our own imaginary, "portable" museums.[40] The mother initially overwrites her children's emotional, liberated archives by replacing their selected objects with what she refers to as "real" things. Yet the shift from the physical to the digital within the museum domain "has blurred the distinction between authentic and virtual: they increasingly overlap," putting the notion of the "real" into question.[41] Indeed, the following "Archive" sections show how her thinking toward archival methods develops through her engagement with a series of other fictional and non-fiction narratives: including the texts by Léger, Sontag, and Camposanto, as well as what she learns from her children's approach. Her own methodological journey thus signals the ways in which digital technologies can be "harnessed to revise empiricist based forms of documentation through new, discursive, relational possibilities, and the ability to store, search, and retrieve vast amounts of data."[42]

In the next "Archive" section, the narrator listens to her sleeping family in the dark and re-writes them as her own archive of experience. She recognizes them through the small sleep sounds that they make, and mentally reconstructs their faces through a patchwork of memories. In creating her family as an imagined archive, she is again writing about herself and about her own creative process, something that is made explicit through her description of reading Nathalie Léger's novella *Suite for Barbara Loden* in this same section. As Léger is asked to write a short entry for a film encyclopedia on Loden's 1970 film *Wanda*, she embarks on a project of truly excessive research which occupies her for months and ultimately fuses subject and object: "I felt like I was managing a huge building site, from which I was going to excavate a miniature model of modernity, reduced to its simplest, most complex form: a woman telling her own story through that of another woman."[43] In the same way, the narrator of *Lost Children Archive* tells the story of disappeared child migrants to the United States through a portrait of her own family built through intertextual references and deep, yet fragmented reflections on her writing process. Léger's mother tries to counter her daughter's obsession with Loden by telling her that because she hasn't experienced the other woman's life, whatever she writes will just be a fiction, and yet the sense of

86   Chapter 4

recognition that the author experiences through the other woman persists. Luiselli's narrator experiences this same identification with Léger via Loden: when the boy wakes up and asks her what the book she is reading is about, in her answer she mixes first- and third-person pronouns in a revealing way: "Nothing really. It's about a woman who's looking for something." "Looking for what?" the boy persists. "*I don't know yet; she doesn't know yet.*"[44] Her testimony thus not only bears witness to the impossibility of telling the story of the child migrants but also tells the story of her own attempts to write (and to write herself into) that same impossibility.[45]

Archiving as intertextual method is thus continuously probed and rethought through the novel, as we see through this lateral analysis of the eight sections entitled "Archive," and particularly of their intertexts. In the third "Archive," the narrator reflects on how to record the present without disrupting it, without transforming it into an already-past moment, and she wishes that she could remember moments through underlining them rather than documenting, referring back to the Léger text that she underlines in the previous "Archive."[46] The intertextual references between sections thus begin to form a supplementary archival thread that fleshes out and illustrates the narrator's ruminations on method. When she does commit to archiving the trip through deciding to take a picture of the two children at play, she feels the sadness of looking through her son's belongings to find the camera instructions.

> Perhaps it's just that belongings often outlive their owners, so our minds can easily place those belongings in a future in which their owner is no longer present. We anticipate our loved ones' future absences through the material presence of all their random stuff.[47]

Once she has taken it, she slips the still undeveloped photograph between two pages of Susan Sontag's early journals, *Reborn*, thus looping in another intertext. It can be no coincidence that the page tells a story about the same sort of "Apache" games her children were playing, through the "Mexican" games played by Sontag's son, yet in Sontag's version of the game, history is reversed "so that Mexico got to keep Texas."[48] The picture is the first Polaroid contained in Box VII in the novel, and the narrator comments, "Though I can't really explain exactly why or how, they look as though they're not really there, like they are being remembered instead of photographed."[49] The image seems to conjure the inventions (and interventions) involved in re-creating archived lives, in which, as Hayden Lorimer puts it, the fact that "lives are always a fiction . . . is what makes the *partiality* of reconstruction so appealing."[50]

In the penultimate "Archive" section, the narrator decides to turn back to her sound project and to create an archive of recorded voice notes about the journey. But when she switches on the recording device, only one sentence emerges: "We're much closer to the end of the trip now than to the starting

Storage

point."[51] Unable to face the finality implicated in the destination to come, she turns to Camposanto's book of *Elegies,* where she has decided to store the growing collection of Polaroids, and records descriptions of the images she sees instead. Then she begins to narrate the book itself so that the two stories (visual and textual) intersect in terms of method. The *Elegies* irrupt into the main narrative, taking control of telling the story of the lost children, and using intertextual methods similar to those employed within *Lost Children Archive*:

> The book is written in a series of numbered fragments . . . each is partly composed using a series of quotes. Throughout the book, these quotes are borrowed from different writers. They are either "freely translated" by the author or "recombined" to the point that some are not traceable back to their original versions. . . . Once I reach the end of the foreword, I reread the first elegy to myself again, and then begin reading the second one, out loud and into my recorder.[52]

From this moment on the *Elegies* begin to encroach more and more insistently into the narration of the story itself. As Luiselli makes clear in the "Works Cited / Notes on Sources" section that follows the novel, the invented *Elegies* text is an integral part of the main narrative, but it is also itself made up of a patchwork of allusions to other literary works about journeys and migration, by authors such as Ezra Pound, Joseph Conrad, Augusto Monterroso, T. S. Eliot, and Jerzy Andrzejewski. "The allusions need not be evident. I'm not interested in intertextuality as an outward, performative gesture, but as a method or procedure of composition."[53] Intertexts in *Lost Children Archive* thus function as a kind of fictive archive which allows for the main narrative thread to take place. As the narrator comments:

> I suppose an archive gives you a kind of valley in which your thoughts can bounce back to you, transformed. You whisper intuitions and thoughts into the emptiness, hoping to hear something back. And sometimes, just sometimes, an echo does indeed return, a real reverberation of something, bouncing back with clarity when you've finally hit the right pitch and found the right surface.[54]

That those echoes are found in a narrative-based archive contributes to Luiselli's sense that we absorb stories and make the narratives we read our own. "It all comes together in the same way that books become part of our own experience without us necessarily having lived those experiences. Literature is like a prosthetic memory."[55] Similarly, in *Suite for Barbara Loden,* the narrator attempts to gain access to Loden's archive in order to complete the narrative she wants to write about her subject. Yet she knows beforehand that the archival search itself is futile.

88   Chapter 4

> I know from experience that to gain access to the dead you must enter this mausoleum that's filled with papers and objects, a sealed place, full to bursting yet completely empty. . . . What will you find there? Boxes, scraps, fakery, piles of things sweating excess and incompleteness and, in spite of brief triumphs, defeat.[56]

The sense encapsulated here is that museums and archives contain what Mike Jones terms "reticent objects," objects that on their own might "communicate little beyond their visible material or textual properties."[57] Such objects require the addition of context through documentation in order to facilitate narrative and interpretation, and museums must "maximise the use of enriched data through cross-linking and filtering to different collection records" to that end.[58] Ultimately, Léger's narrator finds that she comes closer to the story she wants to tell about Loden through reading a novel written by the actress's ex-husband. This sense of "interweaving" data, of following "navigable trails formed by cross-references," thus shapes Luiselli's work as part and product of a collection of intertextual enmeshment.[59] It also aligns the museum novel with new digital methods in the relational museum which, in the words of Fiona Cameron, disrupt singular meanings "in favour of new styles of postmodern texts in which pluralistic narratives arrange information in galaxies of relationships and links."[60]

As we will see in more detail, the location of items—both physical and digital—in museum collections continues to shape how we access information about them.[61] This section has shown how the archival properties of *Lost Children Archive* function both in terms of its structure, and in relation to its intertextual storage system. As the family set off, and every time they move forward on their journey, they repack the trunk of their car with their suitcases, miscellaneous objects, and the seven bankers boxes containing their archive-in-motion. As the boy says, the task of ordering this content falls to him: "I had to make sure (all the boxes) were all in place, together with the rest of our stuff in the trunk. It was like having to solve a puzzle, every time."[62] This statement reminds us that the organization of collections information is always "temporarily situated" knowledge,[63] and also that archives and museums are records not just of historical events but also of record-keeping practices themselves. In the museum, different types of archives coexist: records of museum administration, acquired papers, and object records. All this documentation and information was traditionally kept separate from the objects themselves. Yet in recent years, museums have undertaken "attempts to reconnect artefacts and archives in ways that reflect the complexities of knowledge."[64] Indeed, in the final "Archive" section, the son narrates the burial of a dragonfly that the daughter has accidentally killed. The dragonfly dies suspended in a glass jar, in a way that recalls the unblemished appearance of similar specimens in museum vitrines or displays.[65] The children bury the creature in the hard soil alongside two teaspoons and a penny coin, after

Storage 89

which they assemble pebbles into a circle and sing songs around the grave.[66] The children's creation of ritual, and their understanding of memorialization as an archival practice which is not already rooted in reality but is capable of producing a new layer of reality itself, mirrors the narrator's journey toward a new conceptualization of archival practices, those same practices that are taking place in more open and more relational museum spaces today.

Document

The narrator's anxiety about the worth of documenting experience sees her liken the process of archival accumulation to "contributing one more layer, something like soot, to all the things already sedimented in a collective understanding of the world."[67] Indeed, personalized, and often idiosyncratic, modes of documenting the contents of collections over centuries of acquisitions have led to what we might call a situation of data overload in the museum. Museums work across multiple datasets, both analog and digital, with information spread over "accession registers, catalogue cards, indexes, inventory listings, and (from the 1960s) computer systems, databases, and collections management software."[68] However, they are also reliant on the specialized knowledge of individual curators, which might be lost when people conclude their term of employment in the museum. This complex situation of data management means that countless objects risk falling through the documentation "cracks." When museum and archival specialists talk about these objects, they use terms such as "separation records" to describe the loss of a documented bond between a given object and its record, to processes of disassociation, and they commonly refer to those they can no longer say with confidence how or why they own as "orphaned objects."[69] This powerful image of racks and shelves of orphaned or dissociated objects lining the stores of museums recalls Ariella Azoulay's masterful reconnection of the link between object documentation and the status of the "undocumented" migrant. Azoulay notes the contiguous presence of "millions of objects looted, carefully handled, preserved and displayed in Western museums," objects which are separated from the "millions of people displaced and stripped of possessions." These two groups—once connected through their place in cultural communities of origin—are, in Western discourse, "continuously produced as disconnected, as if it were the nature of artifacts to exist outside of their communities, to come into being as museum objects, to be out of reach of those who felt at home in their midst."[70]

Azoulay also notes the oppositional discourse of care in relation to these two sets of beings: expropriated but highly valued objects, and exploited people routinely excluded from access and resources. Thus, in imperial regimes of occupation, "indigenous communities were often treated as obstacles to be removed, subjects to be converted, partners to be cheated, if not as resources

90   Chapter 4

to be used and abused." People were valueless, yet the objects they had
created, used, and previously cared for were deemed so valuable that they
were looted for display or storage in the Western museum system. Colonization thus "inaugurated the destruction of diverse worlds in order to create
a brand-new world, inaugurated the production of carelessness for people
(and extra care for their expropriated objects)."[71] In the monograph *Potential
History*, but also in her narrated film *Un-documented: Unlearning Imperial
Plunder*, Azoulay reassigns rights to those referred to as "undocumented"
precisely through the objects they were separated from through imperial violence and sees their contemporary migration to Europe and the United States
as akin to a "counter-expedition."

> The film [*Un-documented*] is based on the assumption that there is
> a strong connection between two trajectories of forced migration
> that are thought of as unrelated and are studied separately. The first
> migration is of objects that generated professional care, scrupulous
> documentation, generous hospitality in museums and archives, and
> occasional public display. The second migration is of people who do
> not have, never had, or are unable to obtain the documents without
> which they are banned from access to most kinds of care and hospi-
> tality, and from rebuilding their homes and worlds. These objects are
> those people's documents.[72]

The first section of the film, entitled "The Right to Live Nearby One's
Objects," is narrated by the performance artist and musician Eseohe Arhebamen, also known as Edoheart. Born in Nigeria, Edoheart is a royal descendant
of the Ugu Kingdom of the Benin Empire, which suffered one of the most
brutal instances of imperial looting during the violent sacking of the city
of Benin by British troops in February 1897.[73] Edoheart's powerful, lilting
voice provides a backdrop to the sweeping panoramas of African objects on
display in a museum in Berlin. These are objects, when viewed in close-up,
whose expressions seem indeed to voice the feelings of being unsettled, of
"boredom, pain, longing, disorientation, of decades of being kept in places
they don't know, far from people they know." They appear stifled, congealed
in stillness, yet full of potential animation as they stand ready for a reconcili-
ation with the people who once made and used them, the same people denied
entry to the countries that now store their objects. This broken bond speaks
of the normalization of material violence and, as the film states, "You can see
the harm that was done to people, in the details of objects."

Lost Children Archive provides several material examples of the ramifications of the separation of this bond between objects and people, a
separation which has been enacted through contemporary regimes of border violence that seek to enshrine a lack of rights for those who want or
need to move. Box V, the mother's box, contains a multimedia collection

Storage 91

of maps, clippings, posters, photographs, quotes, and books relating to the migration—particularly of children—across borders. Through these documents, the current movement of Central American migrants is linked to the "orphan trains" that sought to relocate around two hundred thousand homeless children from New York with families around the United States between 1854 and 1930, and to the uncountable numbers of children trafficked to the Americas as part of the transatlantic slave system. The overlapping trails of forced movement mapped out by the mother's documentation thus provide deep historical context to the objects involved. One photograph shows several sealed, clear plastic bags of possessions, which were recovered on migrant trails in the desert of Pima County, Arizona. Following straight after the inclusion of six migrant mortality reports which cover the same territory in the novel, it is not clear whether these objects were discarded by migrants once they were no longer needed, or whether they signal fatalities in and of themselves. The objects are quotidian, mundane: a toothbrush and toothpaste, a mobile phone, a photograph. Whatever the outcome of the journey their owner undertook, the image retains a sense of the haunting claim these objects hold on shifting spheres of land, memory, and attention. They succeed in "making visible what would otherwise stay hidden by the politics of the present."[74]

Yet in a similar fashion to other photography projects, such as Gideon Mendel's *Dzhangal*, Mario Badagliacca's *Frammenti*, and Tom Kiefer's undercover work capturing images of the confiscated possessions of migrants on the US-Mexico border, the collection of objects as an artistic response to migration crises around the world raises ethical questions that link directly back to traditional museum practices.[75] Discussing Mendel's work, Dominique Malaquais comments on the long and violent history of "compiling evidence to account for 'others'" in order to make sense of their difference, which feeds into the "collector's power to examine, name, bracket, and administer" in turn.[76] Museums themselves also "bracket off" objects, bestowing an aura of fragility and difference on them, and thus also replicating border violence. As Didier Maleuvre writes, "The museum is not only the place where art is curated; it is also where art is imprisoned." This "quarantining" functions as a "political gesture" as it defines the objects in terms of their social place, their "mode of integration and their contents."[77] Museums are full of objects no longer integrated within their context. The isolation of museum objects can, in the worst-case scenario, also leave them vulnerable to multiple forms of "custodial neglect," not in terms of the physical deterioration of the objects, but in the loss or misplacement of objects, and the loss of data relating to them. This dissociation in object collections leads to a loss of connections, a loss of meaning, and a loss of value. Retaining, and displaying, objects that have been dissociated from their owners through regimes of border violence, on the other hand, evidences and documents this mismatch between a desire to care for objects and a lack of care for their owners. As

92   Chapter 4

Sara Ahmed has shown, "Colonialism is justified as using what is unused," and colonial occupation, however violent, is habitually "narrated as 'taking care' of *things*."[78] The question is, can this violence be countered through data work, through the gathering of evidence that points to multiple and diverse modes of documentation?

In *Lost Children Archive*, the mother becomes involved in one particular legal case, trying to assist and locate the two daughters of a woman she knows in New York: one eight-year-old and one ten-year-old, who had crossed the border from Mexico and were being held in a detention center in Texas. The girls' situation unfolds against the backdrop of a worsening "crisis" of reception: "More than 80,000 *undocumented* children from Mexico and the Northern Triangle had been detained at the US southern border in just the previous six or seven months."[79] But these girls are not without documentation. Upon leaving, their grandmother had prepared them by packing their backpacks with particular items: "Bible, water bottle, nuts, one toy each, spare underwear."[80] She had also sewn additional identifying data, in the form of their mother's telephone number in New York, onto the dresses they were wearing:

> She had tried to get them to memorize the ten digits, but the girls had not been able to. So she sewed the number onto the collars of their dresses and, over and over, repeated a single instruction: they should never take their dresses off, never, and as soon as they reached America, as soon as they met the first American . . . they would show the inside of the collar to him or her.[81]

The act of sewing here sutures the girls closer to their documentation and points to new ways of conceptualizing the interrelationships between museum objects and their data. Instead of relying on traditional "tree-like structures and branching visualizations of data hierarchies," Mike Jones proposes new, relational models based on nonhierarchical practices such as weaving or yarning.

> When considering the weave of collections, archives are an essential thread. Records link artefacts together, helping us to stitch things into the contextual fabric. Letters tie objects to landscapes and collectors; field notes thread together artefacts, expeditions, communities, and cultural practices; and museum files help us understand how varied items have been wound together by different disciplines, organisational structures, or exhibition narratives over time.[82]

As Trilce Navarrete and John Mackenzie Owen show, "Objects are information carriers."[83] In *Lost Children Archive*, documenting the trails of information that objects embody is a crucial part of constructing and

Storage 93

reconstructing a narrative about multiple forms of loss. Whether this relates to objects and their records, people and their documents, or the story and its intertexts, active documentation is required, as "a positive and creative approach, an insurance policy against the museum (or the novel) becoming a warehouse for unconnected debris."[84]

As stated in the introduction to this chapter, the differences between the couple are enshrined in their oppositional approaches to documentation: the mother self-describes as a "documentarist" (which, she says, makes her more like a chemist), and the father as a "documentarian," or similar to a librarian.[85] Her urgent, politically committed work of documentation leads her toward forming "patchwork solutions" and, inevitably, to deep questioning of method. She comes to see documenting as a collection of

> all the moments that didn't form part of the actual experience. A sequence of interruptions, holes, missing parts, cut out from the moment in which the experience took place. Because experience, plus a document of the experience, is experience minus one. Documents provide a version of the experience that replaces the lived experience, even if what you originally documented were the moments cut from it.[86]

She resolves to "underline" experiences rather than document them in an attempt not to overwrite reality.[87] Yet when she experiences what Patricia Stuelke has diagnosed as a form of Lauren Berlant's "genre flail,"[88] it falls to her son to take over the mantle of documentation, and of the narration of that documentation. He himself writes, "Soon after the beginning of the trip, aside from keeping the trunk neat and tidy, I knew my duty was to keep track of stuff, take pictures of everything important."[89] His plan is to take the most successful elements of both his parents' methods and become both documentarist and documentarian. He is aware that his younger sister will not remember this, their last family trip together, and so in addressing her directly, he says, "I needed to find a way to help you remember, even if it was only through things I documented for you, for the future."[90]

Lost Children Archive shows how the multiform documentation of loss and separation is crucial, and how pursuing archival methodologies can encourage the formation of future networks of relationality between and within stored objects. Much of this recuperative work relates back to the practice of storytelling. As Arlette Farge states, archives show how "narration and fiction are woven together. The resulting cloth is fine-spun, and one cannot easily spot the seams."[91] In this way, the novel's "archival form can be imagined as a method for contributing to an accretion of meaning that develops through recursive attention—through relocations and shufflings."[92] Indeed, as the final section of this chapter will explore, the novel engages in repeated scenes of reenactment through storytelling in order to supplement

94   Chapter 4

the bare data of documentation. As we will see in the next section, however, the novel also warns of the dangers of an overreliance on the documentation of bare data. The dehumanized red dots on the migrant mortality maps the narrator collects point to the risk of digital commodification of objects and people with the museum. The parallel use of the term "cold storage" for both unwanted objects in the museum and border-crossing migrants[93] points to the urgent need for alternative networks of data retrieval and elaboration that the novel and its multiform archival method attempt to respond to.

Inventory

While the first section of this chapter explored the interface between the museum and the archive that *Lost Children Archive* inhabits, here I will focus my analysis on points of divergence between museums and databases that also illuminate the novel's use of storage in terms of both form and content. Working with database theory by Mike Pepi and Lev Manovich, but also with critical elaborations on the idea of the networked novel by Mark McGurl, Debjani Ganguly, and Patricia Stuelke, I will seek to expand on how information is stored and managed both in archival novels such as *Lost Children Archive* "in the age of Amazon" and in the digital museum, and to disentangle the networks that connect things within and across them. Using the sections entitled "Inventory" that span the various accounts in the novel, we will proceed to question which forms of knowledge the database form cannot evidence, and which realities the inventory method cannot show.

In his 1999 essay "Database as Symbolic Form," Manovich takes the position that novels and databases offer oppositional ways for us to make meaning out of the world, and that in the contemporary age, databases are fast encroaching on the primacy of novels, films, and other "traditional" narrative modes as information delivery systems. Part of this opposition has to do with the way users interact with and use the different forms, but it is also —in Manovich's view—due to issues relating to how we experience structure and temporality. The database, unlike the novel, doesn't have a beginning or an end, and in most cases is, in fact, open ended: more data can always be added to a web-based list, meaning that the database is never complete.[94] As Kent Anderson has put it, "The useful archive is the networked archive."[95] Similarly, Manovich argues that the database "represents the world as a list of items it refuses to order," whereas the narrative "creates a cause-and-effect trajectory of seemingly unordered items," making them "natural enemies" in competition for the same territory of human culture.[96] A novel such as *Lost Children Archive* seems to muddle these strict categories set out by Manovich and thus, I would argue, it finds a more natural home within his broad definition of a "new media object." As a narrative that allows its "user" (or reader) to follow multiple links through its networked intertextuality, but

Storage   *95*

also through its inclusion of multiple narrative perspectives, multimedia elements, and relations with other texts on the same topic by the author, it seems most closely to resemble a hyper or interactive narrative that offers "one or more interfaces."[97] As such, it is perhaps closer to occupying a database *logic* than Manovich's strict division between novels and database would seem to suggest on first view.

The first "Inventory" section in the novel details the contents of the family car as they embark on their road trip south:

> In the front seats, he and I. In the glove compartment: proof of insurance, registration, owner's manual, and road maps. In the backseat, the two children, their backpacks, a tissue box, and a blue cooler with water bottles and perishable snacks. And in the trunk: a small duffle bag with my Sony PCM-D50 digital voice recorder, headphones, cables, and extra batteries; a large Porta-brace organizer for his collapsible boom pole, mic, headphones, cables, zeppelin and dead-cat windshield, and the 702T Sound Device. Also: four small suitcases with our clothes, and seven bankers boxes (15" X 12" X 10"), double-thick bottoms and solid lids.[98]

The function of the inventory here needs to be unpicked in order to assess how it relates to the user experience of the inventoried objects as an index. The level of detail is intense, yet everything listed holds equal value, and is reduced to the status of an item (whether it is a person or a tissue box). The inventory provides evidence of the fact that "all of it, us and them, here and there, inside and outside, was registered, collected and archived," but to what end?[99] One of the intertexts that the father packs to take with him is Rosalind E. Krauss's *Perpetual Inventory*, and it is this text that we can perhaps use to illuminate the development of inventory practices in *Lost Children Archive*. In her analysis of André Breton's 1928 novel *Nadja*, Krauss discusses the insertion of photographs into a written text as a way for the author to take critical distance from the material he has authored, offering a sense of authority but also leaving things "open": "Placing himself on the same side of the page as his reader, the writer not only casts his own shadow onto the field of the book, but allows the events unfolding in a future he cannot foresee to cast theirs onto the same space."[100] This style of inventory could thus be seen as an act aimed at the liberation of objects from the author's control, in a way that would allow them to act and to produce meaning with more autonomy as the text develops.

But there are dangers associated with the liberation of objects and images through similar data-driven inventory projects. Mike Pepi is one such critical voice raising the danger that databases and digitization can pose to museums if they engage them in response to the neoliberal, market-driven pressures facing cultural and heritage institutions. Opening his 2014 article "Is the

Museum a Database?" with a dystopian vision based on the vision of artists João Enxuto and Erica Love in which the final iteration of a Google Art Project sees the museum reduced to a virtual events space, Pepi argues that the museum now faces having to adopt a "database logic" which will see it forced to "reformat its content towards structured, indexed, or digitally stored data sets or sets of relations among data."[101] In this way, museums risk becoming nothing more than collections of image files that can be viewed or downloaded off-site by unlimited virtual visitors, transforming the institution into a passive "indexed site of transmission."[102] How does Pepi's reading relate to initiatives such as the Depot Boijmans Van Beuningen app, and do digital media risk becoming extractive, or transforming the museum into the visitors' "personal toy box"? And how does an awareness of this risk temper our reading of *Lost Children Archive* as a storage-led or archival museum novel?

In a novel preoccupied with recording silence as well as sound, it is worth reading the father's project of producing an "inventory of echoes" through Krauss's attention to the implied silence of images in works by Robert Rauschenberg. The father's project, the aim of which is effectively to gather the evidence of absence through reverberations of the past in the present, will create an inventory of "sounds that were present in the time of recording and that, when we listen to them, remind us of the ones that are lost."[103] Krauss points out that Rauschenberg's images often focus on surfaces or the fronts of buildings and objects, which both stand in for the deep space of the "real" as they simultaneously block our vision of it.[104] It is this, Krauss says, that connects Rauschenberg's practice to the idea of an archive, in which "reality is somehow ingested, organized, catalogued, and retrieved."[105] The same sort of survey mentality which links these inventory practices can be identified in the gradual move toward increased automation and the improved organization of collections as a growing concern of museums since the 1960s. In Ross Parry's view, there is a link between the advent of structuralism in cultural studies and the tendency for museums to "think in terms of patterns."[106] This has to do with systems of logistics and naming, and with the turn to encoding the structure of things in writing. This emphasis on the rational order that inventory can produce can also lead to greater relationality and creativity on the part of users, in digital media such as the Depot Boijmans Van Beuningen app. In interactives such as this one, but also in social media and other online formats, the "tagging," commenting on, and manipulation of images and content means that "users themselves became collectors of information, and the act of curatorship itself became open and shared—if conditionally. Compellingly, in this new information space, museums' online users became curators of meaning."[107]

The inventory of stored objects can, in this sense, lead to acts of creative augmentation through thumbnailing, textual descriptions, metadata, and "captioned images" as well as social tagging. It also signals the potential for the sort of liberation of objects described above, since "e-tangible" objects

Storage 97

are considered "in a state of motion, and may occupy or migrate through different states and media" that can produce new, unexpected meaning.[108] This liberation of ownership and meaning can produce anxiety, since it diminishes the trust people place in the museum as a place for "authentic" and "original" objects. But Parry points out that museums are now generally understood to be places where stories are weaved around objects and indeed where interpretation is key to understanding the context and history of the object itself. Virtuality and reality thus merge in the elaboration of the storage spaces of both the digital and physical museum. Indeed, when the son carries out his own inventory of the family's belongings in the car, his focus rests very much more on what each of them does with the objects, rather than on mere lists. Two actions seem to predominate: unknotting and untangling—whether this is in reference to the boy and the father manipulating cables, or to the mother combing the daughter's hair.[109] The son's attention is especially caught by the way that the objects (combs, chargers, cables) bring the family together through the use they make of them, and he unfolds his own narrative from the communal acts the objects facilitate and encourage.

This knotty link between inventory, fiction, and the multiple uses of data cannot help but recall the work of Mark McGurl on novel writing in the "age of Amazon." On the surface, novels provide us with therapeutic ways of processing information about the world. But Amazon, as an inherently "literary" company, which is itself "a vast engine for the production and circulation of stories," reveals sinister uses of this processed information.[110] Its founder, Jeff Bezos, started Amazon as an online bookshop, but as it branched out into all imaginable kinds of retail, it also designed new ways for people to generate and consume narrative: it developed the Kindle e-reader, encourages direct publishing through various Amazon imprints and self-publishing routes for authors, and produces film and television media, book review sites, and audiobooks. McGurl also signals Amazon's more recent move into web services, "where it has become an invisible back-end facilitator."[111] In ways that draw Amazon closer to the central concerns of *Lost Children Archive*, Patricia Stuelke shows how the company also has extensive involvement with violent regimes of border management in terms of migrant detention and deportation:

> Amazon collaborates with both ICE and the data-mining firm Palantir on whose "intelligence system" Investigative Case Management (ICM) ICE relies: ICM "allows ICE agents to access a vast 'ecosystem' of data to facilitate immigration officials in both discovering targets and then creating and administering cases against them." In addition, Amazon also "hosts several of the Department of Homeland Security's other major immigration-related databases and operations, including all the core data systems for USCIS and biometric data for 230 million individuals."[112]

98   Chapter 4

Amazon's active role in producing, farming, and interpreting data in ways that prove deadly to migrants raises the question of "how to write fiction amid the increasing imbrication of the literary sphere, datafication and settler colonial capitalist border surveillance,"[113] a question that Luiselli attempts to tackle through her narrative practices of play and reenactment. In my view, *Lost Children Archive* thus engages the database logic within a fiction-based format in order to illustrate Debjani Ganguly's idea of novel worlds—worlds which are created by what she calls "networked novels." "Novel worlds do not reproduce sociological realities; they generate imaginative approximations of possible worlds through a dynamic reconfiguration of the space-times of the historical or contemporary real."[114] In this way, a networked novel such as *Lost Children Archive* muddles the distinction between text-based narrative and the database proposed by Manovich through its "imagistic constellations" and "plot-generating movements" of play and reenactment,[115] as we will now see in more detail in the final section.

Conclusion: Family Plot

In an article she wrote for the *New Yorker* in 2019, Luiselli describes her trip to the town of Tombstone, Arizona, in the context of what she terms the "period rush" of reenactment culture: in the United States there are apparently over fifty thousand registered Civil War reenactors active today. Reenactments in places in the American Southwest such as Tombstone merge nineteenth-century narratives of the "savage Indian" with those of "illegal immigrants" from Mexico and the Northern Triangle today. Dangers lie in this overlapping of narrative through reenactment, and vigilantism to counter contemporary issues is nourished by repetitions of the myth of the frontier. "It seems plausible that, just as fictions about the Wild West have spilled over into real spaces such as Tombstone, the fiction, repeated endlessly in re-enactments, would somehow spill back into reality, be performed back into existence." In this way, the past is replaced "by a peculiar, repetitive, selective representation of the past."[116]

Various sections of *Lost Children Archive* retell parts of the family story from different perspectives, thus reenacting them through processes of memory that lay bare the act of editing necessary for their repeated narrativization. The way the mother tells the story of how the parents got together is different from the boy's perspective on the same story, and the proliferation of different versions of the same family history is something that preoccupies the mother constantly.

> I don't know what my husband and I will say to each of our children one day. I'm not sure which parts of our story we might each choose to pluck and edit out for them, and which ones we'll shuffle around

Storage 99

and insert back in to produce a final version—even though plucking, shuffling, and editing sounds is probably the best summary of what my husband and I do for a living.[117]

This preoccupation feeds into her anxiety about how to tell the story of the lost children, and leads her to realize that with the same collection of base materials, any reader could formulate completely different narratives:

> Standing in front of the seven bankers boxes, I wonder what any other mind might do with that same collection of bits and scraps, now temporarily archived in a given order inside those boxes. How many possible combinations of all those documents were there? And what completely different stories would be told by their various permutations, shufflings, and reorderings?[118]

We construct narratives ourselves, whether these stories are made of historical fact or family legend, and stories are formed through the choices we make about how to recount them.[119] However, our interlocutors are invested in the versions of the story that they hear and come to know: the narrator's children are committed to the fixity and stability of the stories they are told, demanding the exact same story every time and complaining if there are any alterations in the way the parents tell it, and are described as "anthropologists" studying and recording the family narrative."[120] They take on these family stories, and merge them with the fictional and historical narratives that the parents also share with them during the trip. In so doing, the children transform the stories their father tells them about the Apaches into refugee narratives and make their own "lost children" archive. "But they combine the stories, confuse them. They come up with possible endings and counterfactual histories."[121] This is not a negative outcome in narrative terms, and the narrator is invested in the creative, therapeutic possibilities of following the threads of the children's invented archive. Their stories have the potential to "change our world," dissolving its rational linear organization, and their imagination "destabilizes our adult sense of reality and forces us to question the very grounds of that reality."[122]

Retelling, reimagining, and reenacting stories is thus the only possible method that the narrator identifies as a way to find clarity and seek reckoning for past wrongs committed. As Luiselli states in *Tell Me How It Ends*, the only path toward justice she identifies in her role as a writer is to hear and record stories, and to translate and interpret them in turn.[123] As she says, telling stories is not a solution, a way to "reassemble broken lives. But perhaps it is a way of understanding the unthinkable."[124] The issue that *Lost Children Archive* constantly reenacts is how to tell stories, and particularly, how to tell stories of silences, gaps, and absence. And the conclusion it reaches seems to lie in its acceptance of the patchy, partial nature of the stories we can tell about the past. This patchiness, in the novel, is translated into alternative registers of sound, which manifest most frequently in terms of echoes and stammers. The echoes that the father wants to record merge with the intertextual echoes that construct the mother's narrative. As David James says, her use of the *Elegies* shows how the narrator's "involvement will be temporary and partial, producing no more than an echo of knowledge."[125] The girl's box is a collection of sounds which echo the events recounted in the previous iterations of the story, and recalls her own tendency to stammer.[126] This in turn echoes Luiselli's reception of migrant children's stories as "always shuffled, stuttered, always shattered beyond the repair of a narrative order."[127] This halting, broken way of telling stories, composed through fragments of echoes, recalls Farge's method of archival reading, which she develops "through ruptures and dispersion," and advises that we must form our questions of the available material through no more than "stutters and silences."[128] This method must be repeated over and over again through modes of creative play and reenactment, which, as Stuelke says, are the only way to "somehow access the *stuttering story* behind the data, to allow discrete historical moments of dispossession to touch across space and time."[129] Imaginative reconstruction thus takes on a fundamental role here: in *Lost Children Archive*, Luiselli never tells the stories of migrant children, but rather allows for a reimagination of their story through the protagonist's children's narrative.

Lost Children Archive thus sheds light on the issues of how to story the archive, foregrounding the question of method as one of its primary points of inquiry. It is by searching for information about the past, whether that is through creating narrative, or through searching archives, museum catalogues, and stores, that we create the story we are looking for. As Carolyn Steedman explains, "The object (whether that is an event, story, or a happening in the past) has been altered by the very search for it, and what has been actually lost can never be found. This is not to say that nothing is found, but that the thing is always something else, a creation of the search and the duration of the search."[130] This can happen in our search for material or narrative objects, but it also takes place in acts of retrieval and reelaboration through processes of human memory. But memory cannot, in itself, be relied on to "store" all the material we may wish to retrieve, so we resort to creating what Freud called "permanent memory-traces" in the form of written notes—much as those we might find in archives, catalogues, and other facilities.[131] The limits of memory that Freud explores in his writings on the "Mystic Writing-Pad" show how the human mind functions by oscillating between opposite poles of destruction and retention, in order to be perpetually receptive to new information and, at the same time, to retain and store all the previously received information. There is a clear analogy here to the question of museum storage that this chapter has been engaged with, and the twin processes of accession and deaccession that see its collections absorbed into a "constant dialectic of inscription and erasure."[132] Strands of memory,

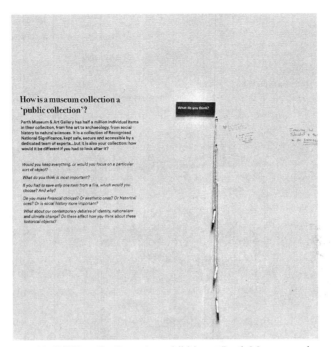

Fig. 12. *Kill Your Darlings*. An exhibition at Perth Museum and Art Gallery. © Anthony Schrag.

archive, and narrative coalesce among stored objects. In each case, the question here is, What do we retain, how do we manage it, and how do we know when and what to let go?

Questions such as these were at the forefront of a recent exhibition held at the Perth Museum and Art Gallery in central Scotland called *Kill Your Darlings* (fig. 12). Based on a residency by visual artist Anthony Schrag, the exhibition queried what a "public" museum collection is, and who it is really for.[133] Schrag was well aware that not everyone is represented in the stories that museums tell about the past, and many people and communities have historically been deliberately excluded from museum narratives. He also wanted to acknowledge that some of the objects in the museum collection were there because they had been expropriated, with varying degrees of force. Finally, his project aimed to highlight that the vast majority of museum collections are inaccessible to those who purportedly own such "public" collections, tucked away in storage that is only open to staff. As Azoulay reminds us, objects should be taken "as proof of one's place in the world, as delegates of people's worlds . . . , and as the grounds out of which the commons and a shared political existence can be reconfigured."[134] But can people and communities really be represented by a museum collection that is mainly confined to storage?

Schrag's initial proposal for his residency was to stage the destruction of one object stored within the museum collections, which was to have been voted on by the public, but this was too radical a step for the museum. Instead, he created an exhibition with three elements: the first was an installation showing a representative sample of objects from the stored collection. The second was the staging of a public vote on which of a selection of eleven objects was the most "valuable," with the public themselves deciding how to assign value to the objects in question. The third and final element was to leave one of the walls in the exhibition blank so that members of public could write about what they thought a museum is and who it should be for directly onto its structure. One Saturday afternoon I visited the exhibition and went on a guided tour of the Perth Museum's stores with the artist and one of the curators. We walked through numerous underground rooms that showcased the pristine storage of the most diverse collection imaginable. In the current status quo, the vast majority of these objects and artworks will never be seen outside the stores. Yet the artistic invention of Schrag's *Kill Your Darlings* succeeded in bringing this issue to light and established playful, creative ways to explore the questions of ownership and accessibility that storage poses for museums. In a similar vein, this chapter has identified a series of interconnected responses to the challenge of how to manage, provide access to, and narrativize storage. For as both the Depot Boijmans Van Beuningen app and the novel *Lost Children Archive* demonstrate, the future of archives and museum stores lies in the stories we tell about them: stories that must be repeatedly told through multiple, shifting perspectives that combine imagination and fact with innovative, creative design.

Chapter 5

Conservation

Introduction

It is perhaps fair to say that no other European capital city is as architecturally defined by its museums as Vienna. The palatial structures housing the imperial collections of art, antiquities, ethnography, and the wonders of the natural world that were initially amassed by Francis I (1708–1765) and his wife Maria Theresa (1717–1780), and then expanded by their descendants, today anchor the spatial grid of the city center. Constructed in the late nineteenth century as part of a never-realized Imperial Forum, the two largest museums—the Naturhistorisches Museum (Natural History Museum) and the Kunsthistorisches Museum (Museum of Fine Arts)—now lie across the Museumsplatz from the newly remodeled MuseumsQuartier, which is home to no fewer than sixty museums and cultural spaces. Vienna's central cityscape is thus defined by the preservation and display of these varied collections, which tell the long history of the Hapsburg city in turn. The Natural History Museum stands directly opposite the Museum of Fine Arts on Maria-Theresien-Platz, housed in almost identical buildings which set up a topographical distinction between nature and culture, and between the animal and human worlds. Both were commissioned and opened by Emperor Franz Joseph I in 1891, and display part of the original collections of the Hapsburg dynasty. The sandstone facade of the Natural History Museum features an inscription dedicated "to the realm of Nature and its exploration," honoring those who have sought to discover and categorize nature for the benefit of human knowledge. Yet in front of the museum stands a small, squat, black elephant statue that faces the Museum of Fine Arts in what appears to be a position of defiance to this distinction, and claiming space for those more-than-human presences that lie inside and simultaneously exceed the magisterial museum structures (fig. 13). It is worth noting further that the MuseumsQuartier itself was constructed out of Vienna's old imperial stables, leaving traces of the animal world in the cultural structures that now draw tourists and residents to visit it by the thousands each year.

103

Fig. 13. The Viennese Elephant. Photograph by Emma Bond.

If you follow the ring road up past the MuseumsQuartier to the north of the city center, you will find another Viennese museum which probes these more-than-human connections across the nature-culture divide in ways that shine light on how posthuman narratives can respond to wider conservation issues in heritage settings. This chapter will explore the depiction of the collection of eighteenth-century anatomical wax models in the Josephinum Medical Museum, and how these and other related relics and specimens have come to be conserved for display within Olga Tokarczuk's 2007 novel *Flights*.[1] The wax models of the Josephinum blend the human and nonhuman in both substance and appearance, making them akin to Rachel Poliquin's taxidermic "animal-objects."[2] As carefully preserved specimens, they will help us to explore the narrative aspects of museum conservation, but they also illuminate broader questions around how museums can respond positively to urgent issues of sustainability and climate change. This is because muddling the human-animal-object divide allows us to rethink Western

Conservation

worldviews that have "historically constructed human beings as distinct, separated from and superior to 'Nature' and, as such, entitled to dominate and exploit the non-human creatures and forces that comprise it."[3] It also offers us the opportunity to reconsider the definition of thingness from an antihumanist standpoint, something which Tokarczuk herself constantly probes through exposing the affective power that her collection of preserved wet and dry specimens, relics, taxidermy, and plastinated body parts amass and deploy throughout the constellation structure of *Flights*.

The concept of relationality is key to how I understand Tokarczuk's ability to resolve an apparent tension in her work between a sensitivity to the significance of more-than-human subjectivities and the power she invests in human capacities of narrative and imagination.[4] The museum-novel represents the perfect place to test out the interconnections between these two imperatives. As Fiona Cameron has argued, museums are ideally positioned to "concretely re-work human subject positions and frame and promote posthuman theories and practices of life through curatorial practice."[5] This possibility opens up not only because museums are trusted sites of knowledge but also because of their unstable cultural ontology. While providing space for public dialogue, museums are in a constant process of self-definition, and their incomplete attempts to categorize and display a holistic, universal view of the world serve as nothing more than a "reminder of the limits of human understanding and influence, but also of the value of working at those limits."[6] The incompleteness of the postmodern museum thus holds an animal element to it, asking us to reconsider museal structures as more-than-human, and to reimagine their investments in "place, permanence, collecting and collections, people and practices" in ways better equipped to support urgent issues such as climate action.[7] Conservation, thingness, and future sustainability are all interlinked issues which find expression in the object collections preserved within the multistranded narrative structure of *Flights*. The constellation structure of the novel disrupts any linear temporality, suggesting new ways of approaching issues of salvage and decay in both heritage management and narrative matters. The material elements of storytelling are key here. As Jennifer Newell has observed, "In a time where something seems to have gone awry in our human relationships with the world, the materiality of objects and collections seems particularly promising, replete with the capacity to reshape and recreate our place in the physical universe."[8] Foregrounding the importance of relationality in contemporary conservation practices will allow me to hold the materiality of the specimens and their figural representation within the creative spaces of the novel and the museum in equal weighting as I proceed through my analysis.

I will start by sketching out a brief history of the Josephinum and its wax model collections before going on to explore their representation both in the museum and in Tokarczuk's novel. I'm interested in linking the wax models to other preserved specimens that abound in the narrative: from religious relics to plastinated body parts, wet and dry animal specimens, and even taxidermied humans. All these "animal-objects" blur the divide between human and more-than-human in ways which confound the taxonomical order of the nineteenth-century museum. As Phillip Blom remarks, these specimens broke down "the last mediation between the human condition and the material world by focusing on the fact that bodies could themselves be objects, dead matter."[9] But rather than casting Tokarczuk's project as a nostalgic journey back in time to the ideals of a Renaissance era cabinet of curiosities, I will use her emphasis on twenty-first-century mobility, connectivity, and relational materiality to show how the narrative showcases the very latest in contemporary museum practice, and in particular, how it reveals an affinity with new conservation practices in museums. From the promotion of modes of "slow" conservation to the privileging of entropy, the meaning of conservation within heritage settings is radically shifting from a belief in the importance of crystallizing the past to an appreciation of "geographical and existential kinesis."[10] This chapter will show how *Flights* provides us with the means to conceptualize those changes in heritage management practices within and by means of a narrative framework of creative relationality.

Anatomies of Conservation

It is hard to overstate the great wealth and influence of the Hapsburg Empire in eighteenth-century Europe and beyond. Rulers of lands that spanned from the Netherlands in the north to parts of Spain and Italy in the south and Hungary and Silesia in the east, the family dynasty also occupied positions of power in other countries through strategically planned marriages. Empress Maria Theresa had succeeded in consolidating the family's power and territorial spread but was a broadly conservative leader. Her son Joseph II was an entirely different character. Although he had been crowned Holy Roman emperor upon the death of his father in 1765, Joseph had to wait until his mother's death in 1780 to be able to unleash his progressive program of social, economic, and political reform. Joseph was also an enthusiastic traveler, visiting his relatives across Europe and identifying successful reforms they themselves had implemented in other countries in order to follow suit at home. During his visit to his sister Marie Antoinette in Versailles and Paris, Joseph had taken great interest in the French hospital system and together with his personal surgeon, Giovanni Brambilla, founded a general hospital in Vienna in 1784. One year later, he opened the Imperial and Royal Joseph Academy of Medicine and Surgery, or—as it became known—the Josephinum.[11]

Upon the Josephinum's opening, the three hundred medical trainees who resided there for their studies would have marveled at the sight of the innovative and artistic teaching aids that Joseph and Brambilla had put at their

Conservation 107

disposal: a collection numbering no fewer than 1,192 anatomical wax models. Joseph had first seen similar wax models on a journey to Bologna in 1769, and when he visited his younger brother Peter Leopold, Grand Duke of Tuscany, in Florence in 1780, he was able to admire similar collections held in the Imperial Regio Museo di Fisica e Storia Naturale, better known as "La Specola." Anatomical wax modeling had started in Italy in the late seventeenth century, and the Florentine museum had amassed the most impressive collection in the world under the direction of Felice Fontana. Joseph was so impressed with what he saw in Italy that he ordered a huge number for his new academy. This was the latest, cutting-edge technology used to understand and display the human anatomy and would be essential for training up Joseph's new fleet of medical surgeons. The Viennese preparations were mostly made from casts stored at La Specola, and they were modeled by Fontana, Clemente Susini, and Paolo Mascagni, although part of the new collection, including the obstetrical preparations, were made from original models. The collection ordered by Joseph II was so vast that it took about five years for the modelers to complete it and send it on to Vienna.[12] The transport alone was no easy task: Karl Holubar describes how the models had to be carried by mules over the Alps and on rafts down the Danube.[13] Yet the process of manufacture of each model was equally laborious. Plaster patterns would be made to provide a negative mold for each wax model, which would then be refined and corrected by hand. The best wax was considered to be "white wax obtained from wild Ukrainian bees," given its high resistance to both low and high temperatures. To this wax, modelers would add "oil, lard and resin (larch and pine)," before applying pigments such as "vermilion, earth pigments and red lead."[14] This list of ingredients and methods shows the inherent blending of human, animal, natural, and chemical elements into the models themselves. Once the base form was finished, "several layers of varnish were applied before blood vessels and tendons were formed and fused together with the model. Where necessary, glass eyes were added and real hair was cut to size to serve as eyelashes."[15] The models thus represent human bodies, but were also partly composed of human elements, and crafted by human hands. The display materials were transported from Italy too, and they form an inherent part of the display assemblage: the rosewood boxes were fitted with Venetian glass covers, inside which the models would recline on pink and cream-colored silk blankets replete with tassels. From the supine perspective of the Josephinum specimens, in their composite amalgamation of human, animal, and inorganic elements, "personhood is recast as a constellation of events and encounters where animal and human lives lose neat beginnings and endings."[16]

Today, the museum stands set back from the busy Viennese ring road, with trams whirring past at speed in both directions. Through the tall, wrought-iron gates lies an oasis of relative peace: the long, symmetrical white building is flanked with trees shaped by topiary, and the roof is embellished with

Fig. 14. The Josephinum, Vienna. External view. Photograph by Emma Bond.

the golden double-headed eagle symbol of the Hapsburg monarchy (fig. 14). Staff in attendance wear white coats that reflect the history of the building as a medical teaching institution. Quiet reigns. The wax model collections are on the first floor, displayed in a series of interconnected rooms. The blinds are drawn to limit the sunlight that would otherwise pour in through the floor-to-ceiling windows and damage the waxworks. Most rooms feature reclining full-height models in glass cases in the center, with smaller models of anatomical features and body parts kept in the shelves of glass cabinets lining the walls. The display echoes the original layout: every wax model is accompanied by an analogous watercolor picture hanging above it that names the body part it represents. Each case also has a pull-out drawer underneath the main display containing a minutely labeled diagram for further consultation.

The appearance of the final room of the right-hand wing is somewhat different: it contains six male figures standing in tall cabinets placed around

Conservation

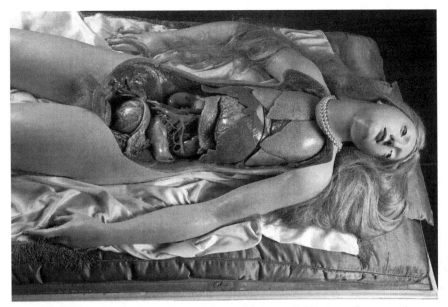

Fig. 15. *Medici Venus*, ca. 1785. Wax model. Josephinum——Ethik, Sammlungen und Gerchichte der Medizin, MedUni Wien.

the side walls, and three female figures reclining in horizontal cases in the middle. In general, the male models are used to showcase networks of muscles, tendons, and skeletal structures, and indeed, in this room, the same male figure is "stripped back" to expose an additional layer of his body in every case. "Skinned," as the narrator of *Flights* comments, "his body pleasingly woven out of muscles and tendons. Openwork."[17] Female models, on the other hand, are used to demonstrate the placement of the internal organs. The three female figures reclining in the last room have organs blooming and overspilling their open cavities. Their faces, however, are serene, even sensual. Blonde hair has carefully been sewn into convincing styles on their heads, their red lips are slightly parted, their eyes half-closed. The middle model has a double string of pearls around her neck. Known as the "Medici Venus," she was modeled on a statue of the Roman goddess in Florence (fig. 15). Her counterpart in La Specola also has a pearl necklace of just one strand; the version in Bologna has three. The Medici Venus in the Josephinum conceals other secrets from the casual viewer. Her organs are all removeable. Once the correct number are lifted off, the viewer can see that she is pregnant, as a tiny four-month-old embryo nestles in her uterus. Unruly tufts of blonde hair, going gray with an age that does not match her face, adorn her pubis. She is at once lovely and monstrous.

The obscene beauty of these models and the extraordinary quality of their craftsmanship means that they exceed our expectations of anatomical specimens and demand to be perceived as artworks in and of themselves. The narrator of *Flights* suggests that they ought to be in a gallery, "because of [their] brilliant execution in wax but also because of the design of the body itself. Who is its creator?"[18] Tokarczuk's visitor to the Josephinum is captivated by the embroidered symmetry of the internal corporeal landscape on display, each model replete with the wonder of its glistening functionality. "Who thought up the human body, and consequently, who holds its eternal copyright?"[19] During her visit she is distracted, though, by the presence of another visitor, "a middle-aged man, wearing wire-rimmed glasses, his hair completely grey."[20] This mysterious man is only interested in one of the models, the Medici Venus, which he examines in detail for a quarter of an hour and then disappears. Afterward, the narrator is left alone in the Josephinum, but the narrative follows the thin, gray-haired man into the next section of the story, entitled "Dr Blau's Travels." Blau is revealed to be a collector of photographs of vaginas, which he takes himself and keeps "in cardboard boxes with patterns, boxes purchased in IKEA."[21] His dream, however, is to create a collection of real-life organs, rather than of mere images. He is fascinated by the "botanical," "petal-like" appearance of the female organ, "beautiful as orchids that draw in insects with their shape and colour."[22] Blau has a perverse obsession with preservation and aims to immortalize the human body in each of its individual configurations through new methods of plastination. He believes that "every body part deserves to be remembered. Every human body deserves to last."[23] Blau's demonic obsession with preservation asks us to rethink the purpose of museum conservation strategies more generally: Who do we conserve for? Are there limits to what we can (and should) keep hold of? And what do we mean by preserving something "forever"?

Conservation Networks

The Josephinum wax models are inserted into a sprawling "cabinet of curiosities" that Tokarczuk assembles through her multiform, multistranded narrative. Indeed, one of the first sections in the book has the title "Cabinet of Curiosities," and the narrator goes on to visit numerous object displays of various kinds throughout her travels. But beyond the content of the novel, Tokarczuk also models a method of novel writing which is similar to the creation of a compendium or encyclopedia, building a case study around her guiding concept of constellationality. *Flights* thus constructs a series of interconnected "pilgrimages" which all aim "at some other pilgrim"—a statement that is repeated throughout the narrative. The narrator claims it is impossible to construct a narrative "with events that succeed one another casuistically and follow from each other."[24] Rather, she argues, it is necessary to "assemble a whole, out of pieces more or less the same size, placed concentrically on

Conservation

the same surface."[25] Indeed, *Flights* comprises no fewer than 116 vignettes of both fictional and nonfictional material. Interviews have recounted how Tokarczuk became deeply immersed in her own research for the book, taking a fellowship at the Vrolik Museum in Amsterdam to study the history of anatomy, and working alongside scholars and anatomists to learn their methods and philosophies.[26] And in describing her constellation methodology to an interviewer, Tokarczuk once likened herself to a tailor making a dress. Wood goes on to state: "When she finished writing *Flights* she gathered all her pages and spent a week studying them spread out on the floor of her living room."[27] The acts of cutting and stitching embedded in these descriptions of her creative process must also recall those of a surgeon, anatomist, or embalmer, or indeed those of a wax modeler melding together multiple genre elements in order to form a composite whole.

Tokarczuk's constellation methodology reminds me of the distinction drawn between preservation and storage by Richard Ovenden in his history of lost library collections around the world.[28] Indeed, the museal techniques of conservation enacted in *Flights* are quite different from the storage strategies analyzed in the previous chapter in this book, on Valeria Luiselli's *Lost Children Archive*. There, the focus was on documentation of histories through processes of archiving, cataloguing, and the ordering of matter into inventories. The potentially creative elements of archiving and storage are certainly foregrounded in Luiselli's work, but the risk remains that of accumulating to excess within an artificially constructed "antiseptic order" of things, which is primarily concerned with preservation for preservation's sake.[29] Tokarczuk, on the other hand, demonstrates a commitment to suggesting more ecological models of conservation, where more-than-human sensitivities lead to the flourishing of oddities within collections that resist order and defy categorization in their openness to decline and decay. The narrator early on expresses her interest in teratology and "freaks" of nature, saying that she is

> drawn to all things spoiled, flawed, defective, broken . . . mistakes in the making of things, dead ends. What was supposed to develop but for some reason didn't; or vice versa, what outstretched the design. Anything that deviates from the norm, that is too small or too big, overgrown or incomplete, monstrous and disgusting. Shapes that don't heed symmetry, that grow exponentially, brim over, bud, or on the contrary, that scale back to the single unit.[30]

This description not only recalls the structure of the novel itself but also reminds us of Jane Bennett's insistence on the material force of objects which allows them to exceed "human meanings, designs, or purposes."[31] Relational collections of more-than-human objects, such as those gathered together in the multistranded vignette constellation of *Flights*, are thus to be conceived of as constituent parts of an "open-ended collective, a non-totalizable sum."[32]

In this sense, it is clear to see why *Flights* has been understood as adhering to a "Renaissance episteme based on unstable metaphysical correspondences between the nonhuman and the human world,"[33] thus bypassing those rationalist taxonomies based on Enlightenment philosophy that characterized the nationalist museum-building projects of the nineteenth century. Yet there is an ecologizing thrust to Tokarczuk's work that I believe embraces future-facing models rather than pointing backward to the past. Such ecologizing experiments, in the words of Fiona Cameron, "aim to consider new ways of handling all the objects of the human and nonhuman as part of a complex, entangled life within the museum by exploring the potential for reworking the possible relations between things and people as new types of museum narratives and practices."[34] In terms of climate sustainability, the distinction I am drawing here between preservation and storage suggests the value in taking a forward-facing (resourcing and empowering) rather than backward-looking (documenting) approach to conservation and collections care in museums.[35]

Building on Latour's work, Cameron also suggests the importance of building a network of what she calls "quasi objects"[36]—hybrid human and nonhuman things—in order to express the entangled complexity of the future-facing museum: something that Tokarczuk achieves in her narrative world through celebrating the hybridity of things that blur the human-animal-object divide. The dismembered human body appears in multiple figurations that maintain their original form but shift function in their preserved state, acquiring new agency as they do so. Religious relics such as "the breasts of Saint Anne, totally intact, kept in a glass jar" are worshipped by pilgrims, in juxtaposition with the neglected contents of museum "drawers full of undocumented pieces of bone, kidney stones, some fossils . . . a mummified armadillo and other animals, a small collection of shrunken Maori heads, masks made out of human skin."[37] Conventional museum storage structures do not allow for sufficient mobility of form and function to express the hybridity of such artifacts, and Tokarczuk provides us with examples of objects which exceed their containers in fabulative, agentic ways. The Flemish surgeon and anatomist Filip Verheyen's amputated leg, kept in a "glass vessel filled with balm of Nantes brandy and black pepper" takes on its own life in its preserved state, "dreaming its own dreams of running, of wet morning grass, of warm sand on the beach."[38] Specimens of hybrid human-animal parts are thus revealed to maintain a certain vital force in their afterlives, confounding narrow interpretative grids of meaning. They become akin to contemporary conceptions of the monstrous as "a rejection of the stifling non/human binary entrapment," since the "monster is not an abstract conceptualization, but an instantaneous, enacted entanglement."[39] Once extracted after his death, Frédéric Chopin's heart is placed in a glass jar and tied to his sister's leg in order to cross national borders in secret, thus fulfilling an emotional and perhaps even political imperative.[40] The mobility of the human organ thus confounds the "establishment of countries and of

Conservation 113

boundaries between them," which demands that the human body "remain in a clearly delineated space" and instead operates the "body's natural desire to roam and to move around."[41]

Tokarczuk uses specimen body parts such as these to blur the human-animal-object divide and, by placing them on display in the museum-novel, she aims to show the artificiality of the distinction between culture and nature that characterizes the traditional museum experience. The formal hybridity of her "animal-objects" allows them to "work toward stitching together the human body and nonhuman realities that appear distant from the domain of visible bodies, and yet share their deep-rooted, affective materiality."[42] Perhaps the most vivid evocation of this within the novel is that of the skinned and stuffed body of the African courtier Angelo Soliman. In his lifetime, Soliman had latterly been a well-respected member of eighteenth-century Viennese society. As a child, however, he had been trafficked to Sicily and enslaved before working as a court Moor for Prince Joseph Wenzel von Lichtenstein, "serving his master's display of power by dressing in exoticized outfits."[43] As Heather Morrison shows, in death his agency was removed, and the "exotic" nature of his outfits was no longer within his own control. "His dress portrayed a free-thinking, self-aware man partaking fully in Vienna's culture—until his death, when the state requisitioned his body and dressed and displayed him to convey the exact opposite."[44] Inserted separately into the vignette structure of the novel are three impassioned letters written by Soliman's daughter Josefine to Emperor Francis I, descendant of Joseph II, begging for the return of his body. "My father was skinned like an animal, stuffed haphazardly with grass, and placed in the company of other stuffed human beings among the remains of unicorns, monstrous toads, two-headed foetuses floating in alcohol and other similar curiosities."[45] It is precisely the juxtaposition of human and animal specimens that offends the sensibility of those who objected to Soliman's body being placed on display, and the organic nature of the figure, its status as once living, that grants it—in the words of Rachel Poliquin—the ability to *haunt*: "By staving off the finality of material dissolution, preservation endows bodily souvenirs with an impoverished yet resolute immortality. They literally are the flagrant emotional drama in which all earthly creatures unavoidably share: of life, its inexplicable terminus, and the materiality that remains."[46]

The hybrid composition of the Josephinum wax models also haunts visitors to the museum today: walking through the stately rooms, I myself was struck by the resemblance of sections of vertebrae to giant centipedes, by the slick circular form of brains to marine creatures, glands to seaweed, and by the sight of blood vessels wafting over the surfaces of organs like mobile coral structures (fig. 16). Tokarczuk's visitor in the museum-novel also notes this striking parallel upon viewing the Medici Venus, remarking that her kidneys appear to "grow out of the bladder like two anemones," and that her kidneys and ureters "look like a mandrake root resting atop her uterus."[47]

Fig. 16. View of wax models in Room 5 of the Josephinum. Josephinum—Ethik, Sammlungen und Gerchichte der Medizin, MedUni Wien.

In this way, the wax models challenge any traditional distinction between "nature" and "culture" because they point to the fact that "relationships between human and nonhuman worlds are inextricably entwined. Such a viewpoint lets animals and artefacts gain agency, and human investigators are obliged to develop an eye for how we collectively shape, and are shaped by, nonhuman existence."[48] Tokarczuk plays with the narrative implications of this entwinement in the structure of *Flights*, replicating the "cells of a honeycomb, the curved arrangement of intestines, the insides of a body, the canals of an ear: spirals, dead-ends, appendixes, soft rounded tunnels" in the novel's constellation structure.[49] But, as the next section of this chapter will show, the representation of these more-than-human artifacts in the novel also reveals a strong affinity with the rapidly shifting conservation paradigm in contemporary museums.

Toward an Alternative Conservation Paradigm

There is evidence that dedicating attention to the preservation of art and material heritage has been a feature of most civilizations ever since humans started to create cultural artifacts. Signs of repair and restoration are evident on even ancient artifacts, and an awareness of how to manage environmental conditions in order to stem future deterioration was not uncommon among those charged with managing collections of various scales in the eighteenth century. Yet conservation practice and theory differ radically between cultures and have evolved exponentially in most museum settings from the nineteenth

Conservation 115

century to today. Scientific technology has, for example, vastly expanded the type and scale of the biological specimens available for preservation: Buttler and Davis have pointed out that until fluid preservation was introduced in the mid-seventeenth century, only dry inert materials could be preserved. Following that, the discovery of formaldehyde at the end of the nineteenth century provided another step change in the quantity and quality of preserved specimens in storage and on display in museums.[50] Yet as technology opened up the possibilities for more complex forms of specimen preservation, the driving force behind the increase in activity seemed to be expanding the scope of *what* could be preserved rather than interrogating *why* things should be preserved at all. Indeed, Tokarczuk's narrator in *Flights* is deeply troubled by what she sees as an unbridled excess of things, knowledge, information, and movement in contemporary society: "There's too much in the world. It would be wiser to reduce it, rather than expanding or enlarging it. . . . We have no choice now but to learn how to endlessly select."[51] Such processes of selection cannot help but recall man's monstrous, unnatural ordering of dead and dislocated specimens in museums. And the irony is that storage and display mechanisms within the museum are often the root cause of much of the object deterioration suffered by collections. Pollutants and contaminants can come from both inside and outside the museum, and can sometimes even originate from specimens themselves (particularly compound ones). Sometimes visitors to the museum can act as contaminants too, bringing in dust, dirt, and chemical traces on their skin and clothes that pose a threat to the safety of object collections. Museums thus hold the seeds of their own dissolution within their very structures and functions, meaning that the conservation paradigm often calls into question the value framework and purpose of the museum itself. Taking this paradox into account, Irit Narkiss has stated that when it comes to conservation, contemporary museums must follow a journey "from science-based guidelines to [a] value-based approach."[52] Such values must include building in the possibility for the reversibility of any preservation action, minimizing intervention, and the preservation of object integrity.[53]

But such paradigm shifts also require us to differentiate between techniques of conservation, preventive conservation, and restoration, and the ethical implications each one holds for our understanding of change management in the museum. Preservation (or conservation) is defined in the Burra Charter as maintaining an object or a place "in its existing state and retarding deterioration," whereas restoration is a much more radical practice and involves returning the artifact or building "as nearly as possible to a known earlier state," "distinguished by the introduction of materials (new or old) into the fabric."[54] Restoration can thus be controversial because it affects the material integrity of an artifact and alters our ideas of what is meant by the term "original." Yet the definition of conservation can be as broad as "the management of change" and the role of preventive conservation simply that of "slowing down the rate of change."[55] Discourses around conservation thus

116   Chapter 5

call forth wider societal issues around temporality, authenticity, and shifting notions of value in relation to culture and heritage. David Lowenthal identifies the desire to slow down change that motivates conservation practice as a psychological manifestation of a nostalgia attributable to cultural amnesia and political manipulations of history, and he sees the phenomenon as most noticeably affecting the most recent generations. As he remarks, "The impulse to preserve is partly a reaction against the increasing evanescence of things and the speed with which we pass them by."[56] The further away we feel from recent history, then, and the more we feel that time is "speeding up" to place ever-greater distance between the present and the past, the more we want to restore material evidence of history to an earlier state of its being. Yet, as we will see in the next chapter, on restitution practices in Maaza Mengiste's novel *The Shadow King*, museums must respond to this conservation impetus by reconciling long-standing Western practices with a new understanding of decolonial praxis. This means rethinking key terms such as "repair" and "conservation" in ways that acknowledge their colonial undertones, since coloniality is expressed "in the denial of the wound and the desire to control."[57] Reparation, in this sense, can be a concept applied to objects, but also to relationships between communities, and to the stories that objects hold within them. This more fluid notion of the conservation of object-stories is identifiable as a feature embedded within the loosely stitched narrative structure of *Flights*. How can we relate this novelistic process of association to questions of climate awareness and the broader discourse around sustainability? As I will illustrate, Tokarczuk's writing shows us that it is precisely in the "concepts of fragility, instability, and impermanence" that the museum and the museum-novel can converge to transform conservation practices, "making them places that are more in keeping with contemporary environmental realities and ethical concerns."[58]

In *Flights* we see the contrast between strictly traditional conservation paradigms focused on preserving everything everywhere, and the new emphasis on allowing space for impermanence and entropy, drawn in the differing representations of the mobile plasticity of object meanings versus the solidifying of things into categories. This mistrust of categorization is evident in descriptions of Dr. Blau's sinister ordering of boxes of genital photography, but also in those of the boxes of holiday photographs taken by a young couple the narrator meets on a train that they keep "safely tucked away in plastic folders, like evidence in a detective's cabinet—evidence that they had been there."[59] When a young mother and child go missing on the small Croatian island of Vis, the father articulates his distress and confusion by unpacking all the objects they had brought with them and photographing them one by one. From his wife's bag he extracts a dark red lipstick, her passport, a little black notebook, a cosmetics bag, an open pack of sanitary napkins, pens, pocket change, a copper pin, sweets, a peg, food crumbs, and a thin scattering of sand. He carefully documents their appearance, trying

Conservation

117

to probe "their constellations, positionings, the directions they point in, the shapes they make," but is unable to parse the narrative they offer him.[60] "He doesn't recognize the writing, doesn't recognize the symbols—it was not a human hand that wrote them, of that he is certain."[61] The mystery of meaning evades those who attempt to possess things through documentation in order to use them as "evidence" of some external fact. In the same way, the narrator also expresses her dislike of touristic guidebooks, claiming that they have "conclusively ruined the greater part of the planet; . . . they have debilitated places, pinning them down and naming them, blurring their contours. The truth is terrible: describing is destroying."[62] Knowledge can only be apprehended through subjective and monadic modes of composition, such as with Wikipedia, which the narrator acknowledges as "mankind's most honest cognitive project. It is frank about the fact that all the information we have about the world comes straight out of our own heads."[63] Such excesses of knowledge that cannot be ordered become, conversely, "inhuman" and take on animal or plant form instead: "the form of a sponge, of deep-sea corals growing over the years until they started to create the most fantastic forms."[64]

It is perhaps no coincidence that Tokarczuk compares the fragility of knowledge blooms to the forms of some of the most endangered parts of the marine ecosystem in her questioning of the preservation paradigm. Conservation practice has always involved weighing different paradigms of risk and balancing the potential trade-offs between intervention and inaction. Once we have assembled a patrimony of cultural heritage that we assign value to, its safeguarding becomes subject to countering the effects of a wide range of what conservators would call "agents of deterioration." Szczepanowska lists ten of the most common agents: "direct physical forces, thieves/vandals and displacers, fire, water, pests, contaminants, radiation, incorrect temperatures, incorrect relative humidity, and custodial neglect."[65] Museums now need to engage in disaster recovery planning and complex operations of monitoring and controlling both their internal environment and external environmental factors, something which is made much more complicated by the ever-worsening climate emergency. Museum conservation is, thus, inextricably linked with questions of sustainability and museum futures. As Suzanne Keene remarks, "Collections force museums to look to the long term" and thus also to plan for climate-sensitive futures.[66] Given that display is the riskiest aspect of an object's life in the museum, part of these considerations is dedicated to attempts to achieve a balance between preservation and allowing collections to be accessed for research or exhibition purposes. We have noted how entry into the museum presupposes a separation of an object's form and function, and in fact, how museum objects take on the specific new function of preserving and displaying "evidence of the past." This signals the final, or "curation phase," of the object's life.[67] Taking this on board, can a museum-novel such as *Flights* counter this potentially reductive role of the museum object as static and evidence based, and offer an example of an alternative conservation structure that allows for a multiplicity of its thing-function, including creative elements released through free-form processes of entropy and decay?

As we have seen at several points through this book, museum conservation practices are traditionally based on a framework that promotes highly subjective ideals of truth, authenticity, and stasis.[68] C. Watkins noted back in 1989 how such conservation values seem to fall neatly into line with the twentieth-century European desire to always appear young and to live a long life: "The museum embodies the denial of death insofar as it is an institution that both preserves and presents objects from the distant past and, through periodic conservation, keeps them in good appearance."[69] The collateral effect of this, however, is that the conservation of the past through objects does not succeed in freezing the past, but actually ends up freezing the present, which, as Alexander Stille says, in turn offers up "a highly distorted, fragmentary version of the past."[70] In *Flights*, free-form travel is offered up as a way to defy this distortion of time through society's attempts to freeze it into preservation. Mobility is celebrated in the original title of the book in Polish as *Bieguni,* or "Wanderers," in reference to a little-known Slavic sect that rejects settled life for an existence of constant movement.[71] One of the vignettes recounts the story of Annushka, a Muscovite who escapes her caring responsibilities one day a week to ride the subway and encounters an oddly dressed woman at her interchange at Kievsky Station. This wandering woman's choice of multiply layered clothing is described as the "haute couture of entropy—fading colours, fraying and falling apart," and the freedom that mobility offers the numerous other subway free riders that Annushka meets allows them to evade categorization and the related ignominy of being "pinned down" like specimens.[72] Working counter to the traditional museum conservation ethos of shoring up stuff in secure storage to avoid running the risk of deterioration, *Flights* thus offers a liberated vision of mobility as an alternative to stasis. The physical energy of mobility is related to active processes of entropy which allow for transformation and change through the "multiplicity of potential arrangements of matter in a given system."[73] The mobility of meaning embodied by material objects is also uniquely able to destabilize anthropocentric assumptions. As Caracciolo writes: "No longer objectified . . . the museum artefact thus becomes a material stand-in for the complexity of the Anthropocene, with its enmeshment of human agency, historically specific responsibilities, and nonhuman materiality."[74] We can thus look to the narrative of the museum-novel to find new ways of conserving these complex object properties in order to better reflect and promote sustainable models of mobility and freedom of form. This is the case even if such practices lead to decay or destruction, since "objects generate meaning not just in their preservation and persistence but also in their destruction and

Conservation   *119*

disposal."[75] As Etienne states, "Instability, change, and loss are sometimes the best ways of caring for a collection."[76]

Conclusion: Narration as Restorative Practice

This chapter has suggested that the representations of the Josephinum wax models and other bodily specimens in *Flights* provide us with examples of posthuman hybridity that can offer new insights into possible methods of future-oriented, sustainable conservation practices in museums. They assemble in Tokarczuk's relational narrative as a composite example of how to "make oddkin," to use Donna Haraway's words: forming "unexpected collaborations and combinations, in hot compost piles" that allow space for processes of entropy and decay as possibilities for object futures.[77] The conservation of animal and compound specimens has often been understood as a mechanism of preserving "liveliness in the face of death," compensating for the passage of time through freezing memories into object form.[78] But the conservation model proposed in *Flights* shows us that while the management of change can allow time to slow down, some level of decay is always inevitable, and entropy is in fact something to be welcomed. Elements of decay, rupture, and composting are locatable throughout the novel and function as models for a kind of future-facing conservation practice that opens up to the possibility of loss and letting go. The narrator states early on that it is precisely the errors and blunders of creation that form the objective of her wanderings.[79] She details poorly preserved mummies in appreciative detail, noting that their "skin was completely blackened, dry," with "torn seagrass spilling out of the seams, which had split apart in places."[80] Objects such as these exceed the strict parameters of their confinement through museum modes of preservation and display, and spill out to form new, often unruly assemblages. In similar fashion, we learn that Professor Ruysch's world-leading collection of wet specimens are bought by Peter I, czar of the Russian Empire, and during their sea voyage back to St. Petersburg the sailors open up the jars to drink the brandy they are preserved in, leaving the specimens "lying around on the floor, submerged in tow and sawdust."[81] The idea in raising these examples here is to look beyond "saving" material heritage and to find alternative ways of relating to the past. As Marilena Alivizatou writes, "The idea is to think beyond concepts of decay, salvage and loss and engage with cultural change as a new heritage value."[82] In *Flights*, these pathways toward alternative value formation are decidedly narrative and forge their way forward by means of connective stories, imaginative wanderings, and fabulative worlds.

Tokarczuk presents us with an elegy for mobility that works against any kind of "frozen order" that would work to "falsify time's passage" in the direction of the past rather than the future.[83] There are lessons here to be learned for museums in their quest to become more sustainable. As we have seen, the narrator of *Flights* expresses her desire to gather a compendium of all that we do not know, and of everything that cannot be captured.[84] Such an assemblage of uncertainty allows her to combine creativity with sustainability in her related discourse on the wasteful nature of paper packaging, and her proposal to use novels and poems instead ("and always in such a way that what is contained and what contains it have some connection").[85] Plasticity of perception as well as form is always fundamental to her vision, as embodied by her appreciation of Dr. Mole's preserved specimens, which are easy to separate and reassemble and thus allow "endless possibilities in terms of travels within the body of the preserved organism."[86] In the same way, although the narrator raises ecological concerns about the use of plastic bags, she can still appreciate their lightness and mobility, commenting that "evolution favours fleeting forms that can flit through the world while at the same time attaining ubiquitousness."[87] Nimble forms of mobility acquire a value that links up with the importance of museums privileging the reparation of relations with communities and their stories rather than the preservation of objects. As Alivizatou states, "Value does not lie in the authenticity of the material, but rather in the knowledge, information, or images that are inherent in their materiality and ultimately reside in human thought and memory."[88]

Tokarczuk was awarded the Nobel Prize in 2019 in recognition of her "narrative imagination that with encyclopedic passion represents the crossing of boundaries as a form of life,"[89] a statement that explicitly acknowledges her interest in creating forms of writing that help us to conceptually cross the human-animal-nature divide. This is also a feature of her other fictional works: in her earlier novel *Drive Your Plow over the Bones of the Dead*, the protagonist collects animal remains in hopes of re-creating them from salvaged DNA in the future. Malgorzata Kowalcze points out that for Tokarczuk, "those shreds of 'dead' matter are permeated with the kind of life that persists even after biological life comes to an end."[90] In *Flights*, too, the journey into and through the human body in its various states of preservation comes to symbolize an ecological and ecologizing drive toward sustainable practices of heritage management that build on her more-than-human sensitivities. In the words of Marco Caracciolo, "By exposing the normally invisible interior of the human body through recurrent patterns of metaphors and similes, Tokarczuk connects it to the abstract reality of our planetary impact."[91] The human body extends transcorporeally into the nonhuman world through the work of narrative—itself a particularly human endeavor. We see bodies in the process of degrading that are compared to plastics, and such a view helps us to appreciate the creative possibilities of decomposition. Watching passersby on the Moscow metro, Annushka sees the "brittleness of arms, the fragility of eyelids, the unstable line of people's lips . . . she sees how weak their hands are, how weak their legs—they will not, cannot,

Conservation

121

carry them to any destination." Their bodies are mechanical composites slowing down toward cessation, their lung sacs described as "dirty plastic bags" as they "wed entropy."[92] The mystery of decay, the joy in these composite, composting constellations are charted in narrative terms and come together in a novelistic imagining of the cooperation of natural biological cycles of growth and decay: "All animate things cooperate in this growth and bursting, supporting one another."[93] Time is measured by change in *Flights*, and space measured by motion. The compound nature of the objects displayed within its multiverse reveals an excess of form that challenges the human-animal-nature divide and renders the rigidity of the traditional preservation paradigm obsolete.

Within the museum sector, Dean Sully has charted a similar shift in conservation practice from "a specialist technical service aimed at preserving heritage, to a mechanism for the creation and re-creation of culture."[94] The creative impulse is thus firmly foregrounded in both the museum and the museum-novel. Instead of crystallizing the past, the aim of contemporary heritage conservation practice is to reflect the "multifaceted plurality of an object's transition through time" in order to envisage potential alternative futures.[95] Time and temporality are threads that annotate concepts of conservation throughout the novel, particularly in the linked sections that discuss "Kairos," the Greek word for time and the name of an ancient Greek god. This word, Kairos, conceals past secrets in the present: on Vis, one of the objects Kunicki extracts from his wife's bag is a museum ticket from Trogir that has K-A-I-R-O-S spelled out on the back of it, "although he's not sure, and doesn't know what that would be."[96] Once home, he decides that it is this word which will explain not only the mystery of his family's disappearance to him but also, by extent, the mystery of human meaning in the universe. He visits the local library, consults dictionaries, and learns the different meanings of the word. When he finds that the link the word has with the museum in Trogir is merely the presence of a statue of the Greek god of the same name ("of little importance, forgotten, Hellenic") in its collections, he believes the search is resolved and abandons his mission.[97] Yet the god Kairos also motivates the next section, which tells the story of an elderly professor of ancient Greek who undertakes a speaking cruise through the Greek islands. His companion, Karen, suggests he give a lecture on "those gods who didn't make it into the pages of the famous, popular books"—gods, that is, like the unknown Kairos. Yet their anonymity allows these figures "a divine volatility and ungraspability, a fluidity of form, an uncertainty of genealogy."[98] These are the ideal figures to populate Tokarczuk's encyclopedia of the unknown, the forgotten, and the poorly preserved for future knowledge. Kairos, as she says, "always operates at the intersection of linear, human and divine time—circular time. And at the intersection between time and space," opening up unique possibilities for contact between moments that connect the linear and the circular.[99] *Flights* shows us that it is objects that hold the power to "bridge spaces and join times" in this way since they conjoin past, present, and future; the known and the unknowable, and "thus they can disrupt linear narratives."[100] In the end it is the narrativization of these objects which performs the ultimate function of preservation: the narrator of *Flights* suggests that in the future "we will reciprocally transform each other into letters and initials, immortalize each other, plastinate each other in formaldehyde phrases and pages."[101] But narrative is also crucial for sustainable futures in museums. As Rob Nixon writes, "In a world awash with data, narrative can play a critical role in shaping environmental publics and environmental policy."[102] Tokarczuk is thus providing the reader with the vision of a form of restoration in which only what is "different" will survive on in creative form to "be resurrected in the end."[103]

With *Flights*, Tokarczuk offers us an excavation site where "forensic dissection unite[s] with unfettered imagination" in a process that Priya Basil has called "fabulography —a practice of projecting freely, associatively into the gaps of the past to retrieve in any form . . . something of what has been lost."[104] The stories that Tokarczuk weaves around more-than-human objects in the novel lend them a potentiality and liveliness that points to alternative, more sustainable futures for museum conservation. Authority is dislodged from the traditional museum values of authenticity, stasis, and preservation, and now resides in the reanimation of remnants, voids, and ruins of material heritage through fabular circles of narrative.

Chapter 6

Restitution

Introduction

As the conclusions to chapter 2 of this book showed, in Claudio Magris's *Blameless*, a missing rifle is the only "evidence" to support the account of Austrian soldier Otto Schimek's heroic refusal to shoot a group of Polish civilians in 1944. On a quest to dig deeper into Schimek's story, the protagonist Luisa meets a research assistant who encourages her to look beyond this (lack of) evidence and to try and understand that the general public's emotional investment in the story lends it an authority that goes beyond the matter of bare facts. He offers her a final piece of information as she leaves, saying, "His rifle was always jamming, a witness says. *That says something.*"[1] If we want to understand what it is that this broken rifle might be saying, we need to wind back to think about how and why we invest objects with the power to tell stories, and what stories *broken* objects in particular can reveal. In order to do so, I want to focus on another malfunctioning gun: this time, the antique Wujigra rifle that belongs to Hirut, the protagonist of Maaza Mengiste's 2019 novel *The Shadow King*. In a novel propelled forward by a peculiar "kinetic force" that manifests in jagged irruptions of past stories into the present action,[2] and in the breached bodies and split subjectivities of its characters, the rupture caused by the revelation of this rifle's brokenness allows new, unexpected narrative avenues to open up and run counter to more conventionally received histories. In this chapter, I will use Hirut's broken Wujigra as a departure point to explore several interrelated questions. How does the novelistic form and focus of *The Shadow King* use this object to stage and restage different elements of the story of colonial breakage (as manifested through practices of occupation, abuse, and violent dispossession), and equally, in what ways can it offer up new potential stories of anti-colonial repair? Can we call on this broken artifact to shed light on the past, present, and future stories of objects stolen from Ethiopia and other lands in the short-lived "empire" of Italian East Africa (Africa Orientale Italiana) that are now held across various museums in Europe and the United States? And finally, can we identify narrative techniques in Mengiste's novel

123

that might indicate how heritage institutions might work more broadly to forge new pathways toward cultural restitution?

As Felwine Sarr and Bénédicte Savoy explain in their 2018 report *The Restitution of African Cultural Heritage*, restitution means to return an item to its original owner, and thus signifies an attempt "to put things back in order, into proper harmony."[3] This chapter will seek to locate this potential for the restoration of order by performing a reparative reading of Mengiste's novel and of the museum objects it evokes. It builds on notions of repair theorized by the French artist Kader Attia and on postcritical literary scholarship by Eve Kosofsky Sedgwick and Rita Felski, among others, to suggest that *The Shadow King* can offer new insight into how to care for objects from lands formerly occupied by Italy that are now held in the collections of museums such as the Museo delle Civiltà in Rome and the Wolfsonian-FIU in Miami. This is not a story of object care through traditional routes of preservation, but of carework which may repair absence through speculating different modes of return: modes that may be as much about "giving up" as they are about "giving back."[4] Ian Chambers remarks:

> If objects, histories, cultures, people were once wrenched out of their context in order to be put on display and exhibited as European knowledge, today this has to be unwound from its colonial premises and handed back to the world it once presumed to define and own. In the harsh light of the gallery space and the illuminated caption, can the *impossibility* of a healing be exposed? Can the modern museum house what amounts to a historical and ontological cut when its collection and criteria are re-routed through a radically diverse accounting of time and space?[5]

Chambers goes on to suggest that the postcolonial museum embodies a cut that "remains uncurable," one that represents an "economy of rupture and becoming that bleeds into the present."[6] In so doing, he alights on something that is also central to Attia's notion of repair as an entanglement of injury and cure, in which the sign of the injury must be maintained, not erased.[7] The deep injury caused by colonialism requires a "response" instead of a "resolution,"[8] and the current chapter will probe precisely the question of how objects in *The Shadow King* can take up this call for response. My analysis will build on Crystal B. Lake's critical attention to found objects and her interest in "old, dirty, rusty, moldy and broken items—the small bits and bobs whose origins or backstories [a]re unknown and whose worth and meaning [is] not self-evident."[9] These items are especially generative precisely because the lack of available information about them opens up the possibility (or necessity) for humans to attempt reconstructions or interpretations of their meaning. This is because, as Sara Ahmed notes, "the failure of things to work creates an incentive to make new things."[10] In narrative terms, these broken

Restitution 125

objects come to assume a dynamism of their own, taking on a "troubling tendency to keep changing their story or to stop talking at the very moments when we need them to say more."[11] In *The Shadow King*, I will show how old, malfunctioning objects of questionable worth such as Hirut's rifle can be read as artifactual insurgents, disrupting any smoothness of the narrative flow and opening up history to divergent perspectives and temporalities that signal possible future routes into repair.

Mengiste's novel opens on the eve of the 1974 revolution that will eventually overthrow the emperor of Ethiopia, Haile Selassie. Hirut, now approaching old age, travels to the capital city, Addis Ababa, to return a box full of photographs, letters, and clippings to its previous owner, the former Italian solider and military photographer Ettore Navarra. Much as the plot of Drndić's *Trieste* followed the trail of items and papers that Haya Tedeschi pulled out of her red basket to narrate her own story of loss and recuperation, *The Shadow King* shows how at first Hirut manually sorts the contents of Ettore's box into a chronological index for the action to follow. The images contained within the boxed photographic record chart the story of Hirut's life before the Italian invasion of Ethiopia in 1935, when she lived as a servant in the house of the military officer Kidane and his wife, Aster. When the Italians invade, the household is mobilized into a rebel unit which establishes camp high in the mountains, spying on and—where possible—attacking the Italian aggressors. The photos also record the subsequent capture of Hirut and Aster by Navarra's unit, led by the violent Colonel Carlo Fucelli, who insists that Navarra document the increasingly frequent and extreme atrocities carried out by the Italians. These photographs are interspersed with Navarra's personal effects—in particular, with letters from his Jewish parents back in Italy. But, as Francesca Capossela, writing in the *Los Angeles Review of Books*, points out, "The book is not only made up of what is documented and preserved; unwritten memories and experiences are recorded alongside Ettore's documents."[12] The photographs do not tell the full story of the facts of war: in fact, more often than not—as the novel shows—they are doctored or falsified to fit the aspirational narrative of Italian imperialism in action.

Indeed, Mengiste is particularly interested in supplementing the existing historical record with the lesser-known story of women's involvement in the Ethiopian resistance to the Italian occupation, women who she says "even today remained no more than errant lines in faded documents."[13] As she explains in the author's note that follows the novel, stories of war most commonly recount the actions and experiences of men, but Mengiste's own great-grandmother defied her parents, took her father's rifle, and enlisted to fight against the Italians.[14] Hers was not an uncommon presence: Hailu Habta and Judith A. Byfield state that approximately one-third of the names that were recorded in the Ethiopian Book of Honor and awarded medals for their contribution to the 1935–1941 war were women.[15] Women were both actors in the war and provided motivation—both symbolic and physical—for it. The Italian colonial era was initially characterized by a dual desire for possession: the possession of new territory became entwined with the fantasy of sexual possession of women in those territories to be conquered. This was seen as righting a double wrong that began in the humiliating defeat of Italian troops by Ethiopian fighters at the Battle of Adwa in 1896, a defeat that was conceptualized in gendered, or even sexualized, terms. As Neelam Srivastana writes, "Mussolini explicitly links the war of aggression to Adwa, a stain on the honour of the nation that needed to be avenged."[16] This new, imperialist war was, then, a revisionist attempt by Italy to "rewrite history, to alter memory, to resurrect their dead and refashion them as heroes."[17] Italy had begun its colonial drive for territorial expansion overseas with the acquisition of land around Assab and Massawa in the 1870s, before forming colonies in Eritrea, Somalia, and Libya, and then enacting the Fascist-era invasions of Ethiopia, Albania, and Greece. These were not peaceable missions. Ruth Ben-Ghiat and Mia Fuller take stock of the "notable primacy in military aggressions" carried out by Italy in its colonial era, "which ranged from old-fashioned savageries (decapitations, castrations, and the burning and razing of civilian quarters) to industrial killing methods (aerial gas bombings, open-grave executions, concentration camps)."[18] Many critics have amply shown the decisive role photography played in justifying the violence involved in the Italian invasion and occupation of Ethiopia, particularly in gendered terms,[19] but, as this chapter will show, there is still more to understand both about how material objects functioned to reinforce an Italian narrative of colonial justification, and about how they can be mobilized to resist that narrative and offer inspiration for alternative stories to emerge from relevant museum collections going forward.

Taking Hold of Objects

Sarr and Savoy open their landmark report by highlighting the colonial "harvesting" of African heritage objects by European nations, which has resulted in over 90 percent of the material cultural legacy of sub-Saharan Africa being "preserved and housed outside of the African continent." The forced absence of these objects is a "wound" that goes beyond their physical removal: the "reserves of energy, creative resources, reservoirs of potentials, forces engendering alternative figures and forms of the real, forces of germination" that were taken alongside them add up to an "incommensurable loss."[20] In particular, Ethiopia was subjected to "extensive foreign looting twice in modern times": first in the punitive British expedition against the fortress of Maqdala in 1868, and second during the Italian occupation of 1935–1941.[21] Richard Pankhurst explains that the Fascist looting had the double objective of on the one hand removing symbols of Ethiopia's ancient independence, and on the other, allowing Mussolini to emulate the imperial looting practices of ancient

Restitution 127

Rome. What is more, Mussolini permitted individual leaders to follow his initiative to loot for their own personal gain:

> The principal fascist leaders were all involved in looting. Pietro Badoglio, the first Italian viceroy, appropriated half the 1,700,000 Maria Theresa dollars found in the Bank of Abyssinia. This enabled him to build a villa in Rome, in which he reportedly installed 300 cases of booty flown from Ethiopia by the Italian Royal Air Force. The second viceroy, Rodolfo Graziani, likewise took back 9 cases of loot, while Attilio Teruzzi, the Minister of Italian Africa, on one visit in 1939, [took] no less than four truck-loads.[22]

This layered story of loss and theft is reflected in the already-mentioned "kinetic force" that sets the narrative action into motion at the start of *The Shadow King*. Prior to Hirut's arrival into her household, Aster, in mourning after the death of her infant son, threw away and burned piles of her own belongings, "her finest dresses and capes and even jewelry," often forgetting exactly what she had destroyed afterward.[23] In searching for a lost necklace, she ransacks the room Hirut shares with the family cook, upends their crate of objects, and unexpectedly finds the rifle Hirut had been gifted by her parents before their deaths. Hirut has memorized the contents of the crate, and they are listed in the novel: "the cook's spare scarf, knotted around three Maria Theresa thalers and two blue buttons; the outgrown dress that Hirut came with; a piece of charcoal she uses for drawing; a broken ceramic plate with pink flowers that is the cook's; the chipped handle of a water jug that is also the cook's; and a bullet that is Hirut's."[24] This is the map of the two servants' shared world shrunk down to fit the contents of a crate, which in turn holds the history of Hirut's identity and heritage within it. The rifle and single bullet are taken by Kidane and Aster to bolster the stock of weapons available to the resistance against the coming Italian invasion. Their loss sends Hirut into a spiral of remembered trauma: her rifle is the only tie she has to her past and to her family, and without this material link she "feels herself disappearing, senses her bones softening and sliding into her skin."[25] Objects matter because they signal belonging and link us to our heritage, our identity, and our communities. They matter perhaps even more once they are gone and exist only in memorial form. Ariella Aïsha Azoulay writes powerfully about her lack of any inherited objects and artifacts relating to her family history in Algeria and Spain, and her consequent struggle to reclaim her identity as a Palestinian Jew rather than an Israeli national.[26] What the present chapter seeks to interrogate is whether the loss or breakage of objects can conversely help us to understand how to create instances of potentiality. And, in a related sense, what can the novelistic form of *The Shadow King* reveal, unlearn, and repair by focusing on the loss of this particular object?

128   Chapter 6

In order to offer some response to these questions, we need to first explore the history of how the objects that tell the stories of the Italian colonial presence in North and East Africa came to be in the collections of the Museo delle Civiltà and the Wolfsonian. The objects I am thinking of in the Museo delle Civiltà originate in the collections of the old Museo coloniale (Colonial Museum), which was opened by Mussolini in 1923 in Palazzo della Consulta, in central Rome. This museum moved locations within the capital and changed names several times before definitively closing in 1971. The objects in its care were then held in storage for forty years, before moving in 2011 to the Museo delle Civiltà complex in Mussolini's new-build EUR district of the city. The original collections once numbered around twelve thousand objects, which were on display to the public across a span of thirty-five rooms. They mainly originated from Ethiopia, though objects representing other Italian colonies were also present. They were collected in phases, and many had been gathered for the various colonial and international exhibitions that Italy staged in the first half of the twentieth century, particularly the Mostra coloniale italiana (Italian Colonial Exhibition) held in Genoa in 1914. The museum had a specific propaganda aim, which was, as Martina Montemaggi writes, "to instruct Italians about their colonial might and civilizational power in Africa while implicitly building national pride and colonial awareness within Italian society."[27] As we will see, the fact that these objects have for so long been hidden in storage lends them a particularly fragmented narrative, as specters in what Francesca Gandolfo has termed a "ghost museum" (*museo fantasma*).[28] At the time of writing, the curators of the Museo delle Civiltà are engaged in a long and complex program aimed at reviving and redisplaying the collection in a new decolonial fashion. One particular challenge they face is the gaps in the knowledge they hold about the collections; this means that a full reconstruction of their history is impossible. As they say, "We know little about these colonial collections, almost no information on who collected the objects, in what context and for what purpose." This makes the museum collections "elusive, mobile material," whose objects—like Lake's artifacts—generate more uncertainty than certainty as the curators attempt to draw meaningful narratives from them.[29]

Objects that tell a differently layered history of Italian colonialism in Africa lie in collections in the somewhat incongruous setting of Miami Beach. As a boy growing up in the 1940s and 1950s in a wealthy international milieu, the museum's founder, Mitchell "Micky" Wolfson Jr., started a lifelong collecting habit that would see him amass over one hundred thousand objects. These objects now fill multiple storehouses and repurposed museum spaces in Miami Beach and in Nervi, a suburb of the northwestern Italian city of Genoa. Wolfson began by collecting hotel room keys, and then gravitated toward collecting design items, with a particular fascination with Nazi and Fascist propaganda. His mantra, "what man makes, makes man," underpins his belief that objects tell us things about human behavior better than any

Restitution   *129*

other form of human expression, and that exploring the design of objects
can teach us about how they work to influence attitudes, actions, and percep-
tions.[30] In 2017 I had the opportunity to spend a month researching Wolfson's
collections of Fascist propaganda relating to Italian colonial expansion into
North and East Africa and the Italian-Ethiopian war of 1935–1941. While
we know all the collection materials were acquired by Wolfson, and often
when, we don't always know why, where, or from whom. Researchers who
visit the collections are thus free to construct their own paths of inquiry into
and around specific items and their linkages, and to reach radically different
outcomes. I arrived at the Wolfsonian at the start of June to a wave of intense
Florida heat and humidity. In between admiring the Art Deco buildings that
punctuated my slow walk along Washington Avenue to the research center
each morning, eating Haitian and Cuban food at lunchtime, and taking long
swims in the warm sea at the end of each day, I looked through reams of
objects, ephemera, and rare printed materials held so far away from where
they were crafted and originally acquired. I initially explored how Italy constructed its colonies as objects of desire, domination, and potential profit, yet I
quickly became drawn to analyzing how the collections are interspersed with
photographs and printed materials from elsewhere in the world, reflecting
their present location in the multilingual, multicultural context of Miami. The
disrupted narratives in the Wolfsonian collections combined with the elusive,
mobile nature of the objects in storage in the Museo delle Civiltà to inspire
my thinking about the different modes of material agency which complicate
any monolinear, propagandistic narrative of Italian empire.

In the analysis that follows I will use narrative techniques showcased in
The Shadow King to suggest approaches to "reading" ways in which cultural
objects are taken hold of by museums such as these, but also ways in which the
same objects hold the potential to "repossess" autonomy of meaning through
diverse forms of restitution. We can see this in how the narrative they embody
changes as they are exchanged, lost, stolen, or recovered. The first way that the
novel intervenes in questions of ownership and belonging is in its attention to
object documentation through acts of listing, cataloguing, and classifying, similar to those we explored in chapter 4 of this book, on Valeria Luiselli's *Lost
Children Archive*. This question of documentation is important when we consider the catastrophic ramifications of the object looting and loss that occur
through colonial occupation and rule. Hirut reflects that "all things, even those
lost, can be put down on paper and measured."[31] But objects might be measured differently, in relation to shifting notions of value that people place on
them. One key example of this is the two separate lists of objects that Hirut
steals from Aster as she searches for her own stolen rifle. Hirut's inventory lists:

> A yellow bead, a swatch of red silk, a golden tassel, five rubber bands,
> six thalers, a broken pencil, a rusted pocket-knife, a torn umbrella,
> a horseshoe, a small amber stone, a hand mirror, and incense burner,

130   Chapter 6

a delicate gold-rimmed coffee cup, an inkpad, a broken compass, a folded map, a leather-bound miniature Bible, two closed amulets, a palm-sized wooden cross, a green wool scarf, a segment of a delicate gold chain, a shiny blue stone, a fragment of soapstone, a silver-handled letter opener, a wine goblet, six matchboxes, two crushed cigarettes, an empty pillbox, a leather bracelet, a strapless watch, a horsehair fly swatter, a collapsible hand fan, an ashtray, a stack of stamped documents, two folded envelopes, a wooden cross pendant, a leather cross pendant, two silver chains, a scrap of black velvet, a spool of discarded cotton, a ball of green yarn, a bent miniature frame, a beaded necklace, a leather satchel, a glass tea cup, a gold-handled spoon, a hand-sized painting of Iyesus Cristos, a child's bracelet, a pince-nez, silver anklets, one gold earring, a black scarf with gold embroidery, binoculars, a plain black scarf, a pair of gold and ruby earrings, a matching bracelet, and a brilliant ruby ring.[32]

Yet what Aster finds is:

Two *crushed* cigarettes, a *broken* pencil, a leather satchel, an *empty* pillbox, a stack of stamped documents, a *strapless* watch, an ink pad and a *broken* compass, a *small* amber stone, a horsehair fly swatter, a *rusted* pocketknife, a collapsible hand fan, two folded envelopes, a wooden cross pendant, two closed amulets, two silver chains wrapped around a silver-handled letter opener, a leather cross pendant, six matchboxes, a *scrap* of black velvet, a blue rock, a gold-handled spoon, a *chipped* piece of sandstone, a knot of *discarded* cotton, one *fake* gold earring, a *scratched* teacup, *small* binoculars, and her necklace.[33]

Hirut ascribes value to her illicit collection where Aster does not see it, and her collection is noticeably larger and more compelling—glinting and shiny—than Aster's dismissive parsing might suggest. What is revealing here is not really the details of the objects themselves, so much as how they shrink and grow according to the desire for their possession and in relation to the strained dynamic between the two women. The divergence in the women's viewpoints on the value of the objects has no material effect on the consequences for Hirut, whom Aster punishes viciously for the theft. Yet as the plot proceeds and such divergences between objects and meaning are activated in order to provide an Ethiopian counternarrative to Italian war propaganda, we start to see more implications for aims of the narrative itself.

Objects are not only subject to physical seizure, though, and were also frequently taken hold of through various modes of documentation, such as photography. As David Forgacs explains, it was in photographs "that colonial fantasies could find ontological anchorage in a face, a body, an event,

Restitution   131

a landscape" and, furthermore, this anchorage in the real functioned to "strengthen the fantasy of possession and the idea of control."[34] History can be manipulated and staged by photographing people as if they were material objects whose identity could be swapped and transformed into multiple and diverse meanings. When Ettore's photos of the captive Aster and Hirut are developed, they are "kept as souvenirs," discussed and distributed around Italy and its African colonies. They are "called many things: Angry Amazon, Woman Warrior, African Giuliette. They are handled and ripped and framed and pasted into albums."[35] Yet, revealingly, when the images find their way back to the women's friends and family, the women are not recognized as themselves. Possession is revealed to be a slippery tool that cannot hold the women in. As Dionne Brand says in relation to a studio portrait of herself as a child, the photographed subject can only be acknowledged as "authored, altered, selected, sorted, from a series of selves for appearance and presentation."[36] This staging mechanism is most forcefully demonstrated within the narrative composition of the so-called Album of the Dead, which Fucelli asks Ettore to fill with images of the Ethiopian prisoners they murder by throwing them off high rocks.[37] This gruesome photo album, contained within Ettore's box, is counteracted by a ledger of the prisoners' names which was written by two Ethiopian women working in the Italian camp, who preserve their names as an alternative memorial for future posterity.[38] In the novel, these two collections—the photo album and the ledger of names—exist on display, side by side. Different ways of documenting objects and collections of objects open up additional gaps in interpretation, revealing what Brand calls a "liminal space between photograph and meaning" which is permeable, and thus easily breached.[39] This permeability manifests not only in their material content but also in how they have been assembled and catalogued within the narrative, and in what else is displayed around them in the text, near or far.

Mengiste has spoken about photographs as offering a "calculated curation of memory" since they act as "tools for amnesia and erasures," as well as providing evidence of the past.[40] And, as Patricia Hayes writes, "Perhaps it is the very disparity between photography and memory that is at times so productive. It triggers a narrative effort to try and mend the breach between the fragmented parts."[41] Where photographs don't exist, remembrances can be molded into narrative, "collecting weight with each backward glance."[42] In turn, photographs, especially when handled as objects, can be labeled falsely in order to make narratives pleasing to their owners or collectors, which has further consequences for memorialization. Hirut remarks, "This is the way it has been written, so this is the way it has been remembered."[43] Yet as James Clifford reminds us, photographs, like objects, can "never be entirely possessed," either by the museum or the novel. "They [are] sites of a historical negotiation, occasions for an ongoing contact."[44] In *The Shadow King*, the narrative itself provides a site for that contact, and thus also for an ongoing negotiation of history. The novel challenges history through juxtaposing the

132   Chapter 6

presence of "different memories," fabulative ones, which exist "regardless of the mathematics."[45] It provides insight into the composition and curation of history by exposing the violence of colonial framing, as well as what lies outside the frame. *The Shadow King* is a fulfillment of a narrative desire to flesh out existing stories of this war with new stories of female prowess, of resistance, of power and bravery, to counteract a narrative of history that privileges Italian perspectives through the preservation of imperial Fascist propaganda, or one that minimizes the force of Ethiopian resistance in order to privilege British involvement in the country's liberation. Mengiste's novel is, in the interpretative key offered by Jean-Christophe Cloutier, a counter-archive of the war, one that gathers up imagined and remembered material that previously had been "unwritten, removed, and lost."[46] And as we will see, by assigning symbolic value to a broken object, we can reread "breakage as a transition moment,"[47] one which proffers a space for possible reparative actions through alternative storied pathways.

Evading Possession

In the seizure of Hirut's rifle by Kidane, her own theft of Aster's belongings, and, more broadly, the capture of unwilling objects and images by colonial invaders, we have seen how things can be taken hold of against the wishes of their makers or former owners. This section will focus on how those objects can still work to evade possession, disrupt narratives, and retain some degree of autonomy after they have been taken. In order to do this, we need to return to the emblematic Wujigra and explore the narrative reasons behind why and how it is revealed to be broken. We don't know that the gun does not work when we first hear mention of it as Hirut's prized possession, but we do know that the idea of repossessing it drives her forward to set off a number of narrative events: her reparative theft of Aster's goods, and her motivation to take on a prominent role in Kidane's army. But when it is lent to another soldier in an ambush on Italian troops, its malfunction leads to his slow and painful death. The Wujigra is without doubt the most emblematic object within the narrative, and once it is taken, a dislocation occurs between the object and its meaning. As a prisoner of the Italian troops, Hirut can no longer remember her own name, but instead recalls the word "Wujigra," "the lone word that points to the singular mistake that led her here."[48] As she repeats the word to Fucelli, Ettore, Ibrahim, and the two Orthodox priests about to be executed, she assigns it a different meaning and emotional load each time: the word no longer signifies the object, but becomes instead her own private language of communication. In its dislocation from the object, the word comes to define and locate Hirut's identity: as an individual, as part of a family, as part of an army, and as part of a nation. Given Hirut's strong bond with the rifle, does the rifle break when it is taken from her, when it passes into hands it

Restitution   *133*

was not meant for? If so, what can this tell us about the signifying status of colonial-era objects that are now held captive in museums located in former colonizing countries? Giulia Grechi cautions that holding on to such things "corrodes the stories that [they] tell, dries up the life intrinsic to them, and nails them into a frozen, faraway fixity. It turns them into *objects* that operate within a discourse, work to illustrate a theory, and function as proof of something. Whether viewed as artefacts or masterpieces, they are prisoners, constrained to be contemplated."[49]

Grechi is one of the consulting members of a team now charged with finding decolonial pathways toward retelling the story of the collections of the former Colonial Museum as it transitions to its new location and assumes a new name: "Museo delle Opacità."[50] In April 2022 I went to the EUR Museum to visit a preliminary installation that the two principal curators, Rosa Anna Di Lella and Gaia Delpino, have created, called *Depositi Aperti* (Open Storage). *Depositi Aperti* has a double aim: first, that of making part of the collections accessible, and counteracting the *occultamento* (concealment) and *rimozione* (repression) of Italy's colonial past that has been facilitated by their removal into closed storage for forty years.[51] Second, it aims to make public the challenges and issues facing the curatorial team in an attempt to open up a space for conversation that visitors can engage with. To this end, the installation is located in two alcoves that flank the main staircase up to the collections of the National Museum of Prehistory and Ethnography, named after its founder, Luigi Pigorini. Objects included in the installation are partially concealed by floor-length semiopaque plastic flaps, printed with the main questions that the curators are grappling with: how to exhibit exploitation, how to exhibit violence, how to display theft, and how to avoid the removal of the colonial experience. Behind these curtains lies a representation of how a sample of the collection objects must have appeared as they lay in storage during the museum's closure. They are displayed wrapped in plastic, partially hidden on shelves and in drawers, unlabeled, with minimal interpretative intervention (fig. 17).

As I explored the installation, I had something of a mixed response: on the one hand, I felt that the work accurately showed the challenges facing the curators as they struggled to make sense of a collection of objects almost devoid of provenance information and tried not to replicate the violence of colonial-era modes of possessing, cataloguing, and displaying objects that were originally taken under duress. On the other, I wondered whether this replication of their concerns really did manage to move the conversation forward and how visitors were expected to engage with the installation or add their own voices in response to the questions posed. I was concerned that displaying objects of extreme colonial violence, such as the infamous face masks taken in Libya by the Fascist anthropologist Lidio Cipriani, without any curatorial intervention, would trigger additional trauma in some of the visitors who came to view them in their uncurated, semistored form.

Fig. 17. *Depositi aperti* exhibition, Museo delle Civiltà, Roma. Photograph by Emma Bond. Courtesy of Museo delle Civiltà, Rome.

One of the most striking objects on display points to ways forward in this impasse. At the entrance to the right-hand alcove stands a slender statue of a man measuring around a meter and a half high, wrapped in clear plastic and with a handwritten label hanging around its neck. The statue is placed next to what might have been its original plinth, which describes it as part of a group of "*statuette del Konso*" (Konso statues) and indicates them as having been part of a gift to the museum by Captain Marescotti Ruspoli in 1927. This identifies it as being one of the famous carved monuments of the Konso people of southern Ethiopia, which are not grave markers (as is sometimes thought), nor objects to be worshipped, but rather represent memorials to worthy ancestors. They are always found in public places (such as on roadsides or at crossroads), in groups, with the central figure representing the deceased man, surrounded by smaller statues of his wife (or wives), enemies

Restitution

135

he might have defeated or killed, children, and big game kills. As Hermann Amborn describes in his richly detailed ethnographic study of the Konso monuments, there is a strong kinetic "tension created through the relationship of these elements to each other and to the surrounding space with other statues and with space."[52] The relationship with the space that surrounds the memorial group of statues is significant and transforms the landscape into a "readable system of meanings"—something that is obviously lost once the statue is placed into a museum context on its own.[53] But what is perhaps most interesting about Amborn's description of the Konso statues, or *waakaa*, is the relationship they form with the observer, too, which means they "are not artifacts that in the end remain external to the human being; rather, they are connected in a common existential context, to which sacredly charged things belong just as much as people."[54] In *Depositi Aperti*, the statue and its former plinth are displayed on top of two light wooden transport boxes marked with arrows to indicate which way up they should be carried, and printed with the word Fragile in large black letters (fig. 18). In the traditional practices of the Konso people, this "fragility" is not a matter of concern—quite the opposite, in fact. As the ancestor represented by the statue is gradually assimilated into the longer lineage of ancestors who have previously passed on, their passage is marked by the decay of the carved statue itself: for this reason it is deliberately left outside in order to be exposed to destruction by the elements. This "decay and transitoriness is deliberate" because the carved "figures are meant to be reproduced" and to be "open to reinterpretation." As Amhorn suggests, "Through this reproduction, a link is set up between past and future generations," as part of an "apparently eternal chain."[55]

What can contemporary museums learn from the relational openness that the Konso statues work to build with their observers? What can their supplementary openness toward their own fragility and future destruction teach us about the ways that colonial-era objects now operate in museums? As Azoulay remarks, "Not all documents and works of art were made to be collected, classified, stored, shown, or studied. These procedures can be advantageous and illuminating in some contexts and invasive and harmful in others."[56] In some cases, as we saw in our discussion of Olga Tokarczuk's novel *Flights* in chapter 5, modes of enforced preservation can thus be conceived of as akin to neglect. Reading the broken Wujigra alongside the fragile Konso statue which remains open to its own future decay allows us to catch sight of the potential latitude that exists in exploring how colonial-era objects can work to evade possession and preservation, and how this evasion is manifested in textual practices of leaving open gaps and frayed uncertainties that position object "meaning" on the outside of prescribed grids of museal interpretation.

This possibility is enacted within the container-like structure of *The Shadow King*: initially, the narrative follows the contents of Ettore's box which have been organized, classified, and arranged into a sequence (his photographs are "labelled neatly by year and placed in chronological order").[57]

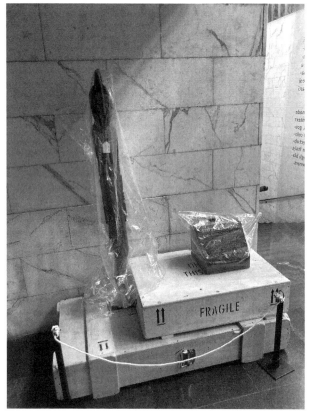

Fig. 18. Konso statue on display in the *Depositi Aperti* exhibition, Museo delle Civiltà, Rome. Photograph by Emma Bond. Courtesy of Museo delle Civiltà, Rome.

At the start of the novel, we bear witness as Hirut looks through the box, so an element of movement is maintained as she tries to "imagine the moments before and the moments after" the camera shutter clicks, "which is what a photograph will often eliminate for us."[58] Stories are cropped out of colonial photographs for aesthetic or propagandistic aims, truncating narrative possibilities.[59] In a photograph of Ettore's battalion arriving in Africa, only half of his body appears; the other half is "cut out of the frame, so no one will ever know that in his disappeared hand, Ettore, too, holds a camera."[60] Yet his own faded occupation of that space persists and the narrative restores what the cameraman cropped out, even adding a caption: "In faint pencil, erased but not completely, he has written, *Guerra!*" This widening of perspective beyond what has been captured for posterity allows for certain malleability in the text, and the potential for resistance to dominant colonial narratives.

Restitution   137

This culminates after the end of the war, when Ettore—still living in Addis Ababa and working as a photographer—has himself "come to care less about the sequence of things," finally understanding that it is "impossible to connect what happened to what will. . . . Everything is happening all at once."[61] History has been bent into a new shape by the process of exhuming the past into the present, transforming the novel into a form of shadow archive: "an affirmation made in the face of the 'wreckage upon wreckage' of centuries of violence"; an archive that through the motion of objects—to borrow Ralph Ellison's famous phrase—"moves not like an arrow but a boomerang."[62]

Resisting Narration

The process of Italian colonial expansion in East Africa was enshrined in and articulated through the production and circulation of written and visual material and objects, many of which were subsequently collected, curated, and displayed in museums around the world. Narrative techniques within *The Shadow King* have so far allowed me to showcase how objects can evade curatorial possession and muddle practices of description in museums and novels alike. In this section, I will show how these same objects can highlight existing counternarratives and resistances to colonial discourses, and perhaps even offer responses to the ethical issues involved in keeping them on display. In particular, I will consider how signs of wear and tear, or other defects and interventions visible on images, objects, and publications kept in the Wolfsonian might work to destabilize the authority of their original message. I will also consider how the juxtaposition of Italian propaganda with material from other countries can redimension and complicate our reception of the story of Italian colonialism. Intertwining these archival findings with object details from Mengiste's novel offers new insight into the material construction of the novel. The first material sign I want to focus on is the scar that marks Hirut's chest, which was the result of an injury sustained when Aster beat her as a punishment for stealing. Described as a "long scar that puckers at the base of her neck and trails over her shoulder like a broken necklace," it is a mark that Hirut attempts to cover up, and that the novel repeatedly puts back on display.[63] Hirut's scar becomes an object of memory, a tactile trace that links her back to the Wujigra that she was looking for when she began to thieve and thus symbolizes the complicated antagonism of her relationship with Aster. The description of the scar as a *broken necklace* also conflates the reason for this scar (the stealing of Aster's necklace) with the physical and psychological ruptures that its seizure caused. Without wishing to collapse Hirut's brief narrative of dispossession and servitude into a broader and graver context of chattel slavery, I think the narrative significance of her scar can nonetheless be illuminated by Marisa Fuentes's painstaking reconstructions of enslaved women's lives in Barbados from archival traces and silences. Fuentes shows how the

138   Chapter 6

scars detailed in reports of missing or fugitive women "disclose more" than the circumstances and conditions of their enslavement and sometimes subsequent escape, "even as they limit their historicization."[64] Through processes of mutilation, inscription, and memorialization, such scars can "produce multiple axes of meaning" and even themselves "turn into . . . stories."[65]

Understanding Hirut's scar as a storied grapheme that can provide supplementary layers of commentary or meaning to her history aligns with the way that Ettore's faded caption on the photograph of Italian troops arriving in Africa persists as a spectral trace within the narrative. The scar points to an alternative narrative that takes in Hirut's motivations for the theft and provides evidence of its ramifications, illustrating Ahmed's understanding of the "scratch as testimony, the wrinkle as expression."[66] It annotates the "official" narrative of her as a thief and, in a sense, replaces the lost Wujigra as a material link back to her own family history. Such supplementary annotations abound in the printed materials held in the Wolfsonian collections, where past owners clearly wanted to contradict or add emphasis or personal comment to the propaganda they were reading. The first instance I noticed of this was some markings in red crayon in the margins of a marketing pamphlet distributed by a pharmaceutical company for Italians seeking to move to Italian East Africa for work. Published in 1936, it predates the legislative decree issued in April of the following year that outlawed personal relations between Italians and native women in the colonies, yet it anticipates the fear of contagion that close contact could engender.[67] However, the previous owner of the guide somewhat bypasses this directive and instead marks with short repeated crayon lines his or her interest in sections on how to check beds for scorpions, tarantulas, and snakes, and the worst times of the day for insect bites. This person's concern regarding the dangers of local fauna is repeated in the section dedicated to "Snakes and Insects," where a single red line curves down the length of the printed writing, where it meets at the bottom the outstretched arm of one of the women in the accompanying illustration, and curls into and then away from her open hand (fig. 19).

These annotations not only reveal details of the reader's emotional investment in the topic but also work to destabilize and undermine the racializing message around hygiene in favor of interests in wildlife and personal safety. Importantly, they also reinforce our sense of the document as a historical object with material properties of its own. This is because, as Ernst Van de Wetering points out, "Signs of ageing and wear help us to orient our understanding of objects."[68] These signs also help us understand some of the diverse ways in which objects can function as communication channels: not just through annotations but also in the supplementary insertion of new materials. While browsing through bound copies of the periodical *L'Italia Coloniale*, I found a torn piece of another magazine image celebrating Italy's victory in a world soccer championship tucked between two pages (fig. 20). When viewed and apprehended as it was found, the insertion overlaid an

Restitution

Fig. 19. Pamphlet, *Norme e consigli per chi va in A. O. Italiana 1*, 1936. Istituto Coloniale Fascista, Rome. S. A. Arti Navarra, Milan. Published with the permission of The Wolfsonian–Florida International University, Miami Beach, Florida, The Mitchell Wolfson Jr. Collection, XB1992.1221.

Fig. 20. Newspaper clipping, *Campioni del Mondo*, 1934. Published with the permission of The Wolfsonian–Florida International University, Miami Beach, Florida, The Mitchell Wolfson Jr. Collection.

article on animals in Somalia, partially concealing photographs of zebras, elephants, and a crocodile that lay behind with cheering sports fans to produce a sort of collage effect.

Collage is created through twin poles of destruction, through actions of cutting or tearing, and creation, through the creative assembly of the composite pieces. It therefore enacts the double act of rupture and repair that is so central to Attia's thought and that challenges Western ideas "about the values of wholeness . . . , authenticity, belonging and otherness."[69] Writing letters to his son Ettore in Ethiopia as a Jew who fled the pogroms in Odesa to find sanctuary in Italy, Leo Navarra senses danger in the air as Mussolini's racial laws come into effect. We later learn that he and his wife were indeed sent to the Risiera di San Sabba, and then to Auschwitz, where they died. Before their deportation, Leo cut up all the letters he had prepared. With scissors in hand, he "held each piece of paper between the sharp silver blades and began to cut. He destroyed every last letter, thoroughly and meticulously, then swept the floor clean."[70] Leo then wrote one final letter, which he sent, and in which Ettore perceives the backdrop of the other letters' destruction. He reads his father as a "broken man," signs of his brokenness persisting "between the words, tucked in every space and margin," asking to be found.[71] As with the inserted scrap picture in *L'Italia Coloniale*, collage pieces signify even when they are left behind. This is something that Emperor Haile Selassie knows well, and the reason why he was determined to leave no trace of himself in England once the time had come for him to return to Ethiopia out of exile:

> He has taken even the hurried scraps of notes he made to himself in the days before departure, picking them up one by one from his rubbish bin, saving them in his pockets, in the corners of his suitcases, in his briefcase, until he is certain he has gotten each one. If he could, he would have scraped every thread, every piece of hair, every drop of water that rolled off his skin onto English ground and brought it back.[72]

Restitution

Remnants such as these function as modes of rebellion that persist to signify—as much in scraps of paper as in sounds and wayward syllables that signal alternative routes into history. Azoulay writes about discovering on her father's birth certificate that her Algerian grandmother's name was Aïsha, and of how she readopted it as her own middle name. She recognizes it as "more than just a name," as a sign of the family's concealed Arabness, and her insistence on holding on to it now as a visible insertion into her name becomes a way of "renewing the precolonial legacy of the family."[73] The "potential" history that still resides in fragments is recycled in the irrepressible sounds of the name that she now splices and collages in textual form: "Aïsha, Aï-sha, Aïeeee-shaaaa, an expression of a sharp pain that erupts with the first syllable (aïeee) and is immediately silenced by the second one ['sha,' a common sound of hushing], as if to appease what could get out of control."[74] Such sounds and syllables cannot be repressed, though, and as they are shared and spread, they occupy a space of rebellion. As the Italian forces stream into Ethiopia, people choose to mispronounce the belligerent emperor's name as "Mussoloni." Mengiste has the character of Haile Selassie note that

> the deliberate mispronunciation has spread across the country, started by those who did not know better and continued by those who do. It is another sign of his people's rebellion, another sign that they are trying to fight in every way that they can.[75]

In misnaming Mussolini, the people redimension the threat that he poses to them, and as Haile Selassie himself adopts the growing trend, he finds that he can no longer form a mental picture of his aggressor.[76] Performing mispronunciation becomes an act of potential history, an unlearning that aims to short-circuit colonial violence by rewinding to before it happened. It does not aim to "mend worlds after violence but rewinds to the moment before the violence occurred and sets off from there."[77] The structural form of *The Shadow King* proceeds in this same fashion, offering the reader a series of potential reversals, rewinding, and returns to consider. In numerous instances the characters are shown how they might resist what has happened in the past as occupying space in a given narrative and how they might open up to alternatives instead. At the point of his decision to rape Hirut, Kidane is offered the chance to set right his previous sexual violence against his wife, Aster: "Go back. Open the bedroom door and send young Aster down the stairs. Place the groom on his feet and draw him away from the bed. Wipe the sheet clean of the bride's blood. All advice has been taken back. . . . Let the minutes stretch."[78] He does not take this chance (since worlds cannot be mended), but another sequence of events persists through the inclusion of a counterfactual alternative. In this instance of extreme bodily repossession at the point of dispossession, Hirut enacts a peculiar, extraordinary resistance to Kidane. She yawns, unnerving and ultimately disabling him. And when

142   Chapter 6

he attempts to protect her on the battlefield, she unlearns language in revolt, and—finally retaking possession of a rifle to replace that which was taken from her—repeats both to Kidane and to Fucelli one single word that stands in the stead of a bullet: "Boom."[79]

Conclusion: Mediating Return

The British looting at Maqdala in 1868 gave rise to what Pankhurst calls the "first request for the restitution of cultural property ever made by an African ruler," in 1872.[80] This request, made by Emperor Yohannes, did in fact result in the return of one manuscript from the British Museum to Ethiopia, making it the first example of an object repatriation of this kind. *The Shadow King* concludes with a restitutive gift of its own. Hirut's initial decision was to return all the contents of Ettore's box, minus the one letter from his father which was his most treasured possession. Her belief was that he "has no right to it because of all that they have lost since he invaded her country" and her retention of it is aimed at correcting "an unnatural balance."[81] Hirut's stated objective here recalls Sarr and Savoy's definition of restitution as the restoration of a harmony lost through previous theft. Yet in an encounter mediated by the surprise appearance of Haile Selassie himself, she changes her mind, alters course, and returns his letter as she slowly speaks out loud the names of all those she fought alongside in Kidane's unit. And as their names fuse past and present conflicts, the letter changes hands. Hirut's narrative journey through the metal box belonging to Ettore has shown that objects can be recuperated and renarrated into present memory as witnesses, for the future purposes of repairing absence.

The repeated requests for the return of the looted obelisk from Aksum, which Mussolini had erected opposite the Ministry of Italian Africa (the present-day Food and Agriculture Organization) in central Rome in 1937, were, however, less successful. The obelisk was eventually returned to Ethiopia in 2005, nearly sixty years after the original postwar agreement between the two countries had been reached. Italian writer Igiaba Scego notes how the obelisk lay in storage in a police warehouse adjacent to a large CIE (Center for Identification and Expulsion), where asylum seekers are held pending repatriation, often for up to two years. During the period of the obelisk's transit there, several inmates of the CIE sewed up their mouths in protest at the length of their own detainment.[82] The wounds caused by European colonialist theft in Africa thus continue to reverberate into the present through the dislocation and lack of care for objects and people alike. Yet the persistent absence of what was once present is, through representations of the interplay between shadow and light, one of the most distinctive and important stylistic features of the novel. As it becomes clear that Emperor Haile Selassie has fled the country and taken refuge abroad, Hirut suggests to Kidane's band that

Restitution

Fig. 21. Mended Roman bust on display in the *Depositi Aperti* exhibition, Museo delle Civiltà, Rome. Photograph by Emma Bond. Courtesy of Museo delle Civiltà, Rome.

they dress a soldier, Minim, in his guise. Minim resembles the emperor in his slight physique, and the illusion of his reappearance promises to reassure the local population and spread word of this display of defiance. As Capossela writes, "The most crucial function of light in the novel is its creation of shadow selves, dark twins for each character." Folding presence into absence and darkness allows for creative dissociation and resistance: the loss of self opens up a space in which to become a double for someone else, and to become oneself "a weapon, a source of power."[83]

On the top shelf of one of the broad flanked wooden cabinets that house the stored objects in *Depositi Aperti* the visitor can make out three Roman busts, shrouded in plastic. One of these has what appears to be a visible mend, large black stitches which crisscross along the base of its neck (fig. 21). Upon seeing it, I couldn't help but think of Hirut's scar and how the sign of injury or damage here adds the potential for the sort of relationality and mediation also embodied by the Konso statue that stands opposite it. The Roman bust can thus be read as one of Stephen Greenblatt's "wounded artifacts" in its ability not only to act as a "witness to the violence of history" but also to display "signs of use, marks of the human touch, and hence links with the openness of touch that was the condition of their creation."[84]

Returning to Attia's work on repair, Grechi makes a useful distinction between two Italian verbs: *guarire* (to heal) and *curare* (to cure). She posits that this idea of "healing" can be seen as an equivalent to Western ideals which aim to "disappear" the original injury and return the object to its former state. "Curing," on the other hand, is understood as a form of reparation or mending that leads to dynamic processes aimed at the creation of new forms, new aesthetics, and new realities.[85] Taking her lead from what she did not find in Italian archives during an extended stay she spent researching for *The Shadow King* in Rome, Mengiste went out into the streets instead, and searched for more quotidian, personal mementos that recalled Italian presences in Ethiopia during the occupation. The photographs that she found in secondhand stalls and junk shops not only guided her formation of the characters in the novel but also gave rise to the creation of a different project: Project 3541, an online archive Mengiste has built of images and memories of the Italo-Ethiopian War.[86] Mengiste's creation of this archive as a space for "new forms, new aesthetics and new realities" is—to borrow Shannon Mattern's words—a form of care work in and of itself, since "to fill in the gaps . . . to draw connections . . . is an act of repair, or, simply, of taking care— connecting threads, mending holes, amplifying quiet voices."[87] The interface between these two creative archival forms—Mengiste's website and *The Shadow King*—allow a space for reworlding, and for repopulation through reclamation, where restitution does not equal return, and where examples of what Fazil Moradi calls "catastrophic art" ("artworks whose worlds the empires destroyed and brutally deported to the imperial metropoles")[88] persist to draw attention to the violence of colonial theft and point toward new ways to respond to the unanswered questions of restitution and reparative justice that preoccupy our postcolonial societies today.

Conclusion

Deaccession

Introduction

As I write, a midsized book with a glossy, terracotta red cover lies on my desk in front of me. The title is *Important Artifacts and Personal Property from the Collection of Lenore Doolan and Harold Morris, Including Books, Street Fashion and Jewelry* (fig. 22). Below this is the date and location of an auction, which we see took place on Saturday, February 14, 2009, in New York. There is no author name on the front cover, but instead the name of an auctioneer company, Strachan & Quinn, which is based in London, New York, and Toronto. The cover illustration is a photograph of one of the auction lots, number 1181: a pair of antique poodle figurines with slightly sinister-looking green jeweled eyes. Deceptively authentic in its appearance, this book by author, illustrator, and designer Leanne Shapton is actually a love story told through the fictionalized auction catalogue of a collection of personal items earmarked for disposal through sale. Three hundred thirty-two lots provide the reader with "evidence" of the key moments of the life cycle of the relationship between the titular characters Doolan and Morris, recounted through the relics of what remains after their breakup. These range from an invitation to the Halloween party where they first met to real estate listings for one-bedroom apartments in different cities as they move out of their shared home. Already in its title it calls into question the "value" of the items in question: who decides what (or even who) is "important" and what is not? As we browse through the differently costed lots, we wonder who gets to assign a monetary or other value to the items for sale, and what criteria they use. On a narrative level this question of value also foregrounds the instability inherent in the relationship between object, text, and image in the book. Which of these three storytelling modes should hold primacy as we look to decode a story made up of deliberately elliptical information? Might it be possible for different narratives to emerge, depending on which of the different modes we turn to for our understanding of events? Shapton's reader has to assume skills of forensic detection, linking images to captions across pages in order to decode the story of Doolan and Morris's relationship, yet although "the pictured objects sited/sighted in the

145

Fig. 22. Front cover of Leanne Shapton, *Important Artifacts and Personal Property from the Collection of Lenore Doolan and Harold Morris, Including Books, Street Fashion and Jewelry*. Courtesy of Bloomsbury Publishing PLC.

auction catalogue trigger questions, . . . only partial answers may be teased out when objects are viewed in relation with other objects."[1]

The auction catalogue format of Shapton's book resembles the mixed media displays of most museum exhibits, which similarly rely on a combination of text, objects, and images in order to construct stories that can be sequenced into a chronology of selected events. The elements of narrative subterfuge in the book's presentation also recall the sometimes less-than-innocent functionality of museum displays. These resemblances already make *Important Artifacts* an important conceptual testing ground for enhancing our understanding of how museums deploy techniques of multimedia narration. The fact that the objects photographed here are for *sale* raises an even

Deaccession

147

more significant series of questions for the contemporary museum: in an era in which most institutions are facing a "crisis of accumulation" of material from the past,[2] how, when, and why should we seek to let go objects from collections? In *Important Artifacts*, it is not the objects themselves that "tell" the story of Doolan and Morris's relationship, but they nonetheless linger in their own recorded ephemerality, existing in a state of suspension before they are dispersed to take up their places in other, new collections. The book thus shows how the "second-hand economies of things, their constellations and their traces of value [are] an integral, rather than peripheral, aspect of history making."[3] Shapton was inspired to create a story in this type of catalogue format after attending an auction of Truman Capote's belongings in New York, some of which she purchased and gave to friends as gifts. But it was not the memory of the objects she acquired or of those she passed on which stayed with her but rather, as she states in an interview on the making of the book, that she became preoccupied with "what gets left behind."[4] In this way *Important Artifacts* celebrates the persistent meaning that resides in what Sarah Wasserman calls "the death of things": forgotten, discarded, or devalued things, things that were not designed for long-term survival.[5] Likewise, the objects pictured in *Important Artifacts* are caught in an in-between space of display before their disposal, which showcases the power of their residual presence. Similar to ghosts from the past haunting the present, these figures of "unfinished disposal" hold, in Kevin Hetherington's words, the power to "fold and unsettle [a] linear sense of represented time by standing outside any knowable sequence of events."[6] These are items that in museum terminology have been deaccessioned, or struck off from the accession register in which they were recorded when they first entered the collection. Deaccession is just one distinct stage in the process of object disposal and occurs before an object is physically removed from the museum "through transfer, repatriation, destruction, or disposal through sale."[7] Deaccessioned objects can sometimes even remain in storage spaces for indeterminate periods of time, becoming what Caitlin DeSilvey and Martin Grünfeld have evocatively called "fringe objects," which persist on the margins of museums as a kind of "residual unculture."[8]

I want to use this concluding chapter of *Curating Worlds* to explore the narrative implications of objects being positioned within this newly "dynamic and uncertain" space of residual unculture. If the things we encounter in books such as *Important Artifacts* can be seen as straddling twin poles of value and waste, and if the instability of the value they are assigned thus allows for conceptual "tinkering," can we use the processes of deaccessioning and disposing of objects from museum collections to shed light on wider innovations taking place within the contemporary literary landscape? The analysis that follows will use the concept of deaccession to address and formulate answers to the issues at stake in several of the previous chapters in this book. Chapter 4 highlighted the growing issue of overburdened museum storage, while chapter 6 dealt with the reparative "loss" of colonial-era objects from museums through acts of restitution and repatriation. Chapter 5 questioned the contemporary validity of the preservation paradigm and suggested generative new ways of understanding natural processes of decay and entropy instead. All three chapters thus showed how literary techniques might be able to help museums articulate modes of response to current issues around cultural and environmental sustainability, and around the crisis of accumulation that faces heritage institutions around the world today. In foregrounding deliberate processes of shedding objects in order to let go of the past, such as deaccession and disposal, this final chapter opens up an interpretative space that asks what postobject futures might look like for museums and literature alike, and what new forms of content will occupy the spaces freed up in their wake. It concludes the book as a whole by identifying a shift in the shape of contemporary fiction and museums that sees both moving in different ways toward "postrepresentativeness" in both their form and their content.[9]

In terms of literature, these new, liminal forms of representation are emerging to occupy a "fringe" position in terms of genre: this time between fiction and nonfiction. These are literary forms "that cross the borders between styles, genres and media, between real-life events and imagined ones."[10] Using a term coined by the Italian author collective Wu Ming, Kate Willman refers to these texts as "unidentified narrative objects," or UNOs; more recently, these same boundary-stretching literary forms have been classified as "post-fictional" by Timothy Bewes. As Bewes states, the postfictional age we are experiencing now bears witness to "an evolution of the novel . . . that involves a replacement of the forms of fiction and fictionality by formally ambiguous modes of writing with ontological implications that extend beyond the practice of literature."[11] *Important Artifacts* is a prime example of this kind of postfictional writing that Bewes sees as destabilizing existing categorizations of literature. A staged narrative, its liminal fictionality is foregrounded not only by the elaborate ruse of the front cover but also by the appearance of acclaimed novelist Sheila Heti in the role of Lenore Doolan in the photographs that accompany the auction lots. In a similar fashion to Orhan Pamuk's *Museum of Innocence*, analyzed in chapter 3, the constructed narrative of *Important Artifacts* is lent authenticity by a collection of material objects that is designed (and yet fails) to act as "evidence" of the authenticity of the underlying story. Some of the objects photographed and displayed belong to Shapton herself, thereby adding overtly autofictional elements into the mix. The aesthetic status of the novel itself thus "denaturalizes the photograph's indexical relationship to reality and, by extension, the object depicted by it."[12] The loosening of ties between the object and its representation in the postfictional novel can be activated to signal a shift in our understanding of the narrative potential of spaces such as museums and other heritage sites that exist "beyond the practice of literature." We can see this shift away from the reliance on objects to signify, to represent, and to store memory as a sign of a growing affinity between literature and museums,

Deaccession

one that helps clarify their conceptual limits in turn. Postfictional texts such as *Important Artifacts* that exist on the fringes of current literary categories can thus also act as a useful vehicle to explore where future concepts of the museum might lie if object collections are deaccessioned into the residual unculture that has been so evocatively charted by Grünfeld and DeSilvey. In this gray area of muddled genres, I see *Important Artifacts* as occupying the same conceptual space as *Extinct*, a colorful compendium of writing about obsolete objects which used to populate the world (such as ashtrays, the Concorde, and minidiscs) but which are now only recorded in textual form. The book is intended to act not so much as a record of the past as one of a once possible future that was anticipated, designed for, and projected toward through now-defunct objects. In charting their disappearance from common use, *Extinct* also pays attention to the "underside of progress: the conflicts, obsolescence, accidents, destruction and failures" that—if attended to with care—can offer a new way of engaging with the material world.[13] Rather than projecting images of the past, "ultimately, every extinct object embodies a vision of the future, a vision that, even if the object itself has been superseded, is still in some way available to us."[14]

Building on such future-led speculations, this concluding chapter will explore whether the postfictional novel can hint at what happens after the primacy of the object collection in the museum has waned. The objects featured in *Important Artifacts* consistently point the reader back toward the text, and indeed it is the notes scribbled on postcards, email printouts, letters, and other written forms that give the most indicative clues of how the narrative of the relationship develops. Idyllic photos of vacations in Venice in lot 1086 show the couple happily eating spaghetti and drinking aperitivi at the Locanda Cipriani, yet a hand-written note in the inside cover of a guidebook in lot 1088 speaks of Doolan crying in the shower while Morris texts, drinks, and smokes alone on the hotel balcony all night.[15] The gaps that open up between different modes of content delivery provide a necessary space for new interpretative work to take place, implicating the reader in its construction. Artifacts themselves offer an "openness to re-meaning; a capacity to carry preferred meaning; a potential for polysemia" which is multiplied when they are inserted into a multimedia landscape such as a museum exhibit or a collaged text.[16] But in the current crisis era of heritage places holding on to "too much stuff," Eilean Hooper-Greenhill's declaration that the "great collecting phase of museums is over" ushers in the idea of the "postmuseum," which will focus on object *use* and enjoyment rather than on the further accumulation of things. The postmuseum is envisaged less as a sited building and more as a scripted process which can be experienced "within a variety of architectural forms."[17] Could one of these forms be the novel, especially in its postfictional form? Wolfgang Ernst has shown how the earliest object collections were designed as a "space of contemplation" or "a cognitive field of ideas": not so much a place, then, as a text, or a semiotic-led space.[18] There are similarities to be marked here with the way writers and critics celebrate our relationship to objects in the ever-popular Object Lessons series, edited by Ian Bogost and Christopher Schaberg.[19] Things such as alarm clocks, coffee, mushrooms, remote controls, and sewers are reconfigured by the authors of this series into pocket-sized books, relieved of their material form and further mediated through evocative textual imaginings.

We have already seen in previous chapters of this book how new models of display and exhibition space are emerging in the era of the postmuseum: from institutions focused on open storage solutions (such as the Boijmans Van Beuningen Museum featured in chapter 4), to literary museums that showcase the fictional (such as Orhan Pamuk's Museum of Innocence in chapter 3, or even the Museum of Jurassic Technology in Los Angeles), and museums that are maximizing the potential for crowdsourced, digital, and traveling forms. Some of these innovations occurred or intensified in the aftermath of the COVID-19 pandemic, but other changes in institutional function are due to post-pandemic financial constraints that have seen museums gain alternative value—for example as community "warm banks" for people struggling to pay energy bills. As we shift away from relying on museums and novels to provide figural representations of reality, new locations for meaning making are emerging within the residual or blank spaces freed up after objects become frail or fail in other ways to deliver. In the analysis that follows, I will probe these ideas in readings of other contemporary books that also interrogate objects in fruitless quests to answer unsolved questions, and in so doing privilege failure, forgetting, and loss over memory, conservation, and positive discovery. Alongside *Important Artifacts* I will read Maria Stepanova's hybrid essay-fiction work *In Memory of Memory* and Judith Schalansky's design-led elegy *An Inventory of Losses*, which I will intersperse with my recollections of a visit to the crowdsourced Museum of Broken Relationships in Zagreb. Can the postmuseum take up the challenge implicit in the postfictional label we assign to books such as these, books that bend genre and expectations in similar measure? Turning to Emily St. John Mandel's *Station Eleven* in conclusion, I find possible answers to this question in a novel which offers a vision of a postpandemic world that is constructed as an archive of experience in and of itself. In anticipating how the fallout from a global virus has shifted our understanding (and our requirements) of heritage, *Station Eleven* shows how the texts and sites this chapter assembles can signal the emergence of the postmuseum text as representative of a world archive in conceptual motion—a motion that has left the primacy of objects in its wake.

"Too Much Stuff"

The museum world was left resolutely shaken by the news of widespread and long-term thefts from the collections of the British Museum by one of

Deaccession 151

its curators in summer 2023. One of the most revealing aspects of the crime was that the disappearance of around two thousand objects had not been noticed because they simply hadn't been catalogued or fully accounted for. Gaps in documentation seem inevitable when dealing with a collection the size of that in the British Museum, estimated to number around eight million objects. But the theft also raised questions about the ability of large national institutions to truly "care" for their objects, and it strengthened calls for the return of some of the museum's more contested collections, the Parthenon marbles first and foremost. This sense of a growing flux and uncertainty in how museum object futures are currently envisioned in the sector has been a long time in the making. Dayna L. Caldwell offers a bleak picture of museums in the grip of an obsessive-compulsive crisis, with their back rooms and basements now resembling "the slowly expanding burden within a hoarder's domain."[20] But how did museums arrive at this pathological state of affairs? The crisis of object accumulation is perhaps best explained by the heritage explosion of the twentieth century, which saw the global number of museums exponentially rise, coupled with an "ethics of memory" which arose in response to the traumas of a century characterized by loss. This combination of factors gave rise to something of a "Noah complex," where museum staff felt compelled to first collect and then retain unsustainable numbers of objects in order to preserve memories of the past.[21] The excess of museums' acquisitions over the second half of twentieth century in particular was due to a number of factors including, in Rodney Harrison's view, the "increasingly broad definition of heritage, the growth of heritage tourism in the global economy and the linked obsession with risk and memorialisation in late modern societies."[22]

Nowadays, a chronic lack of space for storage and display in museums is leading to calls for museums to enforce tough decisions on what can be collected in the present. For decades, museum associations argued that there should be a "strong presumption against disposal of collections because curators hold the material in trust on behalf of the public."[23] Only over the past twenty years have the first steps toward implementing a solid framework for getting rid of objects occurred, spurred by the publication of the National Museum Directors' Conference reports entitled *Too Much Stuff* in 2003, and the issue of a revised Museums Association *Disposal Toolkit* in 2014. Yet curators still have to confront anxieties around which objects to collect in order to preserve a representative sample of the present for the future, since we never know for sure what is going to be valuable, and to whom, beyond our own lifespans. Do we need to whittle down collections of past material in order to make space for the present in the future? On the one hand, museums poised toward disposal risk damaging public trust in their stewardship, thereby putting the notion of museums as institutions bound to survive time into doubt. For if its foundational collections can be dismantled, the museum is no longer a fixed entity for perpetuity. On the other hand, museums have a responsibility to future generations not to become unmanageable. As the *Disposal Toolkit* states, "Museum collections should be developed so that they can provide the best care and opportunities for use and engagement. Curatorially motivated disposal is an integral part of responsible collections management and will ensure that museums are fit for future generations."[24] But what happens to the spaces left behind by objects that are delisted, deaccessioned, and ultimately disposed of, victims of processes of decluttering in public museums and private homes alike? And what sort of narratives emerge in the gaps, the blank spaces, and the empty rooms they leave behind?

As far back as 1968, the Smithsonian-based historian Wilcomb Washburn posed the provocative question that if the primary purpose of the museum is to store and transfer knowledge and information, "need one save objects at all?"[25] In an era of three-dimensional digitization and reproduction through printing, representations of what and how museum objects can *mean* has necessarily been diversified. The focus on the digitized preservation of information rather than objects themselves has seen things transformed into images and the museum become a data bank, "taking apart," as Wolfgang Ernst warns, "the hermeneutic distinction between memory and waste."[26] This overflow affected the modern museum as much as the twentieth-century novel, which is often categorized as functioning like a "storage medium" for the flotsam and jetsam of history.[27] So if the true task of the postmodern museum is "to teach the user how to cope with information,"[28] can postfictional novels show them how to do so? In some of the previous chapters, we have seen how novels "archive, assemble and mine objects for meaning" in order to retain connections to twentieth-century histories of war, migration, loss, and dispossession.[29] Yet in *Important Artifacts*, although the photographs of the couple's things take on the status of objects in and of themselves, they do not relate back to an external reality but merely point to other representations within the text. Objects in the narrative thus help to "invert the fallacy of literature mirroring reality."[30] The stability of information is thrown into doubt, and narrative is required to play a supplementary role in completing the transformation of objects into documentary information. Shapton herself has described how the narrative occupied a position of primacy in her drafting process: "I plotted the story first, then whittled certain moments down to what I thought the residual object might be."[31] Narrative value is further reasserted through the active interpretation of the reader that opens up to a reassessment of the relationship between subject and object. Instead of elevating the object to a status of authoritative autonomy, we are asked to read the narrative "for the imbrication of subject and object, for the messy entanglements between persons and things."[32] The key here is to facilitate the legibility of objects by creating a reading that can "make [them] understandable."[33] Making things understandable does not rely on accurate readings, however, and should not detract from the pleasure there is to be had in piecing things together in speculative mode and fabricating imagined

Deaccession

Fig. 23. The Museum of Broken Relationships, Zagreb. External view. Photograph by Emma Bond.

stories from disparate relics. The reader, and indeed the museum visitor, still has an undisputed role in the interpretation of objects and texts alike.

One of the most popular tourist destinations within the network of cobbled streets that make up Zagreb's picturesque old town is the Museum of Broken Relationships (fig. 23). Housed within a three-story building on the corner of an otherwise nondescript square in the Croatian capital, the museum's cavernous, whitewashed rooms display objects donated by anonymous members of the public. Stories narrativizing the significance of a displayed object to a relationship that has subsequently broken down are summarized in accompanying panels beside them. The Zagreb museum was cofounded by a former couple, Olinka Vištica and Dražen Grubišić, in 2006; it also now has a permanent outpost in Los Angeles, and traveling exhibitions which have reached as far afield as Montenegro to Melbourne and Mexico. Displayed on the entrance panel to the Zagreb museum is a quotation by Roland Barthes: "Every passion, ultimately, has its spectator . . . [there is] no amorous oblation without a final theatre." This citation from *A Lover's Discourse* frames the museum itself—as it does Barthes's work overall—as the "creation of a new literary mode: neither analysis nor autobiography, it sets out the space of an imaginary."[34] The spectator is needed here as active interpreter of the

Fig. 24. Objects on display in the Museum of Broken Relationships, Zagreb. Photograph © Sanja Bistričič. Courtesy of the Museum of Broken Relationships.

objects on display, piecing together the "little scenes, *tableaux*," in the same way that the reader decodes a text made up of "an assembly of citations."[35] The museum's website landing page features an interactive world map made up of pins showing the locations of thousands of relationship breakups. Although some objects from the collection are pictured in the "Collection" tab along with their labels, the main content of the website is composed of 2,829 crowdsourced stories and images featured in a separate "Stories" section. Visitors can log in to either share their breakup story, image, or location in a public forum, or to "time-lock" memories in a secure vault until a specified future moment (caption: "time-lock your memory in the vault: out of sight, out of mind"). Visitors to the website are also encouraged to send objects to the museum while recovering from their loss, thereby contributing to the collection:

> Recently ended a relationship? Wish to unburden the emotional load by erasing everything that reminds you of that painful experience? Don't—one day you may regret it. Instead, send your item to our Museum and take part in the creation of a collective emotional history!

On my own visit to the museum one cold, gray November afternoon, I found that each of the rooms was packed full of enthusiastic visitors. It was

Deaccession   *155*

evident that although people glanced at the objects with interest, delight, and sometimes even disgust (one of the "objects" on display was, for example, tufts of lint taken from a lover's belly button), they spent more time engaging with the stories that donors had provided to "gloss" their objects. Observing people as they interacted with the displays showed me that things in the Museum of Broken Relationships have more of an illustrative than a representational value. Visitors themselves are literally inserted into museum narrative and its physical spaces, since contributions could have come from any one of them, eliding the representational distance between visitor and museum. The Museum of Broken Relationships asks us to reconsider what (or who) is on display in the postmuseum, and what draws people to contribute their personal material to help construct a truly collective display (fig. 24).[36]

Letting Go of the Past

One of the most interesting principles espoused by the Museum of Broken Relationships is the insistence that donating your story or objects to the organization will bring liberation from emotional pain by allowing you to forget what has happened. Much the same could be said for heritage institutions battling with unsustainable numbers of objects on display and in storage that are now turning to deaccession and disposal as a way to "re-work these object 'memories' and to choose to 'forget' some of them."[37] The ability (or indeed the choice) to forget is today becoming one of the most prized personal and institutional capacities in a digitized world where everything can be archived for future reference. This is because fetishizing what remains of history has led to memory becoming akin to a "new religion of the past," as Russian poet and author Maria Stepanova remarks in her astounding, genre-bending book *In Memory of Memory*: "In comparison with a future we don't want to inhabit, what has already happened feels domesticated—practically bearable."[38] The past becomes a safe harbor, a foreign country that can be colonized, modified, and then mobilized for present and future needs. Published by Fitzcarraldo in 2021 in a translation by Sasha Dugdale, the volume has the white cover reserved for nonfiction works rather than the distinctive blue shade of the imprint's fiction range, yet inside, it is characterized—somewhat confusingly—as "Essay/Fiction." It also bears the tantalizing subtitle of *A Romance*. *In Memory of Memory* thus destabilizes our readerly expectations from the get-go: the slash separating but also conjoining genres, the "romance" label providing a bewildering angle. This hybrid labeling anticipates the author's interventionist approach to personal essay-writing that sees her constantly cast doubt on the material she lays before us until we, as readers, are ultimately left grasping at nothing more than her words.

Stepanova's broad mission in *In Memory of Memory* is to oppose any comfortable retreat into the past by consistently showing how her attempts to revive and narrativize her own family history lead to nothing meaningful at all. As she attempts to make sense of her recently deceased Aunt Galya's life by examining the belongings left in her Moscow flat, she quickly feels how the objects actively oppose her quest for meaning: "The meek contents of her apartment, feeling themselves to be redundant, immediately began to lose their human qualities and, in doing so, ceased to remember or mean anything."[39] The narrator then alights on the elderly woman's notebooks, which she carries home to read, "in search of stories, explanations, the oval shape of her life."[40] What she finds instead are astonishingly mundane lists of daily occurrences: what Galya ate on any given day, when she slept and for how long, what she watched on television, and how long she waited for a particular bus. The notebooks are a guide to revealing nothing about personal history, replacing anything of significance with an abundance of detail that allows the writer to achieve "a minute and virtuosic avoidance of content."[41] Guided by Galya's evasive practice, rather than succeeding as a recuperative exercise, Stepanova's work becomes a free-form meditation on the importance of letting go of the search for meaning in the past.

Much of this work of letting go takes place within the relationship the narrator tries to form with objects. By gathering up Galya's belongings into detailed descriptions ("hoards of thermal vests and leggings; new and beautiful jackets and skirts . . . and tiny, ivory brooches, delicate and girlish: a rose, another rose, a crane with wings outstretched") but simultaneously pointing to their lack of transferable meaning, Stepanova uses *In Memory of Memory* to show how postfictional texts can serve as "a particular kind of archive," both for things *and* for their disappearance, thus calling the reader's attention to the generative capacities of loss.[42] Letting go of material remnants thus becomes a creative response to a contemporary necessity, allowing us to let go of particular, comforting fantasies, whether these are of "permanence, of national coherence, of a universal subject, [or] of a particular future."[43] Museums would do well to heed Wasserman's words quoted here. In the same way as the realist novel or the archive, the modern museum has to date represented an "organizational principle for the content of cultural identity and scientific knowledge," one built on principles of collecting, ordering, categorizing, displaying, and preserving past things.[44] It has thus assumed the function of externalizing memory—we can relegate our memorial function to museums, as we can to statues and other memorials, because the physical content of memory is supposedly stored there in perpetuity. Museums, memorials, and even novels are all, in Pierre Nora's felicitous terms, *lieux de mémoire*, or sites of memory, which in effect replace active processes of memorialization "because there are no longer *milieux de mémoire*, real environments of memory."[45] However, faced with the "profusion struggle" of overflowing reserves and storerooms, heritage institutions are now recognizing the need to consciously define the life cycle of objects as bookended by moments of birth and death, foreclosing the possibility of endlessly preserving

Deaccession

memory for future generations.[46] Calls for degrowth in heritage collections thus align museum priorities with economic and social agendas that attend more closely to utility and to the potential future benefits of actions and acquisitions rather than seeing a priori value in the act of accumulation itself.

Can the postmuseum become imagined as a site that will in the future host more temporary objects, objects that will transit in the museum for a defined period and then be let go again? Alongside more traditional, permanent exhibits, can it also become a time-limited home for secondhand, broken, or low-value ephemera, things that were not meant to survive but that might still provide some short-term enjoyment and use for visitors? We have seen how in the Museum of Broken Relationships, the objective "value" of the pieces on display is not a factor of high importance—rather, it is their ability to represent a story that has sentimental power and allows for a connection with visitors' own memories and emotions that counts. Similarly, in Leanne Shapton's work, the "importance" of the artifacts recorded in the auction catalogue is not necessarily economic, but sentimental. Clothes belonging to Doolan and Morris that have holes or stains attesting to wear and tear, objects broken in fights between the two, and photographs with pinhole marks where they were stuck up on walls are all "valued" more highly than expensive artifacts, precisely because they relate to and support the narrative on display. Heritage institutions already give high-value but redundant or out-of-use objects a second life by assigning them high status within the museum collection. By considering this status as nonpermanent and subject to processes of deaccession, disposal, or destruction, we can come to see how "heritage values are ascribed rather than intrinsic."[47] If value is culturally determined then it follows that the formation of a heritage "canon" should always be open to questioning, and, ultimately to revision and change. The value of objects themselves also shifts through processes of accession and deaccession: as Marilena Vecco and Michele Piazzai show, an object can be elevated from the mundane to the collection-worthy when it enters the museum collection, but when it leaves it undergoes a sudden, radical loss of status.[48]

On this note, perhaps the most emblematic object in Stepanova's overflowing archive of textualized stuff is a small white china figurine of a naked young boy with curly hair, one of hundreds she once saw piled up in a box for sale at a Moscow flea market. Every single figurine she sees as she sorts through the collection is broken, but it is exactly their flaws that make them unique: each is "differently mutilated, missing a leg or a face, and all the faces were scarred and chipped."[49] Having chosen one of the figurines to buy, the author then carries this object around with her as she goes in search of a worthwhile narrative about her family history to recount. In its brokenness, the figurine signifies the anticipation of the story's circumscribed ending.

> I already knew that I was carrying the end of my book in my pocket, the hidden answer to a riddle in a puzzle book. My china boy seemed

to embody the way no story reaches us without having its heels chipped off or its face scratched away. And how lacunae and gaps are the constant companions of survival, its hidden engine, fuelling its acceleration.[50]

As the narrator walks around Vienna (where incidentally she visits the wax anatomical models of the Josephinum, analyzed in chapter 5), the china figurine drops out of her pocket and smashes beyond repair, reaffirming the impossibility of her finding a resolution in understanding the past through the storytelling of objects. Throughout this book I have charted similarities and contrasts in the narrative media of novels and museums in an attempt to rethink the relationship between different forms of material memorialization and representations of the past. The fact that the china figurine in Stepanova's *In Memory of Memory*—an object that the narrator initially deploys as an emblem of the potential representation of memory through things— ends up broken may well indicate that this is a relationship beyond repair, one that in its current configuration has reached the end of its utility. With the advent of the postfictional novel and the postmuseum, the old regime of using traditional museal and literary forms as storage emporia for representative memorializations of the past is now changing. This "implosion of the mnemonic museum frame has consequences for the form of representation of the past,"[51] and making difficult decisions about deaccession and disposal can hopefully help us open up space for more sustainable modes of remembering through forgetting in heritage and narrative settings alike.

The twentieth century was characterized by a collective imperative to remember and to salvage memories of the past through "fixing" them in material evidence held in public and private collections. Writing in 1992, Mark Jones remarked that this was a specific feature of the waning century, which was "more uncertain and anxious about its relationship with history than any other previous age. With declining confidence in the present, the urge to conserve and revive the past has become even more frantic."[52] Nowhere is this perhaps more amply felt that in Joe Brainard's midcentury autobiography *I Remember*, which records his childhood memories in a free-flowing list of recollection. In an introduction to the 2012 edition, Paul Auster points out that objects and products are the most frequent indicators for memories in Brainard's text, numbering more than 130 entries ("including driftwood lamps, pop beads, beanbag ashtrays, pearlized plastic toilet seats, jeweled bottle openers, 'Ace' combs, roller skate keys, Aspergum, dented ping-pong balls, and miniature Bibles"[53]). Objects hold the power to evoke the past, and as Paul Connerton has shown, people habitually turn to history to cope with loss (either personal or collective) in the present.[54] Stepanova would say this is because pasts are "submissive": "they reject no interpretation, endure any amount of humiliation."[55] We can re-fashion them however we like. On finding a mystery man's name written on a piece of paper inside a lace purse

Deaccession   *159*

belonging to her grandmother, the narrator pesters her mother for ideas of who it might be: "I wanted to know what to make of it. 'Make of it what you will,' said my mother, and ended the conversation."[56] What are the implications of this refusal of the potential to find meaning in our relationships with objects? Can achieving liberation from such a search allow us to be more creative, and more generative in our interpretation of things? If in the Western tradition to date material objects have been assumed to be able to act as analogues of human memory, then as Adrian Forty shows, they also used to "stand in for memories and thus preserve them."[57] Yet now this is now no longer the case, since in standing in for memories, objects have succeeded in merely substituting them, thereby weakening our ties with the past. The more time Stepanova's narrator spends in her family's archive of objects and photographs, the less she finds she knows or remembers: "The history of a family which I had at the outset learnt at the speed of a straight line was now fragmenting in my head into tesserae, into notes indicating textual omissions, into hypotheses there was no one left to prove."[58] Fact has turned into fiction, and all that remains to her are "unverifiable stories, fables, fairy tale elements, embryos of a novel."[59]

As our reliance on material objects to help us remember wanes, so the emphasis on recognizing the importance of selectively forgetting the past and letting go of associated objects has increased. As Wasserman writes, "Letting go of things and doing away with fantasies of durability means rejecting damaging nostalgia and accepting constant change; it also means recognizing that even temporary formations can carry within them the possibility of real action."[60] Letting go like this fits particularly well into one of the seven different ways of forgetting that Paul Connerton has identified in the contemporary age: annulment, which he sees as a "response to a surfeit of information."[61] Discarding materials and information allows for greater latitude in opening up gaps where creativity might spark new ideas, new connections, and new content. As Leanne Shapton states, "The half story you get forces your imagination to fill in the blanks, and I love that. The information is random, and I love that 'gap-iness.'"[62] In another interview, Shapton speaks of her fascination with the photos that we take endlessly on our mobile phones and then delete. These images excite her, she states, precisely because they are not curated.[63] Forgoing the framework of curation allows for the less structured cultivating of the past as something akin to a garden left free to run wild. This action recalls Caitlin DeSilvey's call for an approach to heritage conservation which makes an asset of incompletion and fragmentation, and even allows for episodes of unexpected beauty, such as in the growth of "ruderal" plants which grow on disturbed ground, such as building sites, wastelands, and waysides.[64] Such "intervals of neglect" that occur when we embrace the idea of entropy and decay—both in the physical landscape of heritage and in the intangible heritage of memory—allow for new sites of value to emerge. This value "centers on the force of the fragment, the remnant, the incongruous juxtaposition of that which persists against that which has been absorbed into other orders."[65] Stepanova would further caution against locating meaning even in rewilded fragments such as these. In visiting the Jewish cemetery in Kherson where she hopes to locate tombstones of as-yet-unknown family members, she finds that the cemetery itself has "given up the ghost, ha[s] allowed the land to consume it."[66] Spikes and thorns tear at her clothes and skin as she searches fruitlessly for nothing in what is now a thick map of thorns: "The fallen tombstones were hidden by wild flowers, burdocks and snail shells, and their surfaces resembled burned skin."[67] Just as the landscape has fallen back into an uncultivated, hostile state, so too can objects revert to something more primordial and less familiar, as the narrator learns when she tries to exit the cemetery, bleeding and frustrated: "Objects falling out of currency slowly lose their defining qualities and turn a new non-human face towards us. They return to the materials from whence they came, wax, paint and clay. The past rewilds itself, oblivion springs out of it like a forest."[68]

In passages such as these, Stepanova not only points toward the failure of objects to help us access the past but also gestures toward the limits of object-based narrative recollection. In similar fashion, in her evocative portrait of the storm-battered Mullion harbor in Cornwall, DeSilvey finds that those same limits to narrative apply, and asks, "If we are looking for ways to let go gracefully, story can provide some solace. But the words that we stack up and ask to do our work are not always enough; they can be unsettled and undermined as surely as a harbor wall."[69] This acceptance of narrative failures and the loss of surety in our reliance on memory as a stable conduit to the past both evoke Michael Taussig's self-stated love of "muted or even defective storytelling as a form of analysis," a defect that can even emerge as an innovative method.[70] For when you cannot locate secure referents to the past, objects become free-floating signifiers that can, in turn, assume *translational* effects. This signals the potential that lies in the "mobilisation of absence."[71] As Cornelius Holtorf explains, "Absent constructions are sites located in between tangible, material forms of heritage and intangible forms of heritage such as story-telling. You look at a very tangible place in front of you but you see something that is present only as a story in your mind—yet, nevertheless, constitutive of the entire experience you have."[72] Early on in her quest for memories Stepanova's narrator takes a trip to the town of Saratov, the birthplace of her great-grandfather, in search of the old family house. When she is shown around by a local guide, she comments:

> The house was unrecognizable, but then I'd never seen it before to recognize it. I spent a good while in the yard just running my hands over the rough Saratov brickwork. Everything was as I'd hoped, perhaps even more so than I'd hoped. I recognized my great-grandfather's yard unhesitatingly. There was no doubt in my mind . . . all of it was mine, all of it instantly part of my family.[73]

Deaccession   *161*

A week after this transformative moment of connection, the narrator receives a call from her colleague in the town to tell her that he'd mixed up the address—the house she had recognized was not hers at all. In episodes such as these Stepanova shows how a coherent family history in the post-Soviet space cannot be reconstructed through the bric-a-brac assembled in the novel. The silence of family memories stored in cupboards, albums, and cemeteries mimics the futility of the narrative drive to complete histories, and speaks instead of the impossibility of saving anything at all. The forgotten art of decomposition means that there is too much past present in the here and now, and the stories we tell about that past are themselves beyond repair. When confronted with her failure to make the mute objects in her family archives communicate, the narrator concludes that in the end nothing revealed itself to her, and "the less I can say about them, the closer they come."[74]

Conclusion: Toward Postobject Futures

We have seen how in *In Memory of Memory* in particular, a "register of narrative certainty gives way to one of crisis and disorientation in which authenticity not only of the account but also of the experience falls into doubt."[75] When read together, *In Memory of Memory*, *Important Artifacts*, and the Museum of Broken Relationships offer a snapshot into a world where preservation at all costs is a concern of the past, and where objects have lost their primacy in our efforts to connect with and memorialize collective and personal pasts. Even narrative efforts at connection are, indeed, also in decline, and evidence the fact that "deflections, refusals, even failures and incapacities are as important to the story of the novel as insights, revelations, intuitions, and enigmas—or more so."[76] It is in this postfictional arena that we can see potential new modes of museum making emerge. Michael Taussig's experimental work of 2004, *My Cocaine Museum*, constructs a make-believe museum which is based on the Gold Museum in Colombia's central bank, but challenges the existing museum's failure to acknowledge the memory of those enslaved Africans forced to mine gold and whose contribution to the country's wealth and development are thus not included in the museum interpretation. Taussig deploys the "show and tell" modality of a museum in his writing to tell the life of present-day gold-mining communities in the rainforests of Colombia's Pacific coast and their imbrication into networks of criminality through the symbiosis of money and drugs. Bypassing the sumptuous objects on display in the Gold Museum, Taussig finds thing power in glimpses of gold on the streets of Bogotá: the foot of a saint in a church rubbed for luck by worshippers, or the flash of cheap metal on the wrist of a street hustler. This, he says, is where "the thingness of things glow[s] in the dark."[77] Taking the museum outside the walls of the institution and into the stories of the streets and rural communities shows how a "'museum' may be any real or imaginary site where the conflict or interaction or simulation of or between personal and collective memory occurs."[78]

In this new era of the postmuseum we thus see how the erosion of object primacy can be redefined as a positive outcome, since objects tie memory down, fixing it into an unnatural stasis that limits its natural capacity for movement. As Michel de Certeau writes, "Memory is a sort of anti-museum: it is not localizable."[79] Perhaps it is in the postfictional grooves of spaces between objects, spaces in which we can move, walk, and think, that we can relocate the meaning of the new museology to come. These spaces of doubt are where the links with contemporary narrative lie, since the "insistent quality of twentieth-century literature is not only refusing to connect the work and the world, but thinking, inhabiting, even forging the space of their disorientation."[80]

Postobject futures as imagined in the postmuseum and postfictional narratives also offer something of a response to urgent issues of sustainability in our planet's fight for climate survival. In an era where the idea "forever pollution" currently haunts our futures, the crisis of accumulation that affects both the public and the private spheres is exacerbated by ever more sophisticated modes of technological hoarding. Postapocalyptic imaginings seem less distant and more imaginable in the aftermath of the COVID-19 pandemic, and narratives such as Emily St. John Mandel's 2014 novel *Station Eleven* provide a glimpse of what our relationships to things might look like in the wake of a disaster to come. When a group of stranded air travelers set up camp in the fictional Severn City Airport after a flu pandemic originating in Georgia eliminates 99 percent of the earth's human population, a lawyer named Clark takes over the Skymiles Lounge with an object collection that becomes known as the Museum of Civilization.

> There seemed to be a limitless number of objects in the world that had no practical use but that people wanted to preserve: cell phones with their delicate buttons, iPads, Tyler's Nintendo consoles, a selection of laptops. There were a number of impractical shoes, stilettoes mostly, beautiful and strange . . . magazines and newspapers, a stamp collection, coins.[81]

News of the airport museum spreads far and wide, with visitors coming to the airport to view, and sometimes add to, the collection on display. But although the objects have a consolatory power for Clark, their curator, the "civilization" they represent is shown to be extinct, replaced by new scales of humanity and inhumanity as those left in the world jostle for survival. Its obsolescence is made clear in the following exchange, where the characters August and Kirsten are asked to explain what the Museum of Civilization is to a passerby: "'I heard it's supposed to be a place where artifacts from

Deaccession   *163*

the old world are preserved,' August said. The man laughed. . . . 'Here's the thing, kids, the entire world is a place where artifacts from the old world are preserved. When was the last time you saw a new car?'"[82] This sense of the world as a holistic archive is ever more relevant in the fight against the climate crisis, for example in tales of parents in the Pacific Marshall Islands naming their children after vanishing landmarks: a favorite reef, an ancient coral head, or a beloved atoll. The Marshallese poet Kathy Jetñil-Kijiner named her daughter after a parcel of land belonging to her mother's family in the hope that using place-based names would help ensure that the legacy of the islands endures, even if the land itself sinks.[83] It is, rightly, the conservation of the planet itself that must concern us now, not the shoring up of individual components of its material contents.

In closing this book it thus seems vital to ask two interrelated questions: Can museums help us to design and envisage new future-oriented practices that will see us transition beyond object dependence? And can literature help to show how they can do so? As Wolfgang Ernst says, "Maybe the task of the museum today is to reflect on the contemporary loss of substance in objects. . . . The materiality of objects is an obstacle to semiotic sublimation, to the attempt at preservation by immaterialization in writing, photography, and other forms of reproduction."[84] My analysis in this chapter has sought to show how literature can offer creative modes of imagining new endings and new beginnings for objects and experience alike. One of these modes can be located in the preamble to Judith Schalansky's *An Inventory of Losses*, which lists all the things that the author knows to have been lost, to have gone extinct, or to have been destroyed during the writing of the book. But the preamble also lists the things that were found or discovered during the same period, including a potentially habitable zone 1,400 light years from our sun.[85] In the twelve chapters that follow, Schalansky goes on to construct literary, fabulative accounts of her own engagement with lost things: things that might only ever have been imagined, the literal stuff of legend. In her attempts to rediscover archival traces of a "phantom island" in the Southern Cook archipelago which was lost in a marine earthquake sometime in the 1840s she finds herself "abandoned by eyewitness accounts," "all alone on deck," and utterly lost in her own conjecture. From that point on her quest alternates between postfictional poles of fantasy and personal memoir. Her account of the now-extinct Caspian tiger imagines the animal's role in arena fights with gladiators in ancient Roman times. In the mountains of the Valais, the author conjures the impossible feat of the physicist Otto von Guericke, who pretended to have re-created a unicorn skeleton from the bones of what were actually ice-age mammals, but she does so through recounting memories of her own, lonely stay in an Alpine chalet.

What would museum exhibits that embrace the modes of loss explored in this chapter look like in practice? And could museum exhibits one day showcase the kind of poetic latitude that absence opens up in texts such as

An Inventory of Losses? The collection of texts and objects I have assembled here have together shown the possible contours of a postmuseal future where the potential of objects is imagined as lying beyond their figural properties. The landscape of ontological doubt sketched by texts such as *In Memory of Memory* further calls into question both the value of the physical space of the museum and the representational powers held within the material contours of the museum object. Recent calls for deaccessioned museum objects and objects marked for disposal to be transformed into art or even into working objects make us further query what the value of static, "forever" collections is now. This value, I would argue, is contingent on factors of external necessity which are constantly changing. Outside the Severn City airport in *Station Eleven*, and thus far from the Museum of Civilization's collection of obsolete objects, lies the graveyard where those who have died there since the outbreak of the Georgia flu pandemic are laid to rest. Between two obsolete runways, a series of airplane tray tables have been repurposed as grave markers, "driven into the ground, details of the deceased carved into the tray's hard plastic."[86] In both literary and museum settings we should be looking for such examples of future-oriented practice in the adaptive reuse of objects that works to find meaning in loss. As Grünfeld and DeSilvey state, "The fringes may get wilder and weedier, and the fringe object itself may appear to disappear, but some residue always remains."[87]

This book has shown that the residues of material and memorial loss exist in multiple forms: in texts, in objects, in modes of intangible heritage, and most of all in stories, whether they are strictly true or even if they are possibly (or probably) false. Kevin Walsh is right when he makes the point that a new museology must involve people "in the production of their own pasts."[88] This is an active process, distinct from any traditional passive experience of didactic learning, or even from the directed learning of an interactive visit in the museum. Reading postfictional literature offers us the tools to produce our own pasts in this way because, as Schalansky says, when all else is lost, or threatened with loss, "writing survives. By writing, as by reading, one can pick one's own ancestors and establish a second, intellectual hereditary line to rival conventional biological heritage."[89] This final chapter has argued that museums can use literary imaginings to find solutions to the challenges to come as we contemplate postobject futures and move beyond current preservation paradigms. Care is reimagined in terms of letting go, of forgetting, and of leaving spaces uncurated in order to spark creative twists and trails of fantasy. The "curating of worlds" imagined in this book's title thus becomes a fabulative project which moves beyond the memorial practices of salvage and repair that characterized cultural forms in the twentieth century and looks forward to envisaging new postobject futures in twenty-first-century museums and literature alike.

NOTES

Introduction

1. Carrie Mae Weems, "Mutual Beliefs" (2009), an interview with Dawoud Bey. *Reflections for Now* (Berlin: Hatje Cantz Verlag, 2023), 30.

2. The Carters, "APES**T," Reservoir Media Music, 2018.

3. See Angelique Chrisafis, "Beyoncé and Jay-Z Help Louvre Museum Break Visitor Record in 2018," *Guardian*, January 3, 2019. The Louvre also capitalized on public interest in the exhibits shown in the video by making a special online visitor guide to the featured highlights, available via the museum website, https://www.louvre.fr/en/explore/visitor-trails/beyonce-and-jay-z-s-louvre-highlights, accessed April 24, 2023.

4. Philip Fisher, "Art and the Future's Past," in *Museum Studies: An Anthology of Contexts*, ed. Bettina Messias Carbonell (Oxford: Wiley-Blackwell, 2012), 465.

5. W. Stanley Jevons, "The Use and Abuse of Museums" (1882), cited in *The Emergence of the Modern Museum. An Anthology of Nineteenth-Century Sources*, ed. Jonah Siegel (Oxford: Oxford University Press, 2005), 289.

6. Allan Hepburn, *Enchanted Objects: Visual Art in Contemporary Fiction* (Toronto: University of Toronto Press, 2010), 42.

7. See Jonah Siegel, *Material Inspirations: The Interests of the Art Object in the Nineteenth Century and After* (Oxford: Oxford University Press, 2020), 4.

8. Matthew Mullins, *Postmodernism in Pieces: Materializing the Social in U.S. Fiction* (Oxford: Oxford University Press, 2016), 30.

9. See Peter Vergo, ed., *The New Museology* (London: Reaktion Books, 1989).

10. Daša Drndić, *Trieste*, trans. Ellen Elias-Bursać (London: MacLehose Press, 2012); Valeria Luiselli, *Lost Children Archive: A Novel* (New York: Alfred A. Knopf, 2019); Claudio Magris, *Blameless*, trans. Anne Milano Appel (New Haven, CT: Yale University Press, 2017); Maaza Mengiste, *The Shadow King: A Novel* (New York: W. W. Norton, 2019); Orhan Pamuk, *The Museum of Innocence. A Novel*, trans. Maureen Freely (London: Faber and Faber, 2009); Maria Stepanova, *In Memory of Memory. A Romance*, trans. Sasha Dugdale (London: Fitzcarraldo, 2021); Leanne Shapton, *Important Artifacts and Personal Property from the Collection of Lenore Doolan and Harold Morris, including Books, Street Fashion, and Jewelry* (London: Bloomsbury, 2009); and Olga Tokarczuk, *Flights*, trans. Jennifer Croft (London: Fitzcarraldo, 2017).

11. Eugenio Donato, "The Museum's Furnace: Notes toward a Contextual Reading of *Bouvard and Pécuchet*," in *Textual Strategies: Perspectives in Post-Structuralist Criticism*, ed. Josue V. Harari (Ithaca, NY: Cornell University Press, 1979), 221, 223.

165

12. Gustave Flaubert, *Bouvard and Pécuchet*, trans. Mark Polizzotti (Chicago: Dalkey Archive Press, 2005), 114.

13. Silke Arnold-de Simine, "Memory Museum and Museum Text: Intermediality in Daniel Libeskind's Jewish Museum and W. G. Sebald's *Austerlitz*," *Theory, Culture and Society* 29, no. 1 (2012): 17.

14. Arnold-de Simine, "Memory Museum and Museum Text," 30.

15. Madhu Dubey, "Museumizing Slavery: Living History in Colson Whitehead's *The Underground Railroad*," *American Literary History* 32, no. 1 (2020): 111.

16. Colson Whitehead, *The Underground Railroad* (London: Little, Brown, 2016), 151.

17. Bill Brown, "Thing Theory," *Critical Inquiry* 28, no. 1 (2001): 5.

18. Peter Schwenger, *The Tears of Things: Melancholy and Physical Objects* (Minneapolis: University of Minnesota Press, 2006), 2, 15.

19. Hepburn, *Enchanted Objects*, 163; emphasis added.

20. Hepburn, *Enchanted Objects*, 172; Mullins, *Postmodernism in Pieces*.

21. For a recent account of the ways in which museums have responded in transformative ways to a series of externally provoked crises, see Samuel J. Redman, *The Museum: A Short History of Crisis and Resilience* (New York: New York University Press, 2022).

22. See https://icom.museum/en/resources/standards-guidelines/museum-definition/, accessed April 24, 2023. In their "Mapping Museums" project, Fiona Candlin and Jamie Larkin have engaged with assemblage theory in order to try and reach a definition, finding that the "notion of a museum both collapses and functions, it is both an impossible and entirely usable term." See "What Is a Museum? Difference All the Way Down," *Museum and Society* 18, no. 2: 123.

23. See https://www.museumsarenotneutral.com, accessed April 24, 2023.

24. My thinking here is in line with Jeanne Canizzo's view of the museum collection as a kind of cultural text, one that can be read in order to "understand the underlying cultural or ideological assumptions that have informed its creation, selection, and display." See "Exhibiting Cultures: 'Into the Heart of Africa,'" *Visual Anthropology Review* 7, no. 1 (1991): 151.

25. See Timothy Ambrose and Crispin Paine, eds., *Museum Basics: The International Handbook* (London: Routledge, 2018), 60.

26. Gaynor Kavanagh, *History Curatorship* (Leicester, UK: Leicester University Press, 1990), 3.

27. Ambrose and Paine, *Museum Basics*, 6.

28. See Lou Stoppard, "Everyone's a Curator Now," *New York Times*, March 3, 2020.

29. "Museums are not supposed to lie to us; this seems a breach of faith. Assuming that our own memories are fallible, we rely on museums as well as historians to get the past 'right' for us. Even if we don't remember every museum experience, we know that the 'straight' version of the past is available to remedy our 'queered' or distorted memories." Susan A. Crane, "Memory, Distortion, and History in the Museum," *History and Theory* 36, no. 4 (1997): 51.

30. Michael Ames, "Cannibal Tours, Glass Boxes and the Politics of Interpretation," in *Interpreting Objects and Collections*, ed. Susan M. Pearce (London: Routledge, 1994), 103.

Notes to Pages 12–15

31. Carol Duncan, "Museums and Citizenship," in *Exhibiting Cultures: The Poetics and Politics of Museum Display*, ed. Ivan Karp and Steven D. Lavine (Washington, DC: Smithsonian Institution, 1991), 92.

32. Svetlana Alpers, "The Museum as a Way of Seeing," in Karp and Lavine, *Exhibiting Cultures*, 26.

33. See Didier Maleuvre, *Museum Memories: History, Technology, Art* (Stanford, CA: Stanford University Press, 1999), 12.

34. See Igor Kopytoff, "The Cultural Biography of Things: Commoditization as Process," in *The Social Life of Things: Commodities in Cultural Perspective*, ed. Arjun Appadurai (Cambridge: Cambridge University Press, 1986), 64–92.

35. James Wood, "*Flights*, a Novel That Never Settles Down," *New Yorker*, September 24, 2018.

36. Peter Pomerantsev, "Russian Memoirs Are Prone to a Particular Kind of Angst," *Spectator*, May 29, 2021.

37. Lorraine Daston and Katharine Park, *Wonders and the Order of Nature, 1150–1750* (New York: Zone Books, 1998), 13.

38. See Stephen Greenblatt, "Resonance and Wonder," in Karp and Lavine, *Exhibiting Cultures*, 51.

39. Phillip Blom, *To Have and to Hold: An Intimate History of Collectors and Collecting* (London: Penguin, 2003), 24.

40. See Maleuvre, *Museum Memories*, 14.

41. Sarah Longair, "Cultures of Curating: The Limits of Authority," *Museum History Journal* 8, no. 1 (2015): 4. See also Elizabeth Crooke's notion of the "active museum," which she employs to describe the new attention given to community engagement within museum thought. "The 'Active Museum': How Concern with Community Transformed the Museum," in *The International Handbook of Museum Studies, part 2, Museum Practice*, ed. Conal McCarthy (Oxford: Wiley, 2015), 481–502.

42. See Susan M. Pearce, "Objects as Meaning; Or Narrating the Past," in Pearce, *Interpreting Objects and Collections*, 26; and Candlin and Larkin on the multifaceted nature of museum visits and the importance of multiple interactions that take place within them ("What Is a Museum?," 124).

43. Canizzo, "Exhibiting Cultures," 151.

44. Angela Naimou, *Salvage Work: U.S. and Caribbean Literatures amid the Debris of Legal Personhood* (New York: Fordham University Press, 2015), 10.

45. Sara Ahmed, *What's the Use? On the Uses of Use* (Durham, NC: Duke University Press, 2019), 21.

46. Greenblatt, "Resonance and Wonder," 43.

47. Ralph Rugoff, foreword to *Kader Attia: The Museum of Emotion* (London: Hayward Gallery, 2019), 4. The salvage and rehabilitation of broken objects performed by Attia also recalls installation works by German Jamaican artist Sonia Elizabeth Barrett, and in particular her Trapani series *Performed Furniture* (2015). The images of ramshackle sea vessels used to bring migrants from North Africa to Sicily haunt the wooden sculptures, which were made from pieces salvaged from municipal waste, and include remnants of eighteenth-century tropical hardwood, thus recalling the multiply layered stories of sea transport and racialized commodification across the centuries. See www.sebarrett.com, accessed April 24, 2023.

48. See Caitlin DeSilvey, "Salvage Memory: Constellating Material Histories on a Hardscrabble Homestead," *cultural geographies* 14, no. 3 (2007): 401–24; Caitlin DeSilvey, *Curated Decay: Heritage beyond Saving* (Minneapolis: University of Minnesota Press, 2017); Crystal B. Lake, *Artifacts: How We Think and Write about Found Objects* (Baltimore: Johns Hopkins University Press, 2020); Sarah Wasserman, *The Death of Things: Ephemera and the American Novel* (Minneapolis: University of Minnesota Press, 2020).

49. See, for example, James Clifford, "The Times of the Curator," in *Curatopia: Museums and the Future of Curatorship*, ed. Philipp Schorch and Conal McCarthy (Manchester, UK: Manchester University Press, 2019), 109–21; Donna Haraway, *When Species Meet* (Minneapolis: University of Minnesota Press, 2008); and Donna Haraway, *Staying with the Trouble: Making Kin in the Chthulucene* (Durham, NC: Duke University Press, 2016).

50. Tokarczuk, *Flights*, 83.

51. Jahan Ramazani, *A Transnational Poetics* (Chicago: University of Chicago Press, 2009), 15.

52. Sharae Deckard, Nicholas Lawrence, Neil Lazarus, Graeme Macdonald, Upamanyu Pablo Mukherjee, Benita Parry, and Stephen Shapiro, *World-Literature in the Context of Combined and Uneven Development* (Liverpool, UK: Liverpool University Press, 2015), 17.

53. Walter Benjamin, "Eduard Fuchs: Collector and Historian," *New German Critique* 5 (1975): (28).

54. Pheng Cheah, *What Is a World? On Postcolonial Literature as World Literature* (Durham, NC: Duke University Press, 2016), 2.

55. Ann Laura Stoler, *Imperial Debris: On Ruins and Ruination* (Durham, NC: Duke University Press, 2013).

56. Stoler, *Imperial Debris*, 8.

57. See Ariella Aïsha Azoulay, *Potential History: Unlearning Imperialism* (New York: Verso, 2019).

58. Stoler, *Imperial Debris*, 8; emphasis added.

59. Cheah, *What Is a World?*, 12.

60. John M. MacKenzie, *Museums and Empire: Hunting, Conservation and British Imperialism* (Manchester, UK: Manchester University Press, 1988), 6–7.

61. George W. Stocking, "Introduction: Essays on Museums and Material Culture," in *Objects and Others: Essays on Museums and Material Culture*, ed. George W. Stocking (Madison: University of Wisconsin Press, 1985), 4.

62. Lake, *Artifacts*, 7.

63. Lake, *Artifacts*, 16.

64. Lake, *Artifacts*, 196.

65. See Gayatri Gopinath, *Unruly Visions: The Aesthetic Practices of Queer Diaspora* (Durham, NC: Duke University Press, 2018).

66. Chris Andrews, "Publishing, Translating, Worldmaking," in *The Cambridge Companion to World Literature*, ed. Ben Etherington and Jarad Zimbler (Cambridge: Cambridge University Press, 2018), 227.

67. DeSilvey, "Salvage Memory," 416.

Notes to Pages 19–23 169

Chapter 1

1. Stefano Furlan was a passionate fan of the Trieste football club who fell into a coma after being beaten by police following a local derby match with Udine in 1984. Furlan died three weeks later at the age of twenty. The murals that memorialize his death are thus another mode of localized memory making that contribute to the complex symbolic landscape of urban Trieste.

2. The walls were part of the creative restructuring of the site by architect Romano Boico for its reopening in 1975. Katia Pizzi notes that "Boico's work is a brutalist and unadorned refitting designed to emphasize vacuity and isolation." "The Granular Texture of Memory: Trieste between Mitteleuropa and the Mediterranean," *Journal of Transcultural Studies* 11, no. 1 (2020): 38. See also Massimo Mucci, *La Risiera di San Sabba: Un'architettura per la memoria* (Gorizia, Italy: Goriziana, 1999).

3. See Francesco Fait, ed., *Civico Museo della Risiera di San Sabba: Monumento Nazionale* (Trieste, Italy: Edizioni Civici musei di storia ed arte, Comune di Trieste, 2016), 19.

4. Pamela Ballinger gives a detailed account of the lives of the refugee families amassed in the cells of the Lager in 1959: "The walls and the beams still bore scratched names, dates, Stars of David, crosses, invocations." *History in Exile: Memory and Identity at the Borders of the Balkans* (Princeton, NJ: Princeton University Press, 2003), 141.

5. "Mi sono proposto di togliere e recintare più che di aggiungere." Cit. Fait, *Civico Museo della Risiera di San Sabba*, 41.

6. Drndić, *Trieste*, 295.

7. Estimates of the number of victims killed in the Risiera are only approximate, and commonly range between two thousand and five thousand people.

8. Drndić, *Trieste*, 142.

9. Katharina Bielenberg, "The Editor's Chair: On Daša Drndić," *Granta*, November 16, 2018.

10. Peter Brooks, *Reading for the Plot: Design and Intention in Narrative* (Cambridge, MA: Harvard University Press, 1984), 4.

11. DeSilvey, *Curated Decay*, 6.

12. DeSilvey, "Salvage Memory," 408.

13. Susan Stewart, *On Longing: Narratives of the Miniature, the Gigantic, the Souvenir, and Collection* (Durham, NC: Duke University Press, 1993), 135.

14. Deborah Tulani Salahu-Din, "Documenting the BLM Movement in Baltimore through Contemporary Collecting: An Initiative of the NMAAHC," *Collections* 15: nos. 2–3 (2019): 102.

15. On the meaning and power of object groupings, see Bruno Latour, *Reassembling the Social: An Introduction to Actor-Network Theory* (Oxford: Oxford University Press, 2005), 28–39. Crystal B. Lake develops Latour's notion into what she calls "artifact network theory" (*Artifacts*, 16). And Jane Bennett's notion of "thing-power" comes from her witnessing a grouping, a collection, a configuration of multiple items, what she calls a "contingent tableau" of objects along with their setting and with her as their observer. *Vibrant Matter: A Political Ecology of Things* (Durham, NC: Duke University Press, 2010), 5.

16. Russell W. Belk, *Collecting in a Consumer Society* (London: Routledge, 1995), 67.

17. Russell W. Belk, "Collectors and Collecting," in *Handbook of Material Culture*, ed. Christopher Tilley et al. (London: SAGE, 2006), 541.

18. Walter Benjamin, "Unpacking my Library: A Talk about Book Collecting," in *Illuminations*, trans. Harry Zorn (London: Pimlico, 1999), 62–63. See also Jean Baudrillard on the narcissistic projection involved in collecting, "whereby the images of the self is extended to the very limits of the collection." "The System of Collecting," in *The Cultures of Collecting*, ed. John Elsner and Roger Cardinal (London: Reaktion Books, 1994), 23.

19. Stewart, *On Longing*, 156.

20. See Stewart, *On Longing*, 151.

21. John Elsner and Roger Cardinal, introduction to Elsner and Cardinal, *Cultures of Collecting*, 10.

22. Brooks, *Reading for the Plot*, 92, 102.

23. Stewart, *On Longing*, 166.

24. Baudrillard, "System of Collecting," 27; emphasis added.

25. "Time has arranged itself in circles. The past is reality, a factual state. But the future offers branching possibilities." Drndić, *Trieste*, 252.

26. Operation Reinhard was divided into three divisions across the territory of the so-called Adriatisches Küstenland: R/1 (Trieste), R/2 (Fiume/Rijeka), and R/3 (Udine).

27. Drndić, *Trieste*, 2.

28. Stewart, *On Longing*, 157. "The collection relies upon the box, the cabinet, the cupboard, the seriality of shelves." Stewart, *On Longing*, 157.

29. Dustin Illingworth, "There Are No Small Fascisms: An Interview with Dasa Drndic," *Paris Review*, August 21, 2017.

30. Brooks, *Reading for the Plot*, 98.

31. Pearce, "Objects as Meaning," 26.

32. Christopher Tilley, "Interpreting Material Culture," 73.

33. Mieke Bal, "Telling Objects: A Narrative Perspective on Collecting," in Elsner and Cardinal, *Cultures of Collecting*, 121. Bal's article shows how we might narrativize collecting rather than seeing collecting as a narrative device in itself, but her attention to temporal framing is of great value to my argument here.

34. Drndić, *Trieste*, 11–12.

35. Drndić, *Trieste*, 19.

36. Drndić, *Trieste*, 108.

37. Drndić, *Trieste*, 16.

38. Drndić, *Trieste*, 116.

39. Carlo Michelstaedter (1887–1910) was a philosopher from Gorizia who committed suicide the day after completing his university thesis, subsequently published as *La persuasione e la retorica*. An English translation has been published by Wilhelm Snyman and Giuseppe Stellardi as *Persuasion and Rhetoric* (Pietermaritzburg, South Africa: University of KwaZulu-Natal Press, 2007). See also Mimmo Cangiano, *The Wreckage of Philosophy: Carlo Michelstaedter and the Limits of Bourgeois Thought* (Toronto: University of Toronto Press, 2018).

40. Drndić, *Trieste*, 114.

41. Bal, "Telling Objects," 121.

42. "Collecting means collecting when it becomes a meaningful sequence." Bal, "Telling Objects," 121.

Notes to Pages 28–31

43. Drndić, *Trieste*, 117.

44. Drndić, *Trieste*, 117.

45. See Bal, "Telling Objects," 122. See also Leo Bersani, *A Future for Astyanax: Character and Desire in Literature* (London: Marion Boyars, 1978), 6.

46. Baudrillard, "System of Collecting," 36.

47. Baudrillard, "System of Collecting," 24.

48. Bal denotes the beginning of the collection to be a "false start" because there is always already another beginning, "which is that of the object itself before it became an object of collecting." "Telling Objects," 122.

49. Stewart, *On Longing*, x.

50. Baudrillard, "System of Collecting," 24.

51. As Peter Brooks puts it, "Repetition speaks in the text of a return which ultimately subverts the very notion of beginning and end, suggesting that the idea of beginning presupposes the end, that the end is a time before the beginning, and hence that the interminable never can be finally bound in a plot." *Reading for the Plot*, 109.

52. Drndić, *Trieste*, 288.

53. James Clifford, "On Collecting Art and Culture," in *The Predicament of Culture: Twentieth-Century Ethnography, Literature, and Art* (Cambridge, MA: Harvard University Press, 1988), 235.

54. Mikhail Bakhtin, *The Dialogic Imagination. Four Essays*, trans. Caryl Emerson and Michael Holquist (Austin: University of Texas Press, 1982), 84.

55. Drndić, *Trieste*, 133.

56. Baudrillard, "System of Collecting," 27; emphasis added.

57. Maleuvre, *Museum Memories*, 12–13.

58. Drndić, *Trieste*, 188.

59. Drndić, *Trieste*, 190–91.

60. Thomas Bernhard, *Gathering Evidence: A Memoir*, trans. David McLintock (London: Vintage, 2003), 85.

61. In fact, Drndić states that the Red Cross helped the Nazis launder the money of their deported victims. See *Trieste*, 86.

62. Drndić, *Trieste*, 237.

63. See Monika Ginzkey Puloy, "High Art and National Socialism, Part I: The Linz Museum as Ideological Arena," *Journal of History of Collections* 8, no. 2 (1996): 201.

64. Lynn H. Nicholas, *The Rape of Europe. The Fate of Europe's Treasures in the Third Reich and the Second World War* (New York: Alfred A. Knopf, 1995), 97.

65. Drndić, *Trieste*, 87.

66. Monika Ginzkey Puloy, "High Art and National Socialism, Part II: Hitler's Linz Collection: Acquisition, Predation and Restitution," *Journal of History of Collections* 10, no. 2 (1998): 207.

67. Drndić, *Trieste*, 247–48.

68. Elsner and Cardinal, *Cultures of Collecting*, 13. In similar fashion, Wolfgang Ernst has described processes of collecting within Nazi death camps as collapsing time into a "mortal real-time relation" in which storerooms filled with objects at the same time as the victims were being exterminated. This "self-referential" musealization means that when "Auschwitz was turned into

a commemorative museum in the postwar era, the essence of the museum had already been inscribed." "Archi(ve)textures of Museology," in *Museums and Memory*, ed. Susan A. Crane (Stanford, CA: Stanford University Press, 2000), 25.

69. As Dora Osborne remarks, there is a "stark contrast between the overwhelming material produced by a hyper-bureaucratized regime and the depleted possessions of its victims." *What Remains: The Post-Holocaust Archive in German Memory Culture* (New York: Camden House, 2020), 8.

70. Drndić, *Trieste*, 314.

71. Drndić, *Trieste*, 294.

72. Drndić, *Trieste*, 344.

73. Drndić, *Trieste*, 316, 335.

74. Drndić, *Trieste*, 351,188, 353.

75. Drndić, *Trieste*, 295. In her recent book on hoarding, Rebecca R. Falkoff describes the condition as a "persistent difficulty discarding or parting with possessions, regardless of their actual value." *Possessed: A Cultural History of Hoarding* (Ithaca, NY: Cornell University Press, 2021), 5.

76. Baudrillard, "System of Collecting," 19.

77. Baudrillard, "System of Collecting," 23.

78. Clifford, "On Collecting Art and Culture," 229.

79. Stewart, *On Longing*, 138, 151.

80. Susan M. Pearce, "Collecting Reconsidered," in Pearce, *Interpreting Objects and Collections*, 195.

81. Kavanagh, *History Curatorship*, 10.

82. Stewart, *On Longing*, 254.

83. Stewart, *On Longing*, 151.

84. Kavanagh, *History Curatorship*, 140.

85. See Rachel Morris, *The Museum Makers: A Journey Backwards—from Old Boxes of Dark Family Secrets to a Golden Era of Museums* (Tewkesbury, UK: September Publishing, 2020), 15.

86. Michael Ames, "Cannibal Tours," 105.

87. Kavanagh, *History Curatorship*, 64.

88. Marilyn Strathern, "Or, Rather, on Not Collecting Clifford," *Social Analysis: The International Journal of Anthropology* 29 (1990): 93.

89. Illingworth, "There Are No Small Fascisms."

90. Drndić, *Trieste*, 1.

Chapter 2

1. See, for example, the editorial in *Burlington Magazine*, "The Victoria and Albert Museum," vol. 163 (April 2021).

2. Hans Ulrich Obrist with Asad Raza, *Ways of Curating* (London: Penguin, 2014), 1.

3. Cheah, *What Is a World?*; Wai Chee Dimock, "Literature for the Planet," *PMLA* 116, no. 1 (January 2001): 173–88; Debjani Ganguly, *This Thing Called the World: The Contemporary Novel as Global Form* (Durham, NC: Duke University Press, 2016); Franco Moretti, *Atlas of the European Novel 1800–1900* (London: Verso, 1998); Rebecca L. Walkowitz, *Born Translated: The Contemporary Novel in an Age of World Literature* (New York: Columbia University Press, 2015).

Notes to Pages 38–42

4. Paul O'Neill, *The Culture of Curating and the Curating of Culture(s)* (Cambridge, MA: MIT Press, 2012), 39.

5. In his author's note to the English translation, Magris discusses how fiction writing is "closely related to finding something real—a story, a character, a detail, something factual." He then names Henriquez as the inspiration for the protagonist of the novel. Magris, *Blameless*, 339.

6. Magris, *Blameless*, 9.

7. Magris, *Blameless*, 17.

8. Magris, *Blameless*, 158.

9. Marianne Hirsch, *The Generation of Postmemory: Writing and Visual Culture after the Holocaust* (New York: Columbia University Press, 2012), 5.

10. Marc Augé's famous formulation of the "nonplace" is part of a wider investigation he carries out into changing anthropological practices in the excessive age of "supermodernity." Augé attributes these changes to what he calls the "acceleration of history," and "the overabundance of events." This overabundance, he says, causes problems because "the density of events over the last few decades threatens to rob (them) of all meaning." His understanding is that this overabundance also drives us toward an "explicit and daily need to give . . . meaning to the world": a need that it would seem explains the cultural turn toward curatorial activities such as selecting, arranging, and assigning value to things and events. See *Non-Places: Introduction to an Anthropology of Supermodernity*, trans. Jon Howe (London: Verso, 1995), 28–29.

11. Magris, *Blameless*, 305.

12. Magris, *Blameless*, 307.

13. Magris, *Blameless*, 306.

14. Dan Hicks, *The Brutish Museums: The Benin Bronzes, Colonial Violence and Cultural Restitution* (London: Pluto Press), xiv.

15. Augé, *Non-Places*, 79.

16. Cheah, *What Is a World?*, 11.

17. Dimock, "Literature for the Planet," 174.

18. Dimock, "Literature for the Planet," 174.

19. David Damrosch, *What Is World Literature?* (Princeton, NJ: Princeton University Press, 2018), 5. See also Ganguly, *This Thing Called the World*, 21.

20. Eric Hayot, *On Literary Worlds* (Oxford: Oxford University Press, 2012), 40.

21. Moretti, *Atlas of the European Novel*, 5.

22. Moretti, *Atlas of the European Novel*, 8.

23. Walkowitz, *Born Translated*, 23–24.

24. Walkowitz, *Born Translated*, 46.

25. Walkowitz, *Born Translated*, 51.

26. Walkowitz, *Born Translated*, 66.

27. Walkowitz, *Born Translated*, 121.

28. Diego Salvadori, "'Quel pezzetto di ippocampo è qualcosa che manca': Scrittura sul corpo in *Non luogo a procedere* di Claudio Magris," *Comparatismi* 4 (2019): 47.

29. Walkowitz, *Born Translated*, 122; emphasis added.

30. Susan M. Pearce, "Museum Objects," in Pearce, *Interpreting Objects and Collections*, 10.

174   Notes to Pages 42–46

31. Cit. Beryl Graham and Sarah Cook, *Rethinking Curating: Art after New Media* (Cambridge, MA: MIT Press, 2015), 10.

32. Graham and Cook, *Rethinking Curating*, 10.

33. Kavanagh, *History Curatorship*, 71.

34. Magris, *Blameless*, 25.

35. Magris, *Blameless*, 81.

36. Magris, *Blameless*, 42.

37. Magris, *Blameless*, 131.

38. Magris, *Blameless*, xii.

39. Claudio Magris, *Alla cieca* (Milan: Garzanti, 2005). Translated into English by Anne Milano Appel as *Blindly*, it also appears in the Yale University Press Margellos series, where it was published in 2012.

40. "La vita di Jorgen è anche una bibliografia sterminata, lacunosa, inaffidabile. Le opere di Jorgen modulano, variano, rimaneggiano di continuo se stesse, si contraggono in un titolo, si dilatano in una prima introduzione a un testo che magari non viene steso oppure viene poco dopo ritoccato, riformulato in una versione che ne capovolge la tesi o semplicemente riannunciato e mai portato a termine o nemmeno iniziato." Fondo Magris, Centro Manoscritti, Università di Pavia, MAG.01.17 *Materiali e appunti di opere di Jorgen*. My translation.

41. Walkowitz, *Born Translated*, 160.

42. Terry Smith, *Thinking Contemporary Curating* (New York: Independent Curators International, 2012), 17.

43. Hans Ulrich Obrist, *Everything You Always Wanted to Know about Curating but Were Afraid to Ask* (London: Sternberg Press, 2011), 129.

44. See David Balzer, *Curationism: How Curating Took over the Art World and Everything Else* (London: Pluto Press, 2014).

45. Graham and Cook, *Rethinking Curating*, 271.

46. Erica Lehrer and Cynthia E. Milton, "'Introduction: Witnesses to Witnessing,'" in *Curating Difficult Knowledge: Violent Pasts in Public Places*, ed. Erica Lehrer, Cynthia E. Milton, and Monica Eileen Patterson (New York, Palgrave Macmillan, 2011), 4.

47. See Jade French, *Inclusive Curating in Contemporary Art. A Practical Guide* (Leeds, UK: ARC Humanities Press, 2020), 80.

48. Kavanagh, *History Curatorship*, 127.

49. Sarah Longair, "Cultures of Curating: The Limits of Authority," *Museum History Journal* 8, no. 1 (2015): 6.

50. Balzer, *Curationism*, 24.

51. Balzer, *Curationism*, 26.

52. Philipp Schorch, Conal McCarthy, and Eveline Dürr, "Introduction: Conceptualizing Curatopia," in Schorch and McCarthy, *Curatopia*, 5.

53. Schorch, McCarthy, and Dürr, "'Introduction: Conceptualizing Curatopia,'" 7.

54. James Clifford, "The Times of the Curator," in Schorch and McCarthy, *Curatopia*, 112. More recent writings by Donna Haraway (I am thinking particularly of *Staying with the Trouble*) have attracted criticism for their adherence to philosophies of population control, which some scholars fear are racially inflected. See, for example, Sophie Lewis, "Cthulhu Plays No Role for Me," *Viewpoint*, May 8, 2017. The artist Alberta Whittle has instead articulated a new vision

of curatorial care that builds on Saidiya Hartman's notion of "waywardness" and involves practices of "self-critique, empathy, friendship, scheming, pleasure, dreaming and rest" that contest the "hegemonic principles of contemporary art that have historically been based on exclusion and erasure." "Biting the Hand That Feeds You: A Strategy of Wayward Curating," *Critical Arts* (2020): 111.

55. Alison Grey, Tim Gardom, and Catherine Booth, *Saying It Differently: A Handbook for Museums Refreshing Their Displays* (London: London Museums Hub, 2006), 59.

56. Grey, Gardom, and Booth, *Saying It Differently,* 36.

57. Grey, Gardom, and Booth, *Saying It Differently*, 38.

58. Magris, *Blameless*, 3.

59. Magris, *Blameless*, 3.

60. Magris, *Blameless*, 324.

61. Magris, *Blameless*, 9.

62. Magris, *Blameless*, 11.

63. Magris, *Blameless*, 10.

64. Magris, *Blameless*, 149.

65. Magris, *Blameless*, 158.

66. Magris, *Blameless*, 226.

67. Magris, *Blameless*, 279.

68. French, *Inclusive Curating in Contemporary Art*, 11. French explains that this is partly because from the 1960s onward, art itself underwent a long process of dematerialization and shifted to a focus on conceptualism and performative elements. This art had arguably a greater need for interpretation and framing by a curatorial figure of authority.

69. French, *Inclusive Curating in Contemporary Art*, 12.

70. Walkowitz, *Born Translated*, 160.

71. Cit. French, *Inclusive Curating in Contemporary Art*, 78.

72. Nicholas Serota, *Experience or Interpretation? The Dilemma of Museums of Modern Art* (London: Thames and Hudson, 2000), 10. Freeman Tilden's classic text, *Interpreting Our Heritage*, also makes this point in the first of his six principles for interpretation: "Any interpretation that does not somehow relate what is being displayed or described to something within the personality or experience of the visitor will be sterile." For this reason, it is more important to ask, "What would the prospective reader wish to read?" than "What is it I wish to say?" (Chapel Hill: University of North Carolina Press, 1977), 9, 59.

73. O'Neill, *Culture of Curating*, 128. Maura Reilly has also discussed recent interest in a more relational approach to curating which is "interested not in a monologue of sameness, but in a multitude or cacophony of voices speaking simultaneously," building on Julia Kristeva's notion of the polylogue. *Curatorial Activism: Towards an Ethics of Curating* (London: Thames and Hudson, 2018), 30.

74. Magris, *Blameless*, 267.

75. See Andrea Witcomb, *Re-imagining the Museum: Beyond the Mausoleum* (London: Routledge, 2003).

76. Magris, *Blameless*, 302.

77. Hicks, *Brutish Museums*, 26.

78. Magris, *Blameless*, 5.

176   Notes to Pages 52–62

79. Magris, *Blameless*, 175.
80. Magris, *Blameless*, 179.
81. Magris, *Blameless*, 191.

Chapter 3

1. Pamuk, *Museum of Innocence*, 681.

2. See Graham Harman, *Guerrilla Metaphysics: Phenomenology and the Carpentry of Things* (Chicago: Open Court, 2005).

3. Tracy Ireland, "Quotidian Utopia: Orhan Pamuk's *The Museum of Innocence* and the Heritage of Love," *Future Anterior* 14, no. 2 (2017): 13.

4. Orhan Pamuk, *The Innocence of Objects*, trans. Ekin Oklap (New York: Abrams Press, 2012), 18.

5. Pamuk, *Innocence of Objects*, 15.

6. Pamuk, *Innocence of Objects*, 17.

7. Pamuk, *Innocence of Objects*, 17.

8. It is worth noting that Kemal observes an emblematic shift in the Westernization of Istanbul when, in later years, the boutique closes and is transformed into a grocery store, and the window that once displayed the emblematic handbag now shows off imported products such as Italian salamis and European brands of salad dressing. See Pamuk, *Museum of Innocence*, 603.

9. Pamuk, *Museum of Innocence*, 5.

10. Pamuk, *Museum of Innocence*, 16.

11. Bennett, *Vibrant Matter*, 24.

12. Bennett, *Vibrant Matter*, 6, 23.

13. Pamuk, *Museum of Innocence*, 4.

14. Susanne Fowler, "Private Peek at Author's Blur of Fact and Fiction," *New York Times*, May 2, 2012.

15. Pamuk, *Museum of Innocence*, 231. Nerval's posthumously published work *Aurélia ou Le Rêve et la Vie* is a hallucinatory account of the writer's descent into madness, which was partly caused by his apparently unrequited passion for Colon. See Gérard de Nerval, *Aurélia and Other Writings*, trans. Geoffrey Wagner (Boston: Exact Change, 1996), 1–70.

16. See Claude Pichois and Michel Brix, *Gérard de Nerval* (Paris: Fayard, 1995), 116–19. I am grateful to Sarah Gubbins for pointing this work out to me, and for additional references to Nerval's own "creative plagiarism" in his travel writing, which includes fictional accounts of journeys to Constantinople. Se: Sarah Gubbins, "Nerval's Journeys in Verse and in Prose," *Nineteenth-Century Contexts* 41, no. 1 (2019): 75–84.

17. See, for example, the essay "Mr. Pamuk, Did All This Really Happen to You?" in Orhan Pamuk, *The Naïve and the Sentimental Novelist. The Charles Norton Lectures, 2009*, trans. Nazim Dikbas (London: Faber and Faber, 2011), 31–56.

18. Pamuk writes, "As Kemal had asked me, I wrote under each and every one of Füsun's cigarette butts the note our protagonist had made about that particular day. This took me the entire summer of 2011. I felt more like a craftsman than a writer. Kemal was the one who had lived and remembered. I, Orhan, was merely transcribing." *Innocence of Objects*, 228.

19. Pamuk, *The Naïve and the Sentimental Novelist*, 80.

Notes to Pages 62–68

20. Pamuk, *The Museum of Innocence*, 545.
21. Fowler, "Private Peek at Author's Blur of Fact and Fiction."
22. Pamuk, *Innocence of Objects*, 61.
23. Pamuk, *Innocence of Objects*, 61.
24. Pamuk, *Museum of Innocence*, 23.
25. Pamuk, *Museum of Innocence*, 40.
26. Pamuk, *Museum of Innocence*, 215–16.
27. Pamuk, *Museum of Innocence*, 698.
28. Ireland, "Quotidian Utopia," 23.
29. Pamuk, *Museum of Innocence*, 577.
30. Gönül Eda Özgül, "The Quest for Home and Identity: Modernity and Innocence in Pamuk's *The Museum of Innocence*," in *Orhan Pamuk: Critical Essays on a Novelist between Worlds*, ed. Taner Can, Berkan Ulu, and Koray Melikoglu (Stuttgart, Germany: Ibidem Press, 2017), 220.
31. Hülya Yagcioglu, "Bridging the Gap between People and Things: The Politics and Poetics of Collecting in Pamuk's *The Museum of Innocence*," in Can, Ulu, and Melikoglu, *Orhan Pamuk: Critical Essays on a Novelist between Worlds*, 190.
32. Yagcioglu, "Bridging the Gap between People and Things," 199.
33. Pamuk, *The Naïve and the Sentimental Novelist*, 123.
34. Ivan Karp, "Culture and Representation," in Karp and Lavine, *Exhibiting Cultures*, 12.
35. Sara Ahmed, *What's the Use?*, 25.
36. Pamuk, *Innocence of Objects*, 246.
37. See Ane Pilegaard, "Through the Lens of the Glass Cabinet: Entering the Material Realm of Museum Objects," *Interiors* 10, no. 3 (2019): 181–82.
38. Pamuk, *Innocence of Objects*, 103.
39. Pamuk, *Museum of Innocence*, 151.
40. Pamuk, *Innocence of Objects*, 144.
41. Pamuk, *The Naïve and the Sentimental Novelist*, 123, 124.
42. Pamuk, *The Naïve and the Sentimental Novelist*, 35.
43. Açalya Allmer, "Orhan Pamuk's Museum of Innocence: On Architecture, Narrative, and the Art of Collecting," *Architectural Research Quarterly* 13, no. 2 (2009): 168.
44. Ireland, "Quotidian Utopia," 16.
45. Pamuk, *Museum of Innocence*, 652.
46. Pamuk, *Museum of Innocence*, 664.
47. The museum objects eventually become akin to trophies in the consolatory power they hold for Kemal: "I may not have 'won' the woman I loved so obsessively, but it cheered me to have broken off a piece of her, however small." Pamuk, *Museum of Innocence*, 511.
48. Zuzanna Jakubowski, "Exhibiting Lost Love: The Relational Realism of Things in Orhan Pamuk's *The Museum of Innocence* and Leanne Shapton's *Important Artifacts*," in *Realisms in Contemporary Culture: Theories, Politics, and Medial Configurations*, ed. Dorothee Birke and Stella Butter (Berlin: De Gruyter, 2013), 143, 140.
49. Pamuk, *Innocence of Objects*, 83.
50. Jakubowski, "Exhibiting Lost Love," 129.

178   Notes to Pages 68–75

51. Charles Simic, *Dime-Store Alchemy: The Art of Joseph Cornell* (New York: New York Review Books, 1992), 19.

52. Rona Cran, *Collage in Twentieth-Century Art, Literature, and Culture: Joseph Cornell, William Burroughs, Frank O'Hara, and Bob Dylan* (Farnham, UK: Ashgate, 2014), 29–32.

53. See Cran, *Collage in Twentieth-Century Art, Literature, and Culture*, 7.

54. Pilegaard, "Through the Lens of the Glass Cabinet," 187.

55. Ane Pilegaard, "Material Proximity: Experimenting with Material Strategies in Spatial Exhibition Design," *Museum World: Advances in Research* 3 (2015: 70.

56. Latour, *Reassembling the Social*, 5.

57. Jakubowski, "Exhibiting Lost Love," 131.

58. Graham Harman, *Guerilla Metaphysics: Phenomenology and the Carpentry of Things* (Chicago: Open Court, 2005), 49.

59. Pamuk, *Museum of Innocence*, 721, 719.

60. Pilegaard, "Through the Lens of the Glass Cabinet," 185.

61. Michael Baxandall, "Exhibiting Intention: Some Preconditions of the Visual Display of Culturally Purposeful Objects," in Karp and Lavine, *Exhibiting Cultures*, 39.

62. Siofra McSherry, "Joseph Cornell's Subversive Materialism," *Comparative American Studies* 11, no. 4 (2014): 376.

63. Gloria Fisk, *Orhan Pamuk and the Good of World Literature* (New York: Columbia University Press, 2018), 2.

64. Stewart, *On Longing*, 22.

65. Pamuk, *Innocence of Objects*, 54.

66. Jodi Hauptman, *Joseph Cornell: Stargazing in the Cinema* (New Haven, CT: Yale University Press, 1999), 20.

67. Pamuk, *Innocence of Objects*, 79, 51–52.

68. Hauptman, *Joseph Cornell*, 25.

69. Mary Ann Caws, ed., *Joseph Cornell's Theatre of the Mind: Selected Diaries, Letters, and Files* (New York: Thames and Hudson, 1993), 136.

70. Caws, *Joseph Cornell's Theatre of the Mind*, 35.

71. Harman, *Guerilla Metaphysics*, 94.

72. Masao Yamaguchi, "The Poetics of Exhibition in Japanese Culture," in Karp and Lavine, *Exhibiting Cultures*, 61.

73. Jakubowski, "Exhibiting Lost Love," 143.

74. Cran, *Collage in Twentieth-Century Art, Literature, and Culture*, 7.

75. Pilegaard, "Through the Lens of the Glass Cabinet," 187.

76. Stewart, *On Longing*, xi.

77. Stewart, *On Longing*, 20–21.

78. Elaine Wright, *Muraqqa': Imperial Mughal Albums from the Chester Beatty Library, Dublin* (Alexandria, VA: Art Services International, 2008), xvii.

79. Wright, *Muraqqa'*, 133.

80. See Wright, *Muraqqa'*, 322–25.

Chapter 4

1. Some examples of present and future open storage in museums include the Visible Storage Center of the Brooklyn Museum, the Glasgow Museums Resource Centre, the new facilities planned for V&A East project in London, a

Notes to Pages 76–83

bespoke new "art factory" for the Centre Pompidou in Massy, Île-de-France, and the National Museum of Modern and Contemporary Art in Cheongju, Korea.

2. Arjun Appadurai, "Archive and Aspiration," in *Information Is Alive: Art and Theory on Archiving and Retrieving Data*, ed. Joke Brouwer and Arjen Mulder (Rotterdam: V2_/NAI, 2003), 16. This is similar to the idea of the museum as a "facilitator of information in digital environments," which provides users with objects and metadata so that they can create their own "personal cultural information space." See Trilce Navarrete and John Mackenzie Owen, "The Museum as Information Space: Metadata and Documentation," in *Cultural Heritage in a Changing World*, ed. K. J. Borowiecki, Neil Forbes, and Antonella Fresa (New York: Palgrave Macmillan, 2016), 118.

3. Steven Lubar, *Inside the Lost Museum: Curating, Past and Present* (Cambridge, MA: Harvard University Press, 2017), 102.

4. Lubar, *Inside the Lost Museum*, 103, 107.

5. Mary Wang, "Valeria Luiselli: 'There Are Always Fingerprints of the Archive in My Books,'" *Guernica*, February 12, 2019.

6. Jean-Christophe Cloutier, *Shadow Archives: The Lifecycles of African American Literature* (New York: Columbia University Press, 2019), 22.

7. Cloutier, *Shadow Archives*, 24.

8. Wang, "Valeria Luiselli."

9. Valentina Montero Román, "Telling Stories That Never End: Valeria Luiselli, the Refugee Crisis at the US-Mexico Border, and the Big, Ambitious, Archival Novel," *Genre* 54, no. 2 (2021): 167; emphasis added.

10. Valeria Luiselli, *Tell Me How It Ends: An Essay in Forty Questions* (London: 4th Estate, 2017), 11.

11. Luiselli, *Tell Me How It Ends*, 30.

12. Antoinette Burton, *Dwelling in the Archive: Women Writing House, Home, and History in Late Colonial India* (Oxford: Oxford University Press, 2003), 26.

13. Burton, *Dwelling in the Archive*, 26.

14. Eric Ketelaar, "Tacit Narratives: The Meanings of Archives," *Archival Science* 1 (2001): 135.

15. Kimberly Orcutt, "The Open Storage Dilemma," *Journal of Museum Education* 36, no. 2 (2011): 209.

16. Luiselli, *Lost Children Archive*, 42.

17. Arlette Farge, *The Allure of the Archives*, trans. Thomas Scott-Railton (New Haven, CT: Yale University Press, 2013), 6.

18. Ray Batchelor, "Not Looking at Kettles," in Pearce, *Interpreting Objects and Collections*, 142.

19. Farge, *Allure of the Archives*, 30.

20. Farge, *Allure of the Archives*, 3.

21. Farge, *Allure of the Archives*, 63–64.

22. Antoinette Burton, ed., *Archive Stories: Facts, Fictions, and the Writing of History* (Durham, NC: Duke University Press, 2005), 7–8.

23. Luiselli, *Lost Children Archive*, 79.

24. Cloutier, *Shadow Archives*, 2.

25. See Sigmund Freud, "Constructions in Analysis" (1937), in *The Standard Edition of the Complete Psychological Works of Sigmund Freud*, vol. 23, ed. and trans. James Strachey (London: Vintage, 2001), 255–69.

180   Notes to Pages 83–87

26. Achille Mbembe, "The Power of the Archive and Its Limits," trans. Judith Inggs, in *Refiguring the Archive*, ed. Carolyn Hamilton et al. (Dordrecht, Netherlands: Kluwer Academic Publishers, 2002), 21.

27. Luiselli, *Lost Children Archive*, 13.

28. Luiselli, *Lost Children Archive*, 12.

29. Luiselli, *Lost Children Archive*, 29.

30. Luiselli, *Lost Children Archive*, 31.

31. Luiselli, *Lost Children Archive*, 20.

32. Luiselli, *Lost Children Archive*, 42.

33. Luiselli, *Lost Children Archive*, 23.

34. Luiselli, *Lost Children Archive*, 24.

35. Luiselli, *Lost Children Archive*, 24.

36. Michael Sheringham and Richard Wentworth, "City as Archive: A Dialogue between Theory and Practice," *Cultural Geographies* 23, no. 3 (2016): 519.

37. Luiselli, *Lost Children Archive*, 32.

38. Enrique Vila-Matas, *A Brief History of Portable Literature*, trans. Anne McLean and Thomas Bunstead (New York: New Directions, 2015), 2.

39. Vila-Matas, *Brief History*, 3.

40. Antonio M. Battro, "From Malraux's Imaginary Museum to the Virtual Museum," in *Museums in a Digital Age*, ed. Ross Parry (London: Routledge, 2010), 143.

41. Klaus Müller, "Museums and Virtuality," in Parry, *Museums in a Digital Age*, 298.

42. Fiona Cameron, "Museum Collections, Documentation, and Shifting Knowledge Paradigms," in Parry, *Museums in a Digital Age*, 85.

43. Nathalie Léger, *Suite for Barbara Loden*, trans. Natasha Lehrer and Cécile Menon (London: Les Fugitives, 2015), 7.

44. Luiselli, *Lost Children Archive*, 44; emphasis added.

45. This also thus recalls Saidiya Hartman's fabulative method, which aims at "exceed[ing] or negotiat[ing] the constitutive limits of the archive": "By advancing a series of speculative arguments and exploiting the capacities of the subjunctive in fashioning a narrative . . . I intended both to tell an impossible story and to amplify the impossibility of its telling." "Venus in Two Acts," *small axe* 26 (2008): 11.

46. Luiselli, *Lost Children Archive*, 60.

47. Luiselli, *Lost Children Archive*, 67.

48. Luiselli, *Lost Children Archive*, 68. An additional intertextual link here is that Sontag's game with her son is played out against the backdrop of the parents' separation (much as in *Lost Children Archive*), so that Sontag and her son are Mexican soldiers and the father is an American soldier. See Susan Sontag, *Reborn: Early Diaries, 1947–1963*, ed. David Rieff (London: Penguin, 2008), 144.

49. Luiselli, *Lost Children Archive*, 68.

50. Hayden Lorimer, "Caught in the Nick of Time: Archives and Fieldwork," in *The SAGE Handbook of Qualitative Geography*, ed. Dydia DeLyser, Steve Herbert, Stuart Aitken, Mike Crange, and Linda McDowell (London, SAGE, 2010), 20.

51. Luiselli, *Lost Children Archive*, 142.

52. Luiselli, *Lost Children Archive*, 143.

53. Luiselli, *Lost Children Archive*, 380.

Notes to Pages 87–92

54. Luiselli, *Lost Children Archive*, 42.

55. Allan Vorda, "The Social Fabric: An Interview with Valeria Luiselli," *Rain Taxi*, 2019.

56. Léger, *Suite for Barbara Loden*, 55.

57. Mike Jones, *Artefacts, Archives, and Documentation in the Relational Museum* (London and New York: Routledge, 2021), 3.

58. Cameron, "Museum Collections, Documentation, and Shifting Knowledge Paradigms," 86.

59. Jones, *Artefacts, Archives, and Documentation*, 97.

60. Cit. Jones, *Artefacts, Archives, and Documentation*, 139.

61. Jones, *Artefacts, Archives, and Documentation*, 9.

62. Luiselli, *Lost Children Archive*, 207.

63. Cameron, "Museum Collections, Documentation, and Shifting Knowledge Paradigms," 87.

64. Jones, *Artefacts, Archives, and Documentation*, 34.

65. Luiselli, *Lost Children Archive*, 223.

66. Luiselli, *Lost Children Archive*, 224.

67. Luiselli, *Lost Children Archive*, 55.

68. Jones, *Artefacts, Archives, and Documentation*, 41.

69. See Katie Rudolph, "Separated at Appraisal: Maintaining the Archival Bond between Archival Collections and Museum Objects," *Archival Issues* 33, no. 1 (2011): 31; Jones, *Artefacts, Archives, and Documentation*, 72; Janet Ulph, "Frozen in Time: Orphans and Uncollected Objects in Museum Collections," *International Journal of Cultural Property* 24, no. 1 (2017): 3–30.

70. Azoulay, *Potential History*, 1–2.

71. Azoulay, *Potential History*, 24–25.

72. Ariella Aïsha Azoulay, *Un-documented: Unlearning Imperial Plunder*, 2020. https://vimeo.com/490778435.

73. See Hicks, *Brutish Museums*.

74. Sarah Mallet and Louise Fowler, "The Dzhangal Archaeology Project and 'Lande': Two Archaeological Approaches to the Study of Forced Migration," in *Material Culture and (Forced) Migration: Materializing the Transient*, ed. Friedemann Yi-Neumann, Andrea Lauser, Antoine Fuhse, and Peter J. Bräunlein (London: UCL Press, 2022), 125.

75. On Tom Kiefer's work, see "Shoes, Pills, Diaries: Objects Seized by Border Officials—in Pictures," *Guardian*, December 11, 2019. Images from Mario Badagliacca's project, which was carried out on the Italian island of Lampedusa in 2013, can be seen on his website: https://www.mariobadagliacca.com/frammenti _2013-r8112, accessed April 24, 2023.

76. Dominique Malaquais, "Forensics: Photography in the Face of Failure," in Gideon Mendel, *Dzhangal* (London: GOST Books, 2017), 73–74.

77. Maleuvre, *Museum Memories*, 39.

78. Sara Ahmed, *What's the Use?*, 47; emphasis added. In related fashion, Krzysztof Pomian comments on the inherent lack of utility represented by museum objects and how that contrasts with the high level of care lavished on them. See "The Collection: Between the Visible and the Invisible," in Pearce, *Interpreting Objects and Collections*, 161.

79. Luiselli, *Lost Children Archive*, 19; emphasis added.

80. Luiselli, *Lost Children Archive*, 18.

81. Luiselli, *Lost Children Archive*, 18. The reference to sewing here also links to an excerpt from Dasa Drndić's novel *Belladonna*, which is included in the same Box V as the other object documentation. The excerpt recounts that in 2002, some sixty migrants held in detention camps sewed their lips together in protest at their incarceration and the delays in processing their applications for authorization to remain (256).

82. Jones, *Artefacts, Archives, and Documentation*, 125.

83. Navarrete and Owen, "Museum as Information Space," 112.

84. Kavanagh, *History Curatorship*, 75.

85. Luiselli, *Lost Children Archive*, 99.

86. Luiselli, *Lost Children Archive*, 102.

87. Luiselli, *Lost Children Archive*, 59–60.

88. "The form that Luiselli arrives at in response to the particularities of her 'flail' is what we might call an archive novel, a novel that explicitly styles itself as an archive, and exposes novel writing as a curatorial practice of research and imagination, laying bare its sources less to offer persuasive evidentiary authority and more to acknowledge the incompleteness of any representational project." Patricia Stuelke, "Writing Refugee Crisis in the Age of Amazon: *Lost Children Archive*'s Reenactment Play," *Genre* 54, no. 1 (2021): 44.

89. Luiselli, *Lost Children Archive*, 210.

90. Luiselli, *Lost Children Archive*, 210.

91. Farge, *Allure of the Archives*, 31. The application of metaphors of tailoring in discussions of archival work is also powerfully evoked by Marisa J. Fuentes in her method of "reading along the bias grain," which allows her to "stretch the archive to accentuate the presence of enslaved women when not explicitly mentioned in certain documents." Marisa J. Fuentes, *Dispossessed Lives: Enslaved Women, Violence, and the Archive* (Philadelphia: University of Pennsylvania Press, 2016), 11; 156.

92. Montero Román, "Telling Stories That Never End," 180.

93. Migrants crossing the Mexico-US border are frequently subjected to freezing conditions in CBP holding cells commonly known as *hieleras*, or freezers. This cold was re-created as part of Alejandro G. Iñárritu's 2017 virtual, immersive installation *Carne y Arena* at the Fondazione Prada in Milan.

94. See Lev Manovich, "Database as Symbolic Form" [1999], in Parry, *Museums in a Digital Age*, 64, 66.

95. Kent Anderson, "The Useful Archive," *Learned Publishing* 15, no. 2 (2002): 86.

96. Manovich, "Database as Symbolic Form" 68.

97. Manovich, "Database as Symbolic Form" 69.

98. Luiselli, *Lost Children Archive*, 7–8.

99. Luiselli, *Lost Children Archive*, 12.

100. Rosalind Krauss, "Perpetual Inventory," *October* 88 (Spring 1999): 101.

101. Mike Pepi, "Is the Museum a Database? Institutional Conditions in Net Utopia," *e-flux* 60 (2014).

102. Pepi, "Is the Museum a Database?"

103. Luiselli, *Lost Children Archive*, 141.

104. Krauss, "Perpetual Inventory," 108.

Notes to Pages 96–104

105. Krauss, "Perpetual Inventory," 108.

106. Ross Parry, *Recoding the Museum: Digital Heritage and the Technologies of Change* (London: Routledge, 2007), 29.

107. Parry, *Recoding the Museum*, 55.

108. Parry, *Recoding the Museum*, 68.

109. Luiselli, *Lost Children Archive*, 196.

110. Mark McGurl, *Everything and Less: The Novel in the Age of Amazon* (London: Verso, 2021), xii.

111. McGurl, *Everything and Less*, 86.

112. Stuelke, "Writing Refugee Crisis in the Age of Amazon," 46.

113. Stuelke, "Writing Refugee Crisis in the Age of Amazon," 48.

114. Ganguly, *This Thing Called the World*, 102.

115. Ganguly, *This Thing Called the World*, 103.

116. Valeria Luiselli, "The Wild West Meets the Southern Border," *New Yorker*, June 3, 2019.

117. Luiselli, *Lost Children Archive*, 5.

118. Luiselli, *Lost Children Archive*, 56–57.

119. As Hayden Lorimer points out, "The intimacies of the self—receding time horizons, muddled chronologies, forced erasures, passionate relations, brief encounters and withering judgements—are what make the *partiality* of reconstruction so appealing." "Caught in the Nick of Time: Archives and Fieldwork," 20.

120. Luiselli, *Lost Children Archive*, 8.

121. Luiselli, *Lost Children Archive*, 75.

122. Luiselli, *Lost Children Archive*, 81, 160.

123. See Luiselli, *Tell Me How It Ends*, 30.

124. Luiselli, *Lost Children Archive*, 69.

125. David James, "Listening to the Refugee: Valeria Luiselli's Sentimental Activism," *Modern Fiction Studies* 67, no. 2 (2021): 400.

126. Luiselli, *Lost Children Archive*, 16.

127. Luiselli, *Tell Me How It Ends*, 7.

128. Farge, *Allure of the Archives*, 94.

129. Stuelke, "Writing Refugee Crisis in the Age of Amazon," 63; emphasis added.

130. Carolyn Steedman, "The Space of Memory: In an Archive," *History of the Human Sciences* 11, no. 4 (1998): 74.

131. Sigmund Freud, "A Note upon the 'Mystic Writing-Pad'" [1925], in *The Standard Edition of the Complete Psychological Works of Sigmund Freud*, vol. 19, ed. and trans. by James Strachey (London: Vintage, 2001), 227.

132. Freud, "A Note upon the 'Mystic Writing-Pad,'" 232.

133. For more information on the project, see Anthony Schrag, "'Kill Your Darlings': What Is a Public Collection and Who Is It For?," *Art.UK*, 2022.

134. Azoulay, *Potential History*, 56.

Chapter 5

1. *Flights* was originally published in Polish with the title *Bieguni* in 2007, by Wydawnictwo Literackie in Kraków. The English-language translation, by Jennifer Croft, was published by Fitzcarraldo Editions, London, in 2017.

2. See Rachel Poliquin, *The Breathless Zoo: Taxidermy and the Culture of Longing* (University Park: Penn State University Press, 2012).

3. Rachel Wehner, "Towards an Ecological Museology," in *Curating the Future: Museums, Communities and Climate Change*, ed. Jennifer Newell, Libby Robin, and Kirsten Wehner (London: Routledge, 2016), 87.

4. "Relationality" is a key term for the field of both nonrepresentational theory and actor-network theory. Vannini identifies the quintessential nonrepresentational style as "that of becoming entangled in relations and objects," and Latour uses actor-network theory to trace relations through registering "the links between unstable and shifting frames of reference." Phillip Vannini, "Non-representational Research Methodologies: An Introduction," in *Non-representational Methodologies: Re-Envisioning Research*, ed. Phillip Vannini (London: Routledge 2015), 15. See also Latour, *Reassembling the Social*, 24.

5. Fiona Cameron, "Posthuman Museum Practices," in *Posthuman Glossary*, ed. Rosi Braidotti and Maria Hlavajova (London: Bloomsbury, 2018), 349.

6. Steve Baker, *The Postmodern Animal* (London: Reaktion Books, 2000), 16.

7. Henry McGhie, *Mobilizing Museums for Climate Action. Tools, Frameworks and Opportunities to Accelerate Climate Action in and with Museums* (London: Museums for Climate Action, 2021), 36.

8. Newell, Robin, and Wehner, introduction to *Curating the Future*, 5.

9. Blom, *To Have and to Hold*, 62.

10. Vannini, "Non-representational Research Methodologies," 3.

11. For a history of the establishment of the Josephinum as part of Joseph II's broader program of reforms, see Barbara Sternthal, Christiane Druml, and Moritz Stipsicz, eds., *The Josephinum: 650 Years of Medical History in Vienna* (Vienna: Brandstätter, 2014).

12. See Alessandro Riva et al., "The Evolution of Anatomical Illustration and Wax Modeling in Italy from the 16th to Early 19th Centuries," *Journal of Anatomy* 216 (2010): 215–16.

13. Karl Holubar, "The Anatomical Wax Preparations in the Josephinum in Vienna, Austria," *Archives of Surgery* 126, no. 4 (1991): 421–22.

14. Sternthal, Druml, and Stipsicz, *Josephinum*, 81.

15. Sternthal, Druml, and Stipsicz, *Josephinum*, 81.

16. Merle Patchett, Kate Foster, and Hayden Lorimer, "The Biographies of a Hollow-Eyed Harrier," in *The Afterlives of Animals: A Museum Menagerie*, ed. Samuel Alberti (Charlottesville: University of Virginia Press), 115.

17. Tokarczuk, *Flights*, 129.

18. Tokarczuk, *Flights*, 129–30.

19. Tokarczuk, *Flights*, 132.

20. Tokarczuk, *Flights*, 129.

21. Tokarczuk, *Flights*, 134.

22. Tokarczuk, *Flights*, 134.

23. Tokarczuk, *Flights*, 135.

24. Tokarczuk, *Flights*, 83.

25. Tokarczuk, *Flights*, 83.

26. Emily Moeck, "Understanding the Fragmentary Nature of *Flights*: An Interview with Olga Tokarczuk," *Consequence*, October 10, 2019.

27. Wood, "*Flights*, a Novel That Never Settles Down."

Notes to Pages 111–115

28. "Storage is not the same thing as preservation." Richard Ovenden, *Burning the Books: A History of Knowledge under Attack* (London: John Murray Press, 2020), 11.

29. Tokarczuk, *Flights*, 137.

30. Tokarczuk, *Flights*, 22–23.

31. Bennett, *Vibrant Matter*, 20.

32. Bennett, *Vibrant Matter*, 24.

33. Marco Caracciolo, "From the Museum of Civilization to *The Octopus Museum*: Curating the Anthropocene in Contemporary Literature," *Textual Practice* 36, no. 9 (2022): 1423.

34. Fiona Cameron, "Ecologizing Experiments: A Method and Manifesto for Composing a Post-humanist Museum," in *Climate Change and Museum Futures*, ed. Fiona Cameron and Brett Neilson (New York: Routledge, 2015), 23.

35. McGhie, *Mobilizing Museums for Climate Action*, 76.

36. Cameron, "Ecologizing Experiments," 23.

37. Tokarczuk, *Flights*, 109, 142–43.

38. Tokarczuk, *Flights*, 200, 201.

39. Nikita Mazurov, "Monster/The Unhuman," in Braidotti and Hlavajova, *Posthuman Glossary*, 262.

40. Tokarczuk, *Flights*, 320–28.

41. Tokarczuk, *Flights*, 271.

42. Caracciolo, "From the Museum of Civilization to *The Octopus Museum*," 1423.

43. Iris Wigger and Spencer Hadley, "Angelo Soliman: Desecrated Bodies and the Spectre of Enlightenment Racism," *Race & Class* 62, no. 2 (2020): 81.

44. Heather Morrison, "Dressing Angelo Soliman," *Eighteenth-Century Studies* 44, no. 3 (2011): 377.

45. Tokarczuk, *Flights*, 270.

46. Poliquin, *Breathless Zoo*, 203.

47. Tokarczuk, *Flights*, 129, 130.

48. Patchett, Foster, and Lorimer, "Biographies of a Hollow-Eyed Harrier," 115.

49. Tokarczuk, *Flights*, 113.

50. Caroline Buttler and Mary Davis, eds., *Things Fall Apart . . . Museum Conservation in Practice* (Cardiff, Wales: National Museum of Wales Books, 2006), 16.

51. Tokarczuk, *Flights*, 65.

52. Irit Narkiss, "Decolonising Museum Conservation Practices: A View from the UK," *Studies in Conservation* 67, supplement 1 (2022): 183.

53. See Hanna M. Szczepanowska, *Conservation of Cultural Heritage: Key Principles and Approaches* (London: Routledge, 2013), 8.

54. Cit. Suzanne Keene, *Managing Conservation in Monuments* (London: Routledge, 2002), 24. The Burra Charter was published in 1992 by ICOMOS (International Council on Museums and Sites) and defines the basic principles and procedures to be followed in the conservation of Australian heritage places. See https://australia.icomos.org/publications/burra-charter-practice-notes/, accessed April 24, 2023.

55. Sarah Staniforth, ed., *Historical Perspectives on Preventative Conservation* (Los Angeles: Getty Conservation Institute, 2013), xiii.

56. David Lowenthal, "The Past Is a Foreign Country," in Staniforth, *Historical Perspectives*, 23.

57. Noémie Etienne, "Who Cares? Museum Conservation between Colonial Violence and Symbolic Repair," *Museums & Social Issues* 15, nos. 1–2 (2021): 68.

58. Etienne, "Who Cares?," 68.

59. Tokarczuk, *Flights*, 28.

60. Tokarczuk, *Flights*, 57.

61. Tokarczuk, *Flights*, 57.

62. Tokarczuk, *Flights*, 75.

63. Tokarczuk, *Flights*, 78.

64. Tokarczuk, *Flights*, 384.

65. Szczepanowska, *Conservation of Cultural Heritage*, 14.

66. Keene, *Managing Conservation in Museums*, 6.

67. Chris Caple, "The History of and an Introduction to Preventive Conservation," in *Preventive Conservation in Museums*, ed. Chris Caple (London: Routledge, 2011), 1.

68. Simon Cane, "Why Do We Conserve? Developing Understanding of Conservation as a Cultural Construct,", Conservation: Principles, Dilemmas, and Uncomfortable Truths, eds. Alison Richmond and Alison Bracker, London: Routledge, 2009, 163.

69. Cit. Miriam Clavir, *Preserving What Is Valued: Museums, Conservation and First Nations* (Vancouver: University of British Columbia Press, 2022), 37.

70. Cit. Buttler and Davis, *Things Fall Apart*, 38.

71. See Wood, "*Flights*, a Novel That Never Settles Down."

72. Tokarczuk, *Flights*, 240.

73. DeSilvey, *Curated Decay*, 10.

74. Caracciolo, "From the Museum of Civilization to *The Octopus Museum*," 1416.

75. DeSilvey, *Curated Decay*, 29.

76. Etienne, "Who Cares?," 61.

77. Haraway, *Staying with the Trouble*, 4.

78. Poliquin, *Breathless Zoo*, 108.

79. Tokarczuk, *Flights*, 24.

80. Tokarczuk, *Flights*, 145.

81. Tokarczuk, *Flights*, 230.

82. Marilena Alivizatou, *Intangible Heritage and the Museum: New Perspectives on Cultural Preservation* (Walnut Creek, CA: Left Coast Press, 2012), 16.

83. Tokarczuk, *Flights*, 268.

84. Tokarczuk, *Flights*, 78.

85. Tokarczuk, *Flights*, 108.

86. Tokarczuk, *Flights*, 160.

87. Tokarczuk, *Flights*, 403.

88. Alivizatou, *Intangible Heritage and the Museum*, 46.

89. See "The Nobel Prize in Literature 2018. Press Release," https://www.nobelprize.org/uploads/2019/10/press-literature2018-2019.pdf.

90. Malgorzata Kowalcze, "The Posthumanist Dimension of the Novel *Drive Your Plow over the Bones of the Dead* by Olga Tokarczuk," *Journal of Posthumanism* 2 (2021): 226.

Notes to Pages 120–126

91. Caracciolo, "From the Museum of Civilization to *The Octopus Museum*, 1424.

92. Tokarczuk, *Flights*, 244.

93. Tokarczuk, *Flights*, 294.

94. Dean Sully, "Conservation Theory and Practice: Materials, Values and People in Heritage Conservation," in *Museum Practice*, ed. Conal McCarthy (Chichester, UK: Wiley Blackwell, 2020), 293.

95. Sully, "Conservation Theory and Practice," 309.

96. Tokarczuk, *Flights*, 52.

97. Tokarczuk, *Flights*, 356.

98. Tokarczuk, *Flights*, 394.

99. Tokarczuk, *Flights*, 394.

100. Gregg Mitman, Marco Armiero, and Robert S. Emmett, *Future Remains: A Cabinet of Curiosities for the Anthropocene* (Chicago: University of Chicago Press, 2017), xi.

101. Tokarczuk, *Flights*, 409.

102. Rob Nixon, "The Anthropocene and Environmental Justice," in Newell, Robin, and Wehner, *Curating the Future*, 31.

103. Tokarczuk, *Flights*, 24.

104. Priya Basil, "Writing to Life," *British Art Studies* 19 (2021).

Chapter 6

1. Magris, *Blameless*, 191; emphasis added.

2. Mengiste, *The Shadow King*, 6.

3. Felwine Sarr and Bénédicte Savoy, *The Restitution of African Cultural Heritage: Toward a New Relational Ethics*, trans. Drew S. Burk (November 2018), 29, accessed April 24, 2023, http://restitutionreport2018.com/sarr_savoy_en.pdf.

4. See Dan Hicks, "UK Welcomes Restitution, Just Not Anti-colonialism," *Hyperallergic*, August 26, 2022.

5. Iain Chambers, "Afterword: After the Museum," in *The Postcolonial Museum: The Arts of Memory and the Pressures of History*, ed. Iain Chambers et al. (Farnham, UK: Ashgate, 2014), 243.

6. Chambers, "Afterword: After the Museum," 243.

7. See "Kader Attia and Ralph Rudoff in Conversation," in Attia, *Museum of Emotion*, 19.

8. Chambers, "Afterword: After the Museum," 243.

9. Lake, *Artifacts*, 4.

10. Sara Ahmed, *What's the Use?*, 25.

11. Lake, *Artifacts*, 6.

12. Francesca Capossela, "The Body Is a Battlefield: On Maaza Mengiste's *The Shadow King*," *Los Angeles Review of Books*, October 23, 2019.

13. Mengiste, *Shadow King*, 425.

14. Mengiste, *Shadow King*, 425.

15. Hailu Habta and Juith A. Byfield, "Fighting Fascism: Ethiopian Women Patriots, 1935–1941," in *Africa and World War II*, ed. Judith A. Byfield et al. (Cambridge: Cambridge University Press, 2015), 384.

16. Neelam Srivastana, *Italian Colonialism and Resistances to Empire, 1930–1970* (New York: Palgrave Macmillan, 2018), 24.

17. Mengiste, *The Shadow King*, 89.

18. Ruth Ben-Ghiat and Mia Fuller, introduction to *Italian Colonialism*, ed. Ruth Ben-Ghiat and Mia Fuller (London: Palgrave Macmillan, 2005), 4.

19. See, in particular, the chapter "Colonies" in David Forgacs, *Italy's Margins: Social Exclusion and Nation Formation since 1861* (Cambridge: Cambridge University Press, 2015), 67–138.

20. Sarr and Savoy, *Restitution of African Cultural Heritage*, 3, 40.

21. Richard Pankhurst, "Ethiopia, the Aksum Obelisk, and the Return of Africa's Cultural Heritage," *African Affairs* 98 (1999): 229.

22. Pankhurst, "Ethiopia, the Aksum Obelisk, and the Return of Africa's Cultural Heritage," 235.

23. Mengiste, *Shadow King*, 14.

24. Mengiste, *Shadow King*, 17.

25. Mengiste, *Shadow King*, 24.

26. Azoulay, *Potential History*, xiii.

27. Martina Montemaggi, "Investigating the Reinstallation of the Museo Coloniale di Roma: A Microcosm of Italian Colonial Memory." Master's thesis, University of Amsterdam, 2018, 2.

28. Francesca Gandolfo, *Il museo coloniale di Roma (1904–1971): Fra le zebra nel paese dell'olio di ricino* (Rome: Gangemi, 2014), 528.

29. Gaia Delpino, Rosa Anna di Lella, and Claudio Mancuso, "Unveiled Storages: How to Imagine a De-colonial Museum?" https://takingcareproject.eu /article/unveiled-storages-how-to-imagine-a-de-colonial-museum.

30. See "The Wolfsonian–FIU Returns to Its Roots with *A Universe of Things: Micky Wolfson Collects*," Media brochure, https://wolfsonian.org/_assets/docs/pr -a-universe-of-things.pdf.

31. Mengiste, *Shadow King*, 16.

32. Mengiste, *Shadow King*, 25.

33. Mengiste, *Shadow King*, 42–43; emphasis added.

34. Forgacs, *Italy's Margins*, 78.

35. Mengiste, *Shadow King*, 359.

36. Dionne Brand, *An Autobiography of Autobiography of Reading* (Edmonton: University of Alberta Press, 2020), 5.

37. Mengiste, *Shadow King*, 279–83.

38. Mengiste, *Shadow King*, 290.

39. Brand, *An Autobiography of Autobiography of Reading*, 6.

40. Zachary Rosen, "Confronting the Weapon of Photography: An Interview with Maaza Mengiste," *Africa Is a Country*, May 22, 2020.

41. Patricia Hayes, Jeremy Silvester, and Wolfram Hartmann, "'Picturing the Past' in Namibia: The Visual Archive and its Energies," in Hamilton et al., *Refiguring the Archive*, 123.

42. Mengiste, *Shadow King*, 58.

43. Mengiste, *Shadow King*, 87.

44. James Clifford, *Routes: Travel and Translation in the Late Twentieth Century* (Cambridge, MA: Harvard University Press, 1997), 194.

45. Mengiste, *Shadow King*, 87.

46. Cloutier, *Shadow Archives*, 2.

47. Ahmed, *What's the Use?*, 31.

Notes to Pages 132–138

48. Mengiste, *Shadow King*, 365.

49. "Corrode le storie che le cose raccontano, asciuga la vita di cui sono intrinse, le inchioda a una fissità algida e lontana. Le fa diventare degli *oggetti*, funzionali a un discorso, illustrazioni di una teoria, prova di qualcosa, artefatti o capolavori, prigionieri in ogni caso della costrizione ad essere contemplate." Giulia Grechi, *Decolonizzare il museo: Mostrazioni, pratiche artistiche, sguardi incarnati* (Milan: Mimesis, 2021), 186. My translation.

50. The initial name proposed for the new museum was the Museo Italo Africano "Ilaria Alpi." Ilaria Alpi was an Italian journalist killed alongside her cameraman in a still unresolved assassination in the Somali capital, Mogadishu, in 1994. It is possible that Alpi was murdered because she was in the process of investigating illegal trafficking of toxic waste from Italy to Africa at the time of her death. Placing Alpi in the name of the new museum, which—as Grechi points out—also made no reference to Italian colonies, appeared to be a further repression of the colonial ideology and history that underpins the original logic behind the collection. See Grechi, *Decolonizzare il museo*, 196.

51. Grechi, *Decolonizzare il museo*, 195.

52. Hermann Amborn, "Concepts in Wood and Stone: Socio-religious Monuments of the Konso of Southern Ethiopia," *Zeitschrift für Ethnologie* 127, no. 1 (2002): 81.

53. Amborn, "Concepts in Wood and Stone," 86.

54. Amborn, "Concepts in Wood and Stone," 84.

55. Amborn, "Concepts in Wood and Stone," 91, 94.

56. Azoulay, *Potential History*, 41.

57. Mengiste, *Shadow King*, 374.

58. Rosen, "Confronting the Weapon of Photography."

59. As Forgacs writes, "The 'tribal' photograph excluded the changes that colonialism brought, often by literally cropping them out of the picture," since "part of the Italian occupiers' collective fantasy was the willed erasure of the fact that the places and people they colonized had already been photographed before they came" (*Italy's Margins*, 90).

60. Mengiste, *Shadow King*, 86.

61. Mengiste, *Shadow King*, 410.

62. Cloutier, *Shadow Archives*, 17. I am also here referencing the title of Maaza Mengiste's article "Bending History," *NKA Journal of Contemporary African Art*, nos. 38–39 (2016): 182–85.

63. Mengiste, *Shadow King*, 3.

64. Fuentes, *Dispossessed Lives*, 14.

65. Fuentes, *Dispossessed Lives*, 14.

66. Ahmed, *What's the Use?*, 31.

67. "L'indigeno non ha neanche la più lontana idea ci ciò che sia igiene. Egli vive con tutta la famiglia sulla stessa stuoia sputando dappertutto. Fare perciò meno vita comune che si può con gli indigeni, è la prima norma per chi vuole conservarsi sano in Africa." (The native does not have the faintest idea what hygiene is. He lives on one mat with all his family, spitting everywhere. Fraternizing the least possible with natives is therefore the first rule for staying healthy in Africa.) *Norme e consigli per chi va in AOI*, Istituto Coloniale Fascista collana gratuita di propaganda 1. Wolfsonian XB1992.1221. My translation.

68. Ernst Van de Wetering, "The Surface of Objects and Museum Style," in *Museum Objects: Experiencing the Properties of Things*, ed. Sandra H. Dudley (London: Routledge, 2012), 105.

69. Rugoff, *Kader Attia: The Museum of Emotion*, 4.

70. Mengiste, *Shadow King*, 296.

71. Mengiste, *Shadow King*, 296.

72. Mengiste, *Shadow King*, 399.

73. Azoulay, *Potential History*, 25.

74. Azoulay, *Potential History*, 25.

75. Mengiste, *Shadow King*, 132.

76. Mengiste, *Shadow King*, 146.

77. Azoulay, *Potential History*, 22.

78. Mengiste, *Shadow King*, 181.

79. Mengiste, *Shadow King*, 301, 310.

80. Pankhurst, "Ethiopia, the Aksum Obelisk, and the Return of Africa's Cultural Heritage," 233.

81. Mengiste, *The Shadow King*, 417.

82. Igiaba Scego and Rino Bianchi, *Roma negata: Percorsi postcoloniali nella città* (Rome: Ediesse, 2014), 95.

83. Francesca Capossela, 'The Body is a Battlefield: On Maaza Mengiste's "The Shadow King," *Los Angeles Review of Books*, October 23, 2019.

84. Greenblatt, "Resonance and Wonder," 44.

85. Grechi, *Decolonizzare il museo*, 191.

86. See "Project 3541," accessed November 3, 2022, https://www.project3541.com. See also Italian Eritrean artist and filmmaker Medhin Paolos's project *Archives of Justice*, which is aimed at "minding the historical gaps" of colonization: https://www.medhinpaolos.com/archives-of-justice/, accessed November 3, 2022.

87. Shannon Mattern, "Maintenance and Care," *Places Journal*, 2018, accessed July 12, 2022, https://placesjournal.org/article/maintenance-and-care/.

88. Fazil Moradi, "Catastrophic Art," *Public Culture* 34, no. 2 (2022): 243–64.

Conclusion

1. Danuta Fjellestad, "Testing the Limits: Leanne Shapton's Ekphrastic Assemblage," *Poetics Today* 39, no. 2 (2018): 349.

2. See Rodney Harrison, "Forgetting to Remember, Remembering to Forget: Late Modern Heritage Practices, Sustainability, and the 'Crisis' of Accumulation of the Past," *International Journal of Heritage Studies* 19, no. 6 (2013): 579–95.

3. Alison J. Clarke, review of *Important Artifacts and Personal Property*, *Journal of Design History* 24, no. 2 (2011): 204.

4. Eliza Honey, "The Exchange: Leanne Shapton," *New Yorker*, February 12, 2009.

5. See Wasserman, *Death of Things*.

6. Kevin Hetherington, "Phantasmagoria/Phantasm Agora: Materialities, Spatialities, and Ghosts," *Space and Culture* 11 (2001): 25.

7. Peter Davies, "Disposals: Debate, Dissent and Dilemma," in *Museums and the Disposals Debate*, ed. Peter Davies (Edinburgh: Museums Etc., 2011), 21.

Notes to Pages 147–155

8. See Martin Grünfeld and Caitlin DeSilvey, "Fringe Objects: Cultivating Residues at the Museum," in *Museale Reste*, ed. Nina Samuel and Felix Sattler (Berlin: De Gruyter, 2022), 35.

9. Harrison, "Forgetting to Remember, Remembering to Forget," 589.

10. Kate Elizabeth Willman, *Unidentified Narrative Objects and the New Italian Epic* (Cambridge, UK: MHRA Legenda, 2019), 1.

11. Timothy Bewes, *Free Indirect: The Novel in a Post-fictional Age* (New York: Columbia University Press, 2022), 9.

12. Fjellestad, "Testing the Limits," 344.

13. Barbara Penner, Adrian Forty, Olivia Horsfall Turner, and Miranda Critchley, introduction to *Extinct: A Compendium of Obsolete Objects*, ed. Barbara Penner et al. (London: Reaktion Books, 2021), 10.

14. Penner et al., *Extinct*, 18.

15. Leanne Shapton, *Important Artifacts and Personal Property from the Collection of Lenore Doolan and Harold Morris, Including Books, Street Fashion, and Jewelry* (London: Bloomsbury, 2009), 34.

16. Eilean Hooper-Greenhill, *Museums and the Interpretation of Visual Culture* (London: Routledge, 2000), 115.

17. Hooper-Greenhill, *Museums and the Interpretation of Visual Culture*, 152.

18. Ernst, "Archi(ve)textures of Museology," 18.

19. See https://www.bloomsbury.com/uk/series/object-lessons/, accessed April 24, 2023.

20. Dayna L. Caldwell, "Disposing Material: Information Lost or New Perspectives Gained?," in Davies, *Museums and the Disposals Debate*, 45.

21. See Cornelius Holtorf, "Averting Loss Aversion in Cultural Heritage," *International Journal of Heritage Studies* 21, no. 4 (2015): 407.

22. Harrison, "Forgetting to Remember, Remembering to Forget," 583.

23. Nick Merriman, "Museum Collections and Sustainability," *Cultural Trends* 17, no. 1 (2008): 4.

24. Museums Association, *Disposal Toolkit: Guidelines for Museums*, 6, https://www.museumsassociation.org/campaigns/collections/disposal-toolkit/.

25. Cit. Bjørnar J. Olsen, "Manker's List: Museum Collections in the Era of Deaccessioning and Disposal," *Nordic Museology* 1 (2018: 67.

26. Ernst, "Archi(ve)textures of Museology," 26.

27. Wasserman, *Death of Things*, 4.

28. Ernst, "Archi(ve)textures of Museology," 18.

29. Wasserman, *Death of Things*, 1.

30. Jakubowski, "Exhibiting Lost Love," 143.

31. Honey, "The Exchange: Leanne Shapton."

32. Wasserman, *Death of Things*, 22.

33. See Salvador Muñoz Viñas, *Contemporary Theory of Conservation* (Oxford: Elsevier Butterworth-Heinemann, 2005), 99.

34. Stephen Heath, "Barthes on Love," *SubStance* 11, no. 4 and 12, no. 1 (1982–1983), 101.

35. Heath, "Barthes on Love," 101.

36. It is interesting to note that even here in the Museum of Broken Relationships, an excess of material donated means that potential contributors are

warned that only 15 percent of the collection can be displayed on an annual basis. I wonder how long the crowdsourced experiment can continue before it is restricted to solely digital submissions?

37. Merriman, "Museum Collections and Sustainability," 3.

38. Stepanova, *In Memory of Memory*, 105.

39. Stepanova, *In Memory of Memory*, 19–20.

40. Stepanova, *In Memory of Memory*, 20.

41. Stepanova, *In Memory of Memory*, 23.

42. Stepanova, *In Memory of Memory*, 19.

43. Wasserman, *Death of Things*, 28.

44. Susan A. Crane, *Museums and Memory*, 2.

45. Pierre Nora, "Between Memory and History: Les Lieux de Mémoire," *Representations* 26 (1989): 7.

46. See Jennie Morgan and Sharon Macdonald, "Degrowing Museum Collections for New Heritage Futures," *International Journal of Heritage Studies* 26, no. 1 (2020): 61.

47. Harrison, "Forgetting to Remember, Remembering to Forget," 586.

48. See Marilena Vecco and Michele Piazzai, "Deaccessioning of Museum Collections: What Do We Know and Where Do We Stand in Europe?," *Journal of Cultural Heritage* 16 (2015): 222.

49. Stepanova, *In Memory of Memory*, 92.

50. Stepanova, *In Memory of Memory*, 93.

51. Ernst, "Archi(ve)textures of Museology," 32.

52. Cit. Muñoz Viñas, *Contemporary Theory of Conservation*, 172.

53. Paul Auster, introduction to *I Remember, by* Joe Brainard, (Honiton, UK: Notting Hill Editions, 2012), xiii.

54. Paul Connerton, *The Spirit of Mourning: History, Memory and the Body* (Cambridge: Cambridge University Press, 2011), 17.

55. Stepanova, *In Memory of Memory*, 133.

56. Stepanova, *In Memory of Memory*, 369.

57. Adrian Forty, introduction to *The Art of Forgetting*, ed. Adrian Forty and Susanne Küchler (Oxford: Berg, 1999), 2.

58. Stepanova, *In Memory of Memory*, 47.

59. Stepanova, *In Memory of Memory*, 47.

60. Wasserman, *Death of Things*, 37.

61. Connerton, *The Spirit of Mourning: History, Memory and the Body*, 38.

62. Mary Wang, "Leanne Shapton: 'The Mix of Proof, Shock and Totally Crappy Images,'" *Guernica*, April 12, 2009.

63. Aida Amaoko, "Interview with Leanne Shapton," *TANK*, April 2019.

64. DeSilvey, *Curated Decay*, 85.

65. DeSilvey, *Curated Decay*, 94.

66. Stepanova, *In Memory of Memory*, 453.

67. Stepanova, *In Memory of Memory*, 454.

68. Stepanova, *In Memory of Memory*, 98.

69. DeSilvey, *Curated Decay*, 50.

70. Michael Taussig, *Walter Benjamin's Grave* (Chicago: University of Chicago Press, 2006), vii.

Notes to Pages 160–164

71. Kevin Hetherington, "Secondhandness: Consumption, Disposal and Absent Presence," *Environment and Planning D: Society and Space* 22 (2004): 167.

72. Holtorf, "Averting Loss Aversion in Cultural Heritage," 410.

73. Stepanova, *In Memory of Memory*, 53.

74. Stepanova, *In Memory of Memory*, 500.

75. Bewes, *Free Indirect*, 2.

76. Bewes, *Free Indirect*, 4.

77. Michael Taussig, *My Cocaine Museum* (Chicago: University of Chicago Press, 2004), x.

78. Crane, "Introduction: Of Museums and Memory," 12.

79. Michel de Certeau, *The Practice of Everyday Life*, trans. Steven Rendall (London: University of California Press, 1984), 108.

80. Bewes, *Free Indirect*, 6.

81. Emily St. John Mandel, *Station Eleven* (London: Picador, 2014), 258.

82. Mandel, *Station Eleven*, 146.

83. See Pete McKenzie, "A Favourite Reef, a Beloved Atoll: Marshall Islands Parents Name Children after Vanishing Landmarks, *Guardian*, March 24, 2023.

84. Ernst, "Archi(ve)textures of Museology," 28.

85. Judith Schalansky, *An Inventory of Losses*, translated by Jackie Smith (London: MacLehose Press, 2020), 7–8.

86. Mandel, *Station Eleven*, 276.

87. Grünfeld and DeSilvey, "Fringe Objects: Cultivating Residues at the Museum," 44.

88. Kevin Walsh, *The Representation of the Past: Museums and Heritage in the Post-Modern World* (London: Routledge, 1992), 161.

89. Schalansky, *An Inventory of Losses*, 24.

BIBLIOGRAPHY

Ahmed, Sara. *What's the Use? On the Uses of Use*. Durham, NC: Duke University Press, 2019.

Alivizatou, Marilena. *Intangible Heritage and the Museum: New Perspectives on Cultural Preservation*. Walnut Creek, CA: Left Coast Press, 2012.

Allmer, Açalya. "Orhan Pamuk's Museum of Innocence: On Architecture, Narrative, and the Art of Collecting." *Architectural Research Quarterly* 13, no. 2 (2009): 163–72.

Alpers, Svetlana. "The Museum as a Way of Seeing." In Karp and Lavine, *Exhibiting Cultures*, 25–32.

Amaoko, Aida. "Interview with Leanne Shapton." *TANK*, April 2019.

Amborn, Hermann. "Concepts in Wood and Stone: Socio-religious Monuments of the Konso of Southern Ethiopia." *Zeitschrift für Ethnologie* 127, no. 1 (2002): 77–101.

Ambrose, Timothy, and Crispin Paine, eds. *Museum Basics: The International Handbook*. London: Routledge, 2018.

Ames, Michael. "Cannibal Tours, Glass Boxes and the Politics of Interpretation." In Pearce, *Interpreting Objects and Collections*, 98–106.

Anderson, Kent. "The Useful Archive." *Learned Publishing* 15, no. 2 (2002): 85–89.

Andrews, Chris. "Publishing, Translating, Worldmaking." In *The Cambridge Companion to World Literature*, edited by Ben Etherington and Jarad Zimbler, 227–40. Cambridge: Cambridge University Press, 2018.

Appadurai, Arjun. "Archive and Aspiration." In *Information Is Alive: Art and Theory on Archiving and Retrieving Data*, edited by Joke Brouwer and Arjen Mulder, 14–25. Rotterdam: V2_/NAI, 2003.

Arnold-de Simine, Silke. "Memory Museum and Museum Text: Intermediality in Daniel Libeskind's Jewish Museum and W. G. Sebald's *Austerlitz*." *Theory, Culture and Society* 29, no. 1 (2012): 14–35.

Attia, Kader. "Kader Attia and Ralph Rudoff in Conversation." In *The Museum of Emotion*. London: Hayward Gallery, 2019.

Augé, Marc. *Non-Places: Introduction to an Anthropology of Supermodernity*. Translated by Jon Howe. London: Verso, 1995.

Auster, Paul. Introduction to *I Remember*, by Joe Brainard, ix-xviii. Honiton, UK: Notting Hill Editions, 2012.

Autry, La Tanya S., and Mike Murawski. "Museums Are Not Neutral." Accessed April 5, 2023. https://www.museumsarenotneutral.com.

Azoulay, Ariella Aïsha. *Potential History: Unlearning Imperialism*. New York: Verso, 2019.

———. *Un-documented: Unlearning Imperial Plunder*. 2020. Film.

Badagliacca, Mario. "Frammenti." Accessed April 5, 2023. https://www.mariobadagliacca.com/frammenti_2013-r8112.

Baker, Steve. *The Postmodern Animal*. London: Reaktion Books, 2000.

Bakhtin, Mikhail. *The Dialogic Imagination. Four Essays*. Translated by Caryl Emerson and Michael Holquist. Austin: University of Texas Press, 1982.

Bal, Mieke. "Telling Objects: A Narrative Perspective on Collecting." In Elsner and Cardinal, *Cultures of Collecting*, 118–35.

Ballinger, Pamela. *History in Exile: Memory and Identity at the Borders of the Balkans*. Princeton, NJ: Princeton University Press, 2003.

Balzer, David. *Curationism: How Curating Took over the Art World and Everything Else*. London: Pluto Press, 2014.

Basil, Priya. "Writing to Life." *British Art Studies* 19 (2021). https://doi.org/10.17658/issn.2058-5462/issue-19/conversation/002.

Batchelor, Ray. "Not Looking at Kettles." In Pearce, *Interpreting Objects and Collections*, 139–43. London: Routledge, 1994.

Battro, Antonio M. "From Malraux's Imaginary Museum to the Virtual Museum." In Parry, *Museums in a Digital Age*, 136–47.

Baudrillard, Jean. "The System of Collecting." In Elsner and Cardinal, *Cultures of Collecting*, xx.

Baxandall, Michael. "Exhibiting Intention: Some Preconditions of the Visual Display of Culturally Purposeful Objects." In Karp and Lavine, *Exhibiting Cultures*, 33–41.

Belk, Russell W. "Collectors and Collecting." In *Handbook of Material Culture*, edited by Chris Tilley, Webb Keane, Susanne Kuechler, Mike Rowlands, and Patricia Spyer, 534–45. London: SAGE, 2006.

———. *Collecting in a Consumer Society*. London: Routledge, 1995.

Ben-Ghiat, Ruth, and Mia Fuller. Introduction to *Italian Colonialism*, edited by Ruth Ben-Ghiat and Mia Fuller, 1–12. New York: Palgrave Macmillan, 2005.

Benjamin, Walter. "Eduard Fuchs: Collector and Historian." *New German Critique* 5 (1975): 27–58.

———. "Unpacking My Library: A Talk about Book Collecting." In *Illuminations*, translated by Harry Zorn. London: Pimlico, 1999.

Bennett, Jane. *Vibrant Matter: A Political Ecology of Things*, Durham, NC: Duke University Press, 2010.

Bersani, Leo. *A Future for Astyanax: Character and Desire in Literature*. London: Marion Boyars, 1978.

Bewes, Timothy. *Free Indirect: The Novel in a Post-fictional Age*. New York: Columbia University Press, 2022.

Bielenberg, Katharina. "The Editor's Chair: On Daša Drndić." *Granta*, November 16, 2018.

Blom, Phillip. *To Have and to Hold: An Intimate History of Collectors and Collecting*. London: Penguin, 2003.

Braidotti, Rosa, and Maria Hlavajova, eds. *Posthuman Glossary*. London: Bloomsbury, 2018.

Brand, Dionne. *An Autobiography of Autobiography of Reading*. Edmonton: University of Alberta Press, 2020.

Bibliography

Brooks, Peter. *Reading for the Plot: Design and Intention in Narrative.* Cambridge, MA: Harvard University Press, 1984.

Brown, Bill. "Thing Theory." *Critical Inquiry* 28, no. 1 (2001): 1–22.

Burton, Antoinette, ed. *Archive Stories: Facts, Fictions, and the Writing of History.* Durham, NC: Duke University Press, 2005.

———. *Dwelling in the Archive: Women Writing House, Home, and History in Late Colonial India.* Oxford: Oxford University Press, 2003.

Buttler, Caroline, and Mary Davis, eds. *Things Fall Apart . . . Museum Conservation in Practice.* Cardiff, Wales: National Museum of Wales Books, 2006.

Caldwell, Dayna L. "Disposing Material: Information Lost or New Perspectives Gained?" In *Museums and the Disposals Debate*, edited by Peter Davies, 44–55. Edinburgh: Museums Etc., 2011.

Cameron, Fiona. "Ecologizing Experiments: A Method and Manifesto for Composing a Post-humanist Museum." In *Climate Change and Museum Futures*, edited by Fiona Cameron and Brett Neilson, 16–33. New York: Routledge, 2015.

———. "Museum Collections, Documentation, and Shifting Knowledge Paradigms." In Parry, *Museums in a Digital Age*, 80–95.

———. "Posthuman Museum Practices." In Braidotti and Hlavajova, *Posthuman Glossary*, 349–52.

Can, Taner, Berkan Ulu, and Koray Melikoglu, eds. *Orhan Pamuk: Critical Essays on a Novelist between Worlds.* New York: Ibidem Press, 2017.

Candlin, Fiona, and Jamie Larkin. "What Is a Museum? Difference All the Way Down." *Museum and Society* 18, no. 2: 115–31.

Cane, Simon. "Why Do We Conserve? Developing Understanding of Conservation as a Cultural Construct." In *Conservation: Principles, Dilemmas, and Uncomfortable Truths*, edited by Alison Richmond and Alison Bracker, 163–176. London: Routledge, 2009.

Cangiano, Mimmo. *The Wreckage of Philosophy: Carlo Michelstaedter and the Limits of Bourgeois Thought.* Toronto: University of Toronto Press, 2018.

Canizzo, Jeanne. "Exhibiting Cultures: 'Into the Heart of Africa.'" *Visual Anthropology Review* 7, no. 1 (1991): 150–60.

Caple, Chris. "The History of and an Introduction to Preventive Conservation." In *Preventive Conservation in Museums*, edited by Chris Caple, 1–15. London: Routledge, 2011.

Capossela, Francesca. "The Body Is a Battlefield: On Maaza Mengiste's *The Shadow King*." *Los Angeles Review of Books*, October 23, 2019.

Caracciolo, Marco. "From the Museum of Civilization to *The Octopus Museum*: Curating the Anthropocene in Contemporary Literature." *Textual Practice* 36, no. 9 (2022): 1413–34.

Carters, The. "APES**T." Reservoir Media Music, 2018.

Caws, Mary Ann, ed. *Joseph Cornell's Theatre of the Mind: Selected Diaries, Letters, and Files.* New York: Thames and Hudson, 1993.

Certeau, Michel de. *The Practice of Everyday Life.* Translated by Steven Rendall. Berkeley: University of California Press, 1984.

Chambers, Iain. "Afterword: After the Museum." In *The Postcolonial Museum: The Arts of Memory and the Pressures of History*, edited by Iain Chambers,

Alessandra De Angelis, Celeste Ianniciello, and Mariangela Orabona, 241–45. Farnham, UK: Ashgate, 2014.

Cheah, Pheng. *What Is a World? On Postcolonial Literature as World Literature.* Durham, NC: Duke University Press, 2016.

Chrisafis, Angelique. "Beyoncé and Jay-Z Help Louvre Museum Break Visitor Record in 2018." *Guardian*, January 3, 2019.

Clarke, Alison J. Review of *Important Artifacts and Personal Property. Journal of Design History* 24, no. 2 (2011): 203–4.

Clavir, Miriam. *Preserving What Is Valued: Museums, Conservation and First Nations.* Vancouver: University of British Columbia Press, 2022.

Clifford, James. "On Collecting Art and Culture." In *The Predicament of Culture: Twentieth-Century Ethnography, Literature, and Art*, 215–51. Cambridge, MA: Harvard University Press, 1988.

———. *Routes: Travel and Translation in the Late Twentieth Century.* Cambridge, MA: Harvard University Press, 1997.

———. "The Times of the Curator." In Schorch and McCarthy, *Curatopia*, 109–21.

Cloutier, Jean-Christophe. *Shadow Archives: The Lifecycles of African American Literature.* New York: Columbia University Press, 2019.

Connerton, Paul. *The Spirit of Mourning: History, Memory and the Body.* Cambridge: Cambridge University Press, 2011.

Cran, Rona. *Collage in Twentieth-Century Art, Literature, and Culture: Joseph Cornell, William Burroughs, Frank O'Hara, and Bob Dylan.* Farnham, UK: Ashgate, 2014.

Crane, Susan A. "Memory, Distortion, and History in the Museum." *History and Theory* 36, no. 4 (1997): 44–63.

Crooke, Elizabeth. "The 'Active Museum': How Concern with Community Transformed the Museum." In *The International Handbook of Museum Studies. Part 2, Museum Practice*, edited by Conal McCarthy, 481–502. Oxford: Wiley, 2015.

Damrosch, David. *What Is World Literature?* Princeton, NJ: Princeton University Press, 2018.

Daston, Lorraine, and Katharine Park. *Wonders and the Order of Nature, 1150–1750.* New York: Zone Books, 1998.

Davies, Peter. "Disposals: Debate, Dissent and Dilemma." In *Museums and the Disposals Debate*, edited by Peter Davies, 20–43. Edinburgh: Museums Etc., 2011.

Deckard, Sharae, Nicholas Lawrence, Neil Lazarus, Graeme Macdonald, Upamanyu Pablo Mukherjee, Benita Parry, and Stephen Shapiro. *World-Literature in the Context of Combined and Uneven Development.* Liverpool, UK: Liverpool University Press, 2015.

Delpino, Gaia, Rosa Anna di Lella, and Claudio Mancuso. "Unveiled Storages: How to Imagine a De-colonial Museum?" Accessed April 5, 2023. https:// takingcareproject.eu/article/unveiled-storages-how-to-imagine-a-de-colonial -museum.

DeSilvey, Caitlin. "Salvage Memory: Constellating Material Histories on a Hard-scrabble Homestead." *cultural geographies* 14, no. 3 (2007): 401–24.

Bibliography

———. *Curated Decay: Heritage beyond Saving*. Minneapolis: University of Minnesota Press, 2017.

Dimock, Wai Chee. "Literature for the Planet." *PMLA* 116, no. 1 (January 2001): 173–88.

Donato, Eugenio. "The Museum's Furnace: Notes toward a Contextual Reading of *Bouvard and Pécuchet*." In *Textual Strategies: Perspectives in Post-Structuralist Criticism*, edited by Josue V. Harari, 213–38. Ithaca, NY: Cornell University Press, 1979.

Drndić, Dasa. *Belladonna*. Translated by Celia Hawkesworth. New York: W. W. Norton, 2017.

———. *Trieste*. Translated by Ellen Elias-Bursać. London: MacLehose Press, 2012.

Dubey, Madhu. "Museumizing Slavery: Living History in Colson Whitehead's *The Underground Railroad*." *American Literary History* 32, no. 1 (2020): 111–39.

Duncan, Carol. "Museums and Citizenship." In Karp and Lavine, *Exhibiting Cultures*, 88–103.

Editorial. "The Victoria and Albert Museum." *Burlington Magazine*, vol. 163 (April 2021).

Elsner, John, and Roger Cardinal, eds. *The Cultures of Collecting*. London: Reaktion Books, 1994.

Ernst, Wolfgang. "Archi(ve)textures of Museology." In *Museums and Memory*, edited by Susan A. Crane, 17–34. Stanford, CA: Stanford University Press, 2000.

Etienne, Noémie. "Who Cares? Museum Conservation between Colonial Violence and Symbolic Repair." *Museums & Social Issues* 15, nos. 1–2 (2021): 61–71.

Fait, Francesco, ed. *Civico Museo della Risiera di San Sabba: Monumento Nazionale*. Trieste, Italy: Edizioni Civici musei di storia ed arte, Comune di Trieste, 2016.

Falkoff, Rebecca R. *Possessed: A Cultural History of Hoarding*. Ithaca, NY: Cornell University Press, 2021.

Farge, Arlette. *The Allure of the Archives*. Translated by Thomas Scott-Railton. New Haven, CT: Yale University Press, 2013.

Fisher, Philip. "Art and the Future's Past." In *Museum Studies: An Anthology of Contexts*, edited by Bettina Messias Carbonell, 457–72. Oxford: Wiley-Blackwell, 2012.

Fisk, Gloria. *Orhan Pamuk and the Good of World Literature*. New York: Columbia University Press, 2018.

Fjellestad, Danuta. "Testing the Limits: Leanne Shapton's Ekphrastic Assemblage." *Poetics Today* 39, no. 2 (2018): 338–57.

Flaubert, Gustave. *Bouvard and Pécuchet*. Translated by Mark Polizzotti. Chicago: Dalkey Archive Press, 2005.

Forgacs, David. *Italy's Margins: Social Exclusion and Nation Formation since 1861*. Cambridge: Cambridge University Press, 2015.

Forty, Adrian. Introduction to *The Art of Forgetting*, edited by Adrian Forty and Susanne Küchler, 1–18. Oxford: Berg, 1999.

Fowler, Susanne. "Private Peek at Author's Blur of Fact and Fiction." *New York Times*, May 2, 2012.

French, Jade. *Inclusive Curating in Contemporary Art. A Practical Guide*. Leeds, UK: ARC Humanities Press, 2020.

Freud, Sigmund. "Constructions in Analysis." In *The Standard Edition of the Complete Psychological Works of Sigmund Freud*. Vol. 23, edited and translated by James Strachey, 255–69. London: Vintage, 2001.

———. "A Note upon the 'Mystic Writing-Pad.'" In *The Standard Edition of the Complete Psychological Works of Sigmund Freud*. Vol. 19, edited and translated by James Strachey, 225–32. London: Vintage, 2001.

Fuentes, Marisa J. *Dispossessed Lives: Enslaved Women, Violence, and the Archive*. Philadelphia: University of Pennsylvania Press, 2016.

Gandolfo, Francesca. *Il museo coloniale di Roma (1904–1971): Fra le zebra nel paese dell'olio di ricino*. Rome: Gangemi, 2014.

Ganguly, Debjani. *This Thing Called the World: The Contemporary Novel as Global Form*. Durham, NC: Duke University Press, 2016.

Ginzkey Puloy, Monika. "High Art and National Socialism, Part I: The Linz Museum as Ideological Arena." *Journal of History of Collections* 8, no. 2 (1996): 201–15.

———. "High Art and National Socialism, Part II: Hitler's Linz Collection: Acquisition, Predation and Restitution." *Journal of History of Collections* 10, no. 2 (1998): 207–24.

Gopinath, Gayatri. *Unruly Visions: The Aesthetic Practices of Queer Diaspora*. Durham, NC: Duke University Press, 2018.

Graham, Beryl, and Sarah Cook. *Rethinking Curating: Art after New Media*. Cambridge, MA: MIT Press, 2015.

Grechi, Giulia. *Decolonizzare il museo: Mostrazioni, pratiche artistiche, sguardi incarnati*. Milan: Mimesis, 2021.

Greenblatt, Stephen. "Resonance and Wonder." In Karp and Lavine, *Exhibiting Cultures*, 42–56.

Grey, Alison, Tim Gardom, and Catherine Booth. *Saying It Differently: A Handbook for Museums Refreshing Their Displays*. London: London Museums Hub, 2006.

Grünfeld, Martin, and Caitlin DeSilvey. "Fringe Objects: Cultivating Residues at the Museum." In *Museale Reste*, edited by Nina Samuel and Felix Sattler, 35–44. Berlin: De Gruyter, 2022.

Gubbins, Sarah. "Nerval's Journeys in Verse and in Prose." *Nineteenth-Century Contexts* 41, no. 1 (2019): 75–84.

Habta, Hailu, and Juith A. Byfield, "Fighting Fascism: Ethiopian Women Patriots, 1935–1941." In *Africa and World War II*, edited by Judith A. Byfield, Carolyn A. Brown, Timothy Parsons, and Ahmad Alawad Sikainga, 383–400. Cambridge: Cambridge University Press, 2015.

Haraway, Donna. *Staying with the Trouble: Making Kin in the Chthulucene*. Durham, NC: Duke University Press, 2016.

———. *When Species Meet*. Minneapolis: University of Minnesota Press, 2008.

Harman, Graham. *Guerrilla Metaphysics: Phenomenology and the Carpentry of Things*. Chicago: Open Court, 2005.

Bibliography

Harrison, Rodney. "Forgetting to Remember, Remembering to Forget: Late Modern Heritage Practices, Sustainability, and the 'Crisis' of Accumulation of the Past." *International Journal of Heritage Studies* 19, no. 6 (2013): 579–95.

Hartman, Saidiya. "Venus in Two Acts." *small axe* 26 (2008): 1–14.

Hauptman, Jodi. *Joseph Cornell: Stargazing in the Cinema*. New Haven, CT: Yale University Press, 1999.

Hayes, Patricia, Jeremy Silvester, and Wolfram Hartmann. "'Picturing the Past' in Namibia: The Visual Archive and its Energies." In *Refiguring the Archive*, edited by Carolyn Hamilton, Verne Hariss, Jane Taylor, Michele Pickover, Graeme Reid, and Razia Saleh, 103–33. Dordrecht, Netherlands: Kluwer Academic Publishers, 2002.

Hayot, Eric. *On Literary Worlds*. Oxford: Oxford University Press, 2012.

Heath, Stephen. "Barthes on Love." *SubStance* 11, no. 4 and 12, no. 1 (1982–1983): 100–106.

Hepburn, Allan. *Enchanted Objects: Visual Art in Contemporary Fiction*. Toronto: University of Toronto Press, 2010.

Hetherington, Kevin. "Phantasmagoria/Phantasm Agora: Materialities, Spatialities, and Ghosts." *Space and Culture* 11 (2001): 24–42.

———. "Secondhandness: Consumption, Disposal and Absent Presence." *Environment and Planning D: Society and Space* 22 (2004): 157–73.

Hicks, Dan. *The Brutish Museums: The Benin Bronzes, Colonial Violence and Cultural Restitution*. London: Pluto Press, 2020.

———. "UK Welcomes Restitution, Just Not Anti-Colonialism." *Hyperallergic*, August 26, 2022. Accessed November 12, 2022. https://hyperallergic.com/756241/uk-welcomes-restitution-just-not-anti-colonialism.

Hirsch, Marianne. *The Generation of Postmemory: Writing and Visual Culture after the Holocaust*. New York: Columbia University Press, 2012.

Holtorf, Cornelius. "Averting Loss Aversion in Cultural Heritage." *International Journal of Heritage Studies* 21, no. 4 (2015): 405–21.

Holubar, Karl. "The Anatomical Wax Preparations in the Josephinum in Vienna, Austria." *Archives of Surgery* 126, no. 4 (1991): 421–22.

Honey, Eliza. "The Exchange: Leanne Shapton." *New Yorker*, February 12, 2009.

Hooper-Greenhill, Eilean. *Museums and the Interpretation of Visual Culture*. London: Routledge, 2000.

ICOM. "Museum Definition." Accessed April 4, 2023. https://icom.museum/en/resources/standards-guidelines/museum-definition/.

ICOMOS. "Burra Charter." 1992. Accessed April 4, 2023. https://australia.icomos.org/publications/burra-charter-practice-notes/.

Illingworth, Dustin. "There Are No Small Fascisms: An Interview with Dasa Drndic." *Paris Review*, August 21, 2017.

Ireland, Tracy. "Quotidian Utopia: Orhan Pamuk's *The Museum of Innocence* and the Heritage of Love." *Future Anterior* 14, no. 2 (2017): 13–26.

Jakubowski, Zuzanna. "Exhibiting Lost Love: The Relational Realism of Things in Orhan Pamuk's *The Museum of Innocence* and Leanne Shapton's *Important Artifacts*." In *Realisms in Contemporary Culture: Theories, Politics, and Medial Configurations*, edited by Dorothee Birke and Stella Butter, 124–45. Berlin: De Gruyter, 2013.

James, David. "Listening to the Refugee: Valeria Luiselli's Sentimental Activism." *Modern Fiction Studies* 67, no. 2 (2021): 390–417.

Jones, Mike. *Artefacts, Archives, and Documentation in the Relational Museum.* London and New York: Routledge, 2021.

Karp, Ivan. "Culture and Representation." In Karp and Lavine, *Exhibiting Cultures,* 11–24.

Karp, Ivan, and Steven D. Lavine, eds. *Exhibiting Cultures: The Poetics and Politics of Museum Display,* Washington, DC: Smithsonian Institution, 1991.

Kavanagh, Gaynor. *History Curatorship.* Leicester, UK: Leicester University Press, 1990.

Keene, Suzanne. *Managing Conservation in Museums.* London: Routledge, 2002.

Ketelaar, Eric. "Tacit Narratives: The Meanings of Archives." *Archival Science* 1 (2001): 131–41.

Kiefer, Tom. "Shoes, Pills, Diaries: Objects Seized by Border Officials—in Pictures." *Guardian,* December 11, 2019.

Kopytoff, Igor. "The Cultural Biography of Things: Commoditization as Process." In *The Social Life of Things: Commodities in Cultural Perspective,* edited by Arjun Appadurai, 64–92. Cambridge: Cambridge University Press, 1986.

Kowalcze, Malgorzata. "The Posthumanist Dimension of the Novel *Drive Your Plow over the Bones of the Dead* by Olga Tokarczuk." *Journal of Posthumanism* 2 (2021): 225–28.

Krauss, Rosalind. "Perpetual Inventory." *October* 88 (Spring 1999): 86–116.

La Force, Thessaly. "Leanne Shapton: Studio Visit." *Paris Review,* February 16, 2012.

Lake, Crystal B. *Artifacts: How We Think and Write about Found Objects.* Baltimore: Johns Hopkins University Press, 2020.

Latour, Bruno. *Reassembling the Social: An Introduction to Actor-Network Theory.* Oxford: Oxford University Press, 2005.

Léger, Nathalie. *Suite for Barbara Loden.* Translated by Natasha Lehrer and Cécile Menon. London: Les Fugitives, 2015.

Lehrer, Erica, and Cynthia E. Milton. "Witnesses to Witnessing." Introduction to *Curating Difficult Knowledge: Violent Pasts in Public Places,* edited by Erica Lehrer, Cynthia E. Milton, and Monica Eileen Patterson, 1–19. New York, Palgrave Macmillan, 2011.

Longair, Sarah. "Cultures of Curating: The Limits of Authority." *Museum History Journal* 8, no. 1 (2015): 1–7.

Lorimer, Hayden. "Caught in the Nick of Time: Archives and Fieldwork." In *The SAGE Handbook of Qualitative Geography,* edited by Dydia DeLyser, Steve Herbert, Stuart Aitken, Mike Crange, and Linda McDowell, 248–73. London: SAGE, 2010.

Lowenthal, David. "The Past Is a Foreign Country." In *Historical Perspectives on Preventative Conservation,* edited by Sarah Staniforth, 19–25. Los Angeles: Getty Conservation Institute, 2013.

Lubar, Steven. *Inside the Lost Museum: Curating, Past and Present.* Cambridge, MA: Harvard University Press, 2017.

Luiselli, Valeria. *Lost Children Archive: A Novel.* New York: Alfred A. Knopf, 2019.

Bibliography

———. *Tell Me How It Ends: An Essay in Forty Questions*. London: 4th Estate, 2017.

———. "The Wild West Meets the Southern Border." *New Yorker*, June 3, 2019.

MacKenzie, John M. *Museums and Empire: Hunting, Conservation and British Imperialism*. Manchester, UK: Manchester University Press, 1988.

Magris, Claudio. *Alla cieca*. Milan: Garzanti, 2005.

———. *Blameless*. Translated by Anne Milano Appel. New Haven, CT: Yale University Press, 2017.

———. *Blindly*. Translated by Anne Milano Appel. New Haven, CT: Yale University Press, 2012.

Malaquais, Dominique. "Forensics: Photography in the Face of Failure." In *Dzhangal*, by Gideon Mendel, 73–74. London: GOST Books, 2017.

Maleuvre, Didier. *Museum Memories: History, Technology, Art*. Stanford, CA: Stanford University Press, 1999.

Mallet, Sarah, and Louise Fowler, "The Dzhangal Archaeology Project and 'Lande': Two Archaeological Approaches to the Study of Forced Migration." In *Material Culture and (Forced) Migration: Materializing the Transient*, edited by Friedemann Yi-Neumann, Andrea Lauser, Antoine Fuhse, and Peter J. Bräunlein, 125–46. London: UCL Press, 2022.

Mandel, Emily St. John. *Station Eleven*. London: Picador, 2014.

Manovich, Lev. "Database as Symbolic Form." In Parry, *Museums in a Digital Age*, 64–71.

Mattern, Shannon. "Maintenance and Care." *Places Journal*, 2018. Accessed July 12, 2022. https://placesjournal.org/article/maintenance-and-care/.

Mazurov, Nikita. "Monster/The Unhuman." In Braidotti and Hlavajova, *Posthuman Glossary*, 262–64.

Mbembe, Achille. "The Power of the Archive and Its Limits." Translated by Judith Inggs. In *Refiguring the Archive*, edited by Carolyn Hamilton, Verne Harris, Jane Taylor, Michele Pickover, Graeme Reid, and Razia Saleh, 19–26. Dordrecht, Netherlands: Kluwer Academic Publishers, 2002.

McGhie, Henry. *Mobilizing Museums for Climate Action. Tools, Frameworks and Opportunities to Accelerate Climate Action in and with Museums*. London: Museums for Climate Action, 2021.

McGurl, Mark. *Everything and Less: The Novel in the Age of Amazon*. London: Verso, 2021.

McKenzie, Pete. "A Favourite Reef, a Beloved Atoll: Marshall Islands Parents Name Children after Vanishing Landmarks." *Guardian*, March 24, 2023.

McSherry, Siofra. "Joseph Cornell's Subversive Materialism." *Comparative American Studies* 11, no. 4 (2014): 374–86.

Mengiste, Maaza. "Bending History." *NKA Journal of Contemporary African Art, nos.* 38–39 (2016): 182–85.

———. "Project 3541." Accessed November 3, 2022. https://www.project3541.com.

———. *The Shadow King: A Novel*. New York: W. W. Norton, 2019.

Merriman, Nick. "Museum Collections and Sustainability." *Cultural Trends* 17, no. 1 (2008): 3–21.

Michelstaedter, Carlo. *Persuasion and Rhetoric*. Translated by Wilhelm Snyman and Giuseppe Stellardi. Pietermaritzburg, South Africa: University of KwaZulu-Natal Press, 2007.

Mitman, Gregg, Marco Armiero, and Robert S. Emmett. *Future Remains: A Cabinet of Curiosities for the Anthropocene*. Chicago: University of Chicago Press, 2017.

Moeck, Emily. "Understanding the Fragmentary Nature of *Flights*: An Interview with Olga Tokarczuk." *Consequence*, October 10, 2019.

Montemaggi, Martina. "Investigating the Reinstallation of the Museo Coloniale di Roma: A Microcosm of Italian Colonial Memory." Master's thesis, University of Amsterdam, 2018. Accessed April 5, 2023. https://scripties.uba.uva.nl/document/662093.

Montero Román, Valentina. "Telling Stories That Never End: Valeria Luiselli, the Refugee Crisis at the US-Mexico Border, and the Big, Ambitious, Archival Novel." *Genre* 54, no. 2 (2021): 167–93.

Moradi, Fazil. "Catastrophic Art." *Public Culture* 34, no. 2 (2022): 243–64.

Moretti, Franco. *Atlas of the European Novel 1800–1900*. London: Verso, 1998.

Morgan, Jennie, and Sharon Macdonald. "Degrowing Museum Collections for New Heritage Futures." *International Journal of Heritage Studies* 26, no. 1 (2020): 56–70.

Morris, Rachel. *The Museum Makers: A Journey Backwards—from Old Boxes of Dark Family Secrets to a Golden Era of Museums*. Tewkesbury, UK: September Publishing, 2020.

Morrison, Heather. "Dressing Angelo Soliman." *Eighteenth-Century Studies* 44, no. 3 (2011): 361–82.

Mucci, Massimo. *La Risiera di San Sabba: Un'architettura per la memoria*. Gorizia, Italy: Goriziana, 1999.

Müller, Klaus. "Museums and Virtuality." In Parry, *Museums in a Digital Age*, 295–305.

Mullins, Matthew. *Postmodernism in Pieces: Materializing the Social in U.S. Fiction*. Oxford: Oxford University Press, 2016.

Muñoz Viñas, Salvador. *Contemporary Theory of Conservation*. Oxford: Elsevier Butterworth-Heinemann, 2005.

Museums Association. "Disposal Toolkit: Guidelines for Museums." Accessed April 5, 2023. https://www.museumsassociation.org/campaigns/collections/disposal-toolkit/.

Naimou, Angela. *Salvage Work: U.S. and Caribbean Literatures amid the Debris of Legal Personhood*. New York: Fordham University Press, 2015.

Narkiss, Irit. "Decolonising Museum Conservation Practices: A View from the UK." *Studies in Conservation* 67, supplement 1 (2022): 183–91.

Navarrete, Trilce, and John Mackenzie Owen. "The Museum as Information Space: Metadata and Documentation." In *Cultural Heritage in a Changing World*, edited by Karol Jan Borowiecki, Neil Forbes, and Antonella Fresa, 112–23. New York: Palgrave Macmillan, 2016.

Nerval, Gérard de. *Aurélia and Other Writings*. Translated by Geoffrey Wagner. Boston: Exact Change, 1996.

Newell, Jennifer, Libby Robin, and Kirsten Wehner, eds. *Curating the Future: Museums, Communities and Climate Change*. London: Routledge, 2016.

Bibliography

———. Introduction to Newell, Robin, and Wehner, *Curating the Future*, 1–16.

Nicholas, Lynn H. *The Rape of Europe. The Fate of Europe's Treasures in the Third Reich and the Second World War.* New York: Alfred A. Knopf, 1995.

Nixon, Rob. "The Anthropocene and Environmental Justice." In Newell, Robin, and Wehner, *Curating the Future*, 23–31.

Nora, Pierre. "Between Memory and History: Les Lieux de Mémoire." *Representations* 26 (1989): 7–24.

O'Neill, Paul. *The Culture of Curating and the Curating of Culture(s).* Cambridge, MA: MIT Press, 2012.

Obrist, Hans Ulrich. *Everything You Always Wanted to Know about Curating but Were Afraid to Ask.* London: Sternberg Press, 2011.

———, with Asad Raza. *Ways of Curating.* London: Penguin, 2014.

Olsen, Bjørnar J. "Manker's List: Museum Collections in the Era of Deaccessioning and Disposal." *Nordic Museology* 1 (2018): 62–73.

Orcutt, Kimberly. "The Open Storage Dilemma." *Journal of Museum Education* 36, no. 2 (2011): 209–16.

Osborne, Dora. *What Remains: The Post-Holocaust Archive in German Memory Culture.* New York: Camden House, 2020.

Ovenden, Richard. *Burning the Books: A History of Knowledge under Attack.* London: John Murray Press, 2020.

Özgül, Gönül Eda. "The Quest for Home and Identity: Modernity and Innocence in Pamuk's *The Museum of Innocence.*" In Can, Ulu, and Melikoglu, *Orhan Pamuk: Critical Essays on a Novelist between Worlds*, 203–30.

Pamuk, Orhan. *The Innocence of Objects.* Translated by Ekin Oklap. New York: Abrams Press, 2012.

———. *The Museum of Innocence. A Novel.* Translated by Maureen Freely. London: Faber and Faber, 2009.

———. *The Naïve and the Sentimental Novelist. The Charles Norton Lectures, 2009.* Translated by Nazim Dikbas. London: Faber and Faber, 2011.

Pankhurst, Richard. "Ethiopia, the Aksum Obelisk, and the Return of Africa's Cultural Heritage." *African Affairs* 98 (1999): 229–39.

Paolos, Medhin. "Archives of Justice." Accessed November 3, 2022. https://www.medhinpaolos.com/archives-of-justice/.

Parry, Ross, ed. *Museums in a Digital Age.* London: Routledge, 2010.

———. *Recoding the Museum: Digital Heritage and the Technologies of Change.* London: Routledge, 2007.

Patchett, Merle, Kate Foster, and Hayden Lorimer. "The Biographies of a Hollow-Eyed Harrier." In *The Afterlives of Animals: A Museum Menagerie*, edited by Samuel Alberti, 110–33. Charlottesville: University of Virginia Press.

Pearce, Susan M., ed. *Interpreting Objects and Collections.* London: Routledge, 1994.

———. "Museum Objects." In Pearce, *Interpreting Objects and Collections*, 9–11.

———. "Objects as Meaning; Or Narrating the Past." In Pearce, *Interpreting Objects and Collections*, 19–29.

———. "Collecting Reconsidered." In Pearce, *Interpreting Objects and Collections*, 193–204.

Penner, Barbara, Adrian Forty, Olivia Horsfall Turner, and Miranda Critchley. Introduction to *Extinct: A Compendium of Obsolete Objects*, edited by Barbara Penner, Adrian Forty, Olivia Horsfall Turner, and Miranda Critchley, 9–18. London: Reaktion Books, 2021.

Pepi, Mike. "Is the Museum a Database?: Institutional Conditions in Net Utopia." *e-flux* 60 (2014).

Pichois, Claude, and Michel Brix. *Gérard de Nerval*. Paris: Fayard, 1995.

Pilegaard, Ane. "Material Proximity: Experimenting with Material Strategies in Spatial Exhibition Design." *Museum World: Advances in Research* 3 (2015): 69–85.

———. "Through the Lens of the Glass Cabinet: Entering the Material Realm of Museum Objects." *Interiors* 10, no. 3 (2019): 172–90.

Pizzi, Katia. "The Granular Texture of Memory: Trieste between Mitteleuropa and the Mediterranean." *Journal of Transcultural Studies* 11, no. 1 (2020): 34–47.

Poliquin, Rachel. *The Breathless Zoo: Taxidermy and the Culture of Longing*. University Park: Penn State University Press, 2012.

Pomerantsev, Peter. "Russian Memoirs Are Prone to a Particular Kind of Angst." *Spectator*, May 29, 2021.

Pomian, Krzysztof. "The Collection: Between the Visible and the Invisible." In Pearce, *Interpreting Objects and Collections*, 160–74.

Ramazani, Jahan. *A Transnational Poetics*. Chicago: University of Chicago Press, 2009.

Redman, Samuel J. *The Museum: A Short History of Crisis and Resilience*. New York: New York University Press, 2022.

Reilly, Maura. *Curatorial Activism: Towards an Ethics of Curating*. London: Thames and Hudson, 2018.

Riva, Alessandro, Gabriele Conti, Paola Solinas, and Francesco Loy. "The Evolution of Anatomical Illustration and Wax Modeling in Italy from the 16th to Early 19th Centuries." *Journal of Anatomy* 216 (2010): 209–22.

Rosen, Zachary. "Confronting the Weapon of Photography: An Interview with Maaza Mengiste." *Africa Is a Country*, May 22, 2020. Accessed September 13, 2022. https://africasacountry.com/2020/05/confronting-the-weapon-of -photography.

Rudolph, Katie. "Separated at Appraisal: Maintaining the Archival Bond between Archival Collections and Museum Objects." *Archival Issues* 33, no. 1 (2011): 25–39.

Rugoff, Ralph. Foreword to *Kader Attia: The Museum of Emotion*. London: Hayward Gallery, 2019.

Salvadori, Diego. "'Quel pezzetto di ippocampo è qualcosa che manca": Scrittura sul corpo in *Non luogo a procedere* di Claudio Magris." *Comparatismi* 4 (2019): 44–63.

Sarr, Felwine, and Bénédicte Savoy. *The Restitution of African Cultural Heritage: Toward a New Relational Ethics*. Translated by Drew S. Burk. November 2018. http://restitutionreport2018.com/sarr_savoy_en.pdf.

Scego, Igiaba, and Rino Bianchi. *Roma negata: Percorsi postcoloniali nella città*. Rome: Ediesse, 2014.

Bibliography

Schalansky, Judith. *An Inventory of Losses*. Translated by Jackie Smith. London: MacLehose Press, 2020.

Schorch, Philipp, and Conal McCarthy, eds. *Curatopia: Museums and the Future of Curatorship*. Manchester, UK: Manchester University Press, 2018.

Schorch, Philipp, Conal McCarthy, and Eveline Dürr. "Introduction: Conceptualizing Curatopia." In Schorch and McCarthy, *Curatopia*, 1–16.

Schrag, Anthony. "'Kill Your Darlings': What Is a Public Collection and Who Is It For?" *Art.UK*, 2022.

Schwenger, Peter. *The Tears of Things: Melancholy and Physical Objects*. Minneapolis: University of Minnesota Press, 2006.

Serota, Nicholas. *Experience or Interpretation? The Dilemma of Museums of Modern Art*. London: Thames and Hudson, 2000.

Shapton, Leanne. *Important Artifacts and Personal Property from the Collection of Lenore Doolan and Harold Morris, Including Books, Street Fashion, and Jewelry*. London: Bloomsbury, 2009.

Sheringham, Michael, and Richard Wentworth. "City as Archive: A Dialogue between Theory and Practice." *Cultural Geographies* 23, no. 3 (2016): 517–23.

Siegel, Jonah, ed. *The Emergence of the Modern Museum. An Anthology of Nineteenth-Century Sources*. Oxford: Oxford University Press, 2005.

———. *Material Inspirations: The Interests of the Art Object in the Nineteenth Century and After*. Oxford: Oxford University Press, 2020.

Simic, Charles. *Dime-Store Alchemy: The Art of Joseph Cornell*. New York: New York Review Books, 1992.

Smith, Terry. *Thinking Contemporary Curating*. New York: Independent Curators International, 2012.

Sontag, Susan. *Reborn: Early Diaries, 1947–1963*. Edited by David Rieff. London: Penguin, 2008.

Srivastana, Neelam. *Italian Colonialism and Resistances to Empire, 1930–1970*. New York: Palgrave Macmillan, 2018.

Staniforth, Sarah, ed. *Historical Perspectives on Preventative Conservation*. Los Angeles: Getty Conservation Institute, 2013.

Steedman, Carolyn. "The Space of Memory: In an Archive." *History of the Human Sciences* 11, no. 4 (1998): 65–83.

Stepanova, Maria. *In Memory of Memory. A Romance*. Translated by Sasha Dugdale. London: Fitzcarraldo, 2021.

Sternthal, Barbara, Christiane Druml, and Moritz Stipsicz, eds. *The Josephinum: 650 Years of Medical History in Vienna*. Vienna: Brandstätter, 2014.

Stewart, Susan. *On Longing: Narratives of the Miniature, the Gigantic, the Souvenir, the Collection*. Durham, NC: Duke University Press, 1993.

Stocking, George W. "Introduction: Essays on Museums and Material Culture." In *Objects and Others: Essays on Museums and Material Culture*, edited by George W. Stocking, 3–14. Madison: University of Wisconsin Press, 1985.

Stoler, Ann Laura. *Imperial Debris: On Ruins and Ruination*. Durham, NC: Duke University Press, 2013.

Stoppard, Lou. "Everyone's a Curator Now." *New York Times*, March 3, 2020.

Strathern, Marilyn. "Or, Rather, on Not Collecting Clifford." *Social Analysis: The International Journal of Anthropology* 29 (1990): 88–95.

Stuelke, Patricia. "Writing Refugee Crisis in the Age of Amazon: *Lost Children Archive*'s Reenactment Play." *Genre* 54, no. 1 (2021): 43–66.

Sully, Dean. "Conservation Theory and Practice: Materials, Values and People in Heritage Conservation." In *Museum Practice*, edited by Conal McCarthy, 293–314. Chichester, UK: Wiley Blackwell, 2020.

Szczepanowska, Hanna M. *Conservation of Cultural Heritage: Key Principles and Approaches*. London: Routledge, 2013.

Taussig, Michael. *My Cocaine Museum*. Chicago: University of Chicago Press, 2004.

———. *Walter Benjamin's Grave*. Chicago: University of Chicago Press, 2006.

Thomas, Bernhard, *Gathering Evidence: A Memoir*. Translated by David McLintock. London: Vintage, 2003.

Tilden, Freeman. *Interpreting Our Heritage*. Chapel Hill: University of North Carolina Press, 1977.

Tilley, Christopher. "Interpreting Material Culture." In Pearce, *Interpreting Objects and Collections*, 67–75.

Tokarczuk, Olga. *Flights*. Translated by Jennifer Croft. London: Fitzcarraldo, 2017.

Tulani Salahu-Din, Deborah. "Documenting the BLM Movement in Baltimore through Contemporary Collecting: An Initiative of the NMAAHC." *Collections* 15, nos. 2–3 (2019): 101–12.

Ulph, Janet. "Frozen in Time: Orphans and Uncollected Objects in Museum Collections." *International Journal of Cultural Property* 24, no. 1 (2017): 3–30.

Van de Wetering, Ernst. "The Surface of Objects and Museum Style." In *Museum Objects: Experiencing the Properties of Thing*s, edited by Sandra H. Dudley, 103–8. London: Routledge, 2012.

Vannini, Phillip. "Non-representational Research Methodologies: An Introduction." In *Non-representational Methodologies: Re-envisioning Research*, edited by Phillip Vannini, 1–18. London: Routledge 2015.

Vecco, Marilena, and Michele Piazzai. "Deaccessioning of Museum Collections: What Do We Know and Where Do We Stand in Europe?" *Journal of Cultural Heritage* 16 (2015): 221–27.

Vergo, Peter, ed. *The New Museology*. London: Reaktion Books, 1989.

Vila-Matas, Enrique. *A Brief History of Portable Literature*. Translated by Anne McLean and Thomas Bunstead. New York: New Directions, 2015.

Vorda, Allan. "The Social Fabric: An Interview with Valeria Luiselli." *Rain Taxi*, 2019.

Walkowitz, Rebecca L. *Born Translated: The Contemporary Novel in an Age of World Literature*. New York: Columbia University Press, 2015.

Walsh, Kevin. *The Representation of the Past: Museums and Heritage in the Postmodern World*. London: Routledge, 1992.

Wang, Mary. "Leanne Shapton: 'The Mix of Proof, Shock and Totally Crappy Images.'" *Guernica*, April 12, 2009.

Wang, Mary. "Valeria Luiselli: 'There Are Always Fingerprints of the Archive in My Books.'" *Guernica*, February 12, 2019.

Wasserman, Sarah. *The Death of Things: Ephemera and the American Novel*. Minneapolis: University of Minnesota Press, 2020.

Bibliography

Weems, Carrie Mae. "Mutual Beliefs. An Interview with Dawoud Bey." In *Reflections for Now*. Berlin: Hatje Cantz Verlag, 2023.

Wehner, Rachel. "Towards an Ecological Museology." In Newell, Robin, and Wehner, *Curating the Future*, 85–100.

Whitehead, Colson. *The Underground Railroad*. London: Little, Brown, 2016.

Whittle, Alberta. "Biting the Hand That Feeds You: A Strategy of Wayward Curating." *Critical Arts* (2020): 110–23.

Wigger, Iris, and Spencer Hadley. "Angelo Soliman: Desecrated Bodies and the Spectre of Enlightenment Racism." *Race & Class* 62, no. 2 (2020): 80–107.

Willman, Kate Elizabeth. *Unidentified Narrative Objects and the New Italian Epic*. Cambridge, UK: MHRA Legenda, 2019.

Witcomb, Andrea. *Re-imagining the Museum: Beyond the Mausoleum*. London: Routledge, 2003.

Wolfsonian–FIU. "The Wolfsonian–FIU Returns to Its Roots with *A Universe of Things: Micky Wolfson Collects*." Media brochure. https://wolfsonian.org/_assets/docs/pr-a-universe-of-things.pdf.

Wood, James. "*Flights*, a Novel That Never Settles Down." *New Yorker*, September 24, 2018.

Wright, Elaine. *Muraqqa': Imperial Mughal Albums from the Chester Beatty Library, Dublin*. Alexandria, VA: Art Services International, 2008.

Yagcioglu, Hülya. "Bridging the Gap between People and Things: The Politics and Poetics of Collecting in Pamuk's *The Museum of Innocence*." In Can, Ulu, and Melikoglu, *Orhan Pamuk: Critical Essays on a Novelist between Worlds*, 185–201.

Yamaguchi, Masao. "The Poetics of Exhibition in Japanese Culture." In Karp and Lavine, *Exhibiting Cultures*, 57–67.

INDEX

Page locators in italics indicate illustrations.

absence: gaps left by deaccession, 152, 156, 162–64; of lives lost, 21–22; looted African heritage, 123–24, 126–29; mobilization of, 160–61; narrativized, 39–40, 48, 50, 52–53, 69, 74, 96, 99, 122, 142–43; repaired by carework/restitution, 123–24, 136–38, 142

accumulation. *See* crisis of accumulation; overaccumulation

active museum, 167n41

actor-network theory, 55–56, 69–70, 72, 184n4

Ahmed, Sara, 14, 64, 92, 124, 138

Alivizatou, Marilena, 119–20

Allmer, Açalya, 67

Alpers, Svetlana, 12

Alpi, Ilaria, 189n50

Altes Museum Berlin, 13

Amazon (company), 94, 97–98

Amborn, Hermann, 135

Ambrose, Timothy, 11

Ames, Michael, 12

anatomical wax models, 104–5, 107–10, *109*, 113–14, *114*, 119, 158

Anderson, Kent, 94

Andrews, Chris, 17

Andrzejewski, Jerzy, 84, 87

Anthropocene, 118

"APES**T" (Carters), 3–4, *4*

Appadurai, Arjun, 76, 80

Appel, Anne Milano, 38, 43

archive: digital/online, 144, 155; experience of visiting, 43–44, 82; fragmentation of, 85–87, 125, 137–38; as future-oriented/creative process, 76, 84–85, 98–100; historical vs. fictional/constructed, 80–83, 85–88; human-object bonds separated in,

86–90, 101; as intertextual method, 84–88, 100; literature as, 10–11, 80, 152, 156; vs. museum, 16, 42–43, 77–78, 82; as narrative structure, 78–81, 88, 93–94, 96, 100, 111; Nazi, 30–31; shadow/counter-, 132, 136–38; sound, 78, 83–84, 86–87, 96, 100; as unreliable/partial, 80–83, 86, 125. *See also* documentation; storage

Aristotle, 62

Arnold-de Simine, Silke, 6–7

Attia, Kader, 15, 124, 140, 144

Augé, Marc, 173n10

Auschwitz, 29, 33, 140, 171n68

Auster, Paul, 158

Austerlitz (Sebald), 6–7

authenticity: discourses/values of, 14–15, 115, 118, 120, 122, 140; of displayed objects, 59–64, 71–72, 80, 97, 148, 163; fictionalized appearance of, *59*, 74, 145; vs. virtual, 84–85, 96–97

Autry, La Tanya S., 9

Azoulay, Ariella Aïsha, 16, 89–90, 101, 127, 135, 141

Badagliacca, Mario, 91

Bal, Mieke, 26, 170n42, 171n48

Ballinger, Pamela, 169n4

Balzer, David, 45–46

Barrett, Sonia Elizabeth, 167n47

Barthes, Roland, 23–24, 49, 153

Basil, Priya, 122

Batchelor, Ray, 82

Battro, Antonio M., 85

Baudrillard, Jean, 31, 170n18

Belk, Russell, 23

Belladonna (Drndić), 80, 84, 182n81

Ben-Ghiat, Ruth, 126

211

212 Index

Benjamin, Walter, 23, 84–85
Bennett, Jane, 111, 169n15
Berlant, Lauren, 93
Bernhard, Thomas, 29
Bewes, Timothy, 148
Beyoncé, 3–4, *4*
Bezos, Jeff, 97
Black Lives Matter, 8
Blameless (Magris): curatorial work in, 38–40, 42–45, 47–49, 52–53; on facts vs. stories, 52–53, 123; real-life Museo and, 38–39, 49–52, *51*; Risiera di San Sabba in, 39–40, 43, 48, 50
Blindly (Magris), 43–44
Blom, Phillip, 106
Bogost, Ian, 150
Boico, Romano, 20–21, 169n2
Bolts, Willem, 44
Booth, Catherine, 46–47
Bouvard and Pécuchet (Flaubert), 6
Brainard, Joe, 158
Brambilla, Giovanni, 106–7
Brand, Dionne, 131
Breton, André, 95
British Museum (London), 13, 77, 142, 150–51
Brooklyn Museum (New York), 178n1
Brooks, Peter, 21, 23, 171n51
Brown, Bill, 7
Burra Charter, 115
Burton, Antoinette, 80–82
Buttler, Caroline, 115
Byfield, Judith A., 125

cabinets of curiosities, 13, 76, 106, 110
Caldwell, Dayna L., 151
Cameron, Fiona, 88, 105, 112
Campioni del Mondo (newspaper clipping), 138, 140, *140*
Candlin, Fiona, 166n22
Canizzo, Jeanne, 14, 166n24
Capossela, Francesca, 125, 143
Capote, Truman, 147
Caracciolo, Marco, 118, 120
Cardinal, Roger, 30–31
care: conservation as, 10, 104–5, 111–12, 116, 118, 151; curation as, 14–15, 45–46, 52, 151–52; in display/arrangement, 71–72; of expropriated objects vs. exploited people,

89–92, 101, 128–29, 131, 142; letting go/forgetting as, 155–61, 164; memorialization as, 88–89; repair as, 124, 140, 144; restitution as, 123–24. *See also* conservation; curating/curation; restitution
carpentry of things, 58, 68
Carters (Beyoncé and Jay-Z), 3–4, *4*
cemeteries, 19, 27, 160–61, 164
Centre Pompidou (Massy, France), 178n1
Centro Manoscritti (University of Pavia), 43–44
Certeau, Michel de, 162
Chambers, Ian, 124
Chatwin, Bruce, 7–8
Cheah, Pheng, 15–16, 38, 41
Chester Beatty Library (Dublin), 63, 73–74, *73*
Chopin, Frédéric, 112
chronotope, 28–29
Cipriani, Lidio, 133
classifying/classification, 6, 13, 22, 30–32, 82, 106, 112–13
Clifford, James, 28, 46, 131
Cloutier, Jean-Christophe, 83, 132
collage: Cornell's artwork, 56, 58, 68–69, 71–74; museum display as, 61, 64–65, 69, 71–74; narrative form as, 7, 140–41, 149. *See also* fragmentariness
collecting/collections: container's role in, 24–25, *25*, 28, 32, 125, 135–36; as control, 23, 31, 58, 67–68, 91–92, 130–31; crowdsourced, 150, 154–55, *154*; as extractive/colonial, 83–84, 89, 91–92, 112–13, 123–24, 133–34, 151; fascist obsession with, 20–22, 29–31, 123–24, 126–29, 131, 137, 142; history composed by, 23, 28–34; as imperial process, 16, 103, 107, 123–24, 133, 137, 142; of miniatures, 13, 84–85; museum defined as space of, 8–9, 13, 22–23, 32, 76–77, 156; percent in storage, 77, 101, 191n36; prolific collectors, 38–39, 47, 49–50, *51*, 105–7; recollecting and, 22, 24, 27, 39, 60–64, 158; as reframing/storying, 21–22, 71, 73; temporality of, 23–24, 34; violence of, 8–9, 20–22,

89–92, 101, 124, 126–27, 133, 144; visitor-reader's active role in, 25–26. *See also* classifying/classification

Colon, Jenny, 60–61, 63

colonialism/colonization: as breakage/injury, 123–24, 126–27, 132–33, 141–44; collecting practices of, 8, 16, 83–84, 89, 91–92, 112–13, 128, 133; conservation practices and, 112–13, 116; in Ethiopia, 123, 125–34; looting of African heritage, 123–24, 126–29, 131, 133–37, *134*, *136*, 142; persistence of, 16–17, 89, 97–98, 142, 161; racist discourses of, 138, *139*. *See also* decolonialism/decolonization

Connerton, Paul, 158–59

Conrad, Joseph, 87

conservation: entropy/impermanence and, 106, 116–21, 134–35, *136*, 159–61; future-facing/creative models of, 111–12, 117–22, 164; human/animal/insect specimens, 88, 112–13, 115, 118–20; paradigm shifts in, 71, 110, 112, 114–18, 121, 148, 156–57, 161, 164; preservation techniques, 104–6, 114–15, 119; repair/reparation/restoration, 5, 10, 14–15, 114–16, 120, 122, 144; sustainability/climate action and, 104–5, 112, 116–20, 122, 148, 162–63. *See also* care; decay/ruination; restitution

constellations: Luiselli/Pamuk/Shapton and, 72–73, 98, 147; personhood as, 107; as theoretical framework, 7, 15, 40–41, 52; Tokarczuk's *Flights* and, 15, 105, 110–11, 114, 120–21

Cook, Sarah, 45

Cornell, Joseph, 56, 58, 68–69, 71–72, 74

COVID-19 pandemic, 11, 37, 150, 162

Crane, Susan A., 166n29

crisis of accumulation, 147–49, 151, 162

Crooke, Elizabeth, 167n41

crowdsourcing, 150, 154–55, *154*

curating/curation: of absented/destroyed materials, 39–40, 48, 50, 52–53; author-curator's role, 38, 42–43, 46–49, 89, 182n88; bias in, 8, 12, 101; as care, 14–15, 45–46,

151–52; conceptualized, 37–38, 42, 45–47; as creating, 45–46, 49, *59*, 82, 99, 140; decolonial efforts at, 128, 133–41, *134*, *136*, *139–40*; as imperial process, 16, 103, 137; vs. less structured cultivating, 159–61, 164; popular understanding of, 11, 45, 49; as proactive interpretation, 17, 42–45, 49, 96–97, 133; shifting stories/narratives and, 50–53, 98–100, 131; as translation, 41, 43, 46, 48–49; world literature and, 38, 40–45. *See also* care; orientation devices

Damrosch, David, 41

Davis, Mary, 115

deaccession: auction catalogues, 145–47, *146*; as forgetting/erasure, 77, 100, 155–61, 164; postobject futures and, 148–49, 152, 161–64. *See also* disposal

decay/ruination: broken objects, 123–25, 127, 132–33, 135, 157–58; caused by storage/display, 31, 62, 114–15, 117; custodial neglect, 91, 117, 119; entropy, 106, 116–21, 134–35, *136*, 159–61; foregrounded in museum design, 19–21, *20*; meaning generated in, 118–22, 135, 137–38, *139*; openness to, 14–15, 111–13, 119–22, 135, 148, 159; rewilding, 159–61, 164; signs of wear, 138, *139*, 143–44, *143*, 157

decolonialism/decolonization: of institutions, 8–9, 11, 128; as repair, 123–24, 140–44; supplementary annotations as acts of, 138–41, *139–40*; visibilizing of repressions, 133–38, *134*, *136*, 161. *See also* colonialism/colonization

deictic storytelling, 55, 57–64

Delpino, Gaia, 133

Depositi Aperti (Museo delle Civiltà), 133–35, *134*, *136*, 143–44, *143*

Depot Boijmans Van Beuningen (Rotterdam), 75–76, *76*, 85, *96*, 102, 150

Derrida, Jacques, 80

DeSilvey, Caitlin, 15, 18, 22, 147, 149, 159–60, 164

digitization/digital realms: Amazon (company), 94, 97–98; archives, 144, 155; dangers of, 95–98, 155, 162; databases, 77–78, 81, 89, 94–98, 152, 154; museums, 11, 81, 94, 96–97, 152; records/objects, 75–77, 81, 85, 88–89, 95–97, 150, 152, 154. *See also* technology

Di Lella, Rosa Anna, 133

Dimock, Wai Chee, 38, 41

displacement, 6, 16–17, 72, 101. *See also* migrants/refugees/asylum seekers

display: of anatomical wax models, 107–10, *109*, 113–14, *114*; cabinets of curiosities, 13, 76, 106, 110; as cause of object deterioration, 114–15, 117–19; craftsmanship in, 55–56, 61–66, 70–72, 107–10, *109*; curator's work of, 45–47; deictic storytelling in, 55, 57–64; ethics of, 91–92, 133–35, *134*, *136*, 137; human/animal/insect specimens, 88, 112–13; as imperial process, 16, 89–91, 103, 107, 123–24, 137, 142; of in/authentic objects, 60–64, 71–72, 148; interpretive freedom of, 67–71, 73; in novel vs. museum, 59–63, 72–73; role of framing in, 64–66, 71–74, 107–8, 132, 136; self-fulfillment through, 58, 64–65; technology used in, 40, 47–49, 56, 65–67, 70, 72; as world-building, 64–66. *See also* collage

disposal, 118, 145, 147–48, 151–52, 155–58, 164. *See also* deaccession

Disposal Toolkit (Museums Association), 151–52

documentation: accession registers/catalogues, 8, 77, 89, 100; of atrocities, 30–31, 125–26, 131; digitized, 75–77, 81, 85, 88–89, 95–97, 150, 152; driven by fiction, 79, 80, 86; vs. dynamic archiving, 84–85, 112; vs. impermanence/entropy, 116–18, 135; inventories, 77, 94–98, 127, 129–30, 156, 158, 163; ledger of names, 21, 24, 27–28, 131, 142; of loss/separation, 90–93, 155–56, 163; partiality of, 80–81, 86, 125, 151; photography as, 126, 130–31,

135–37, 148; "undocumented" migrants and, 89–92, 94. *See also* archive; storage

Drabble, Barnaby, 42

Drive Your Plow over the Bones of the Dead (Tokarczuk), 120

Drndić, Daša, 21, 25, 33; in Luiselli's *Lost Children Archive*, 80, 84, 182n81. *See also Trieste*

Dubey, Madhu, 7

Duchamp, Marcel, 84–85

Dugdale, Sasha, 155

Duncan, Carol, 12

Dzhangal (Mendel), 91

Edoheart (Eseohe Arhebamen), 90

Eliot, T. S., 87

Ellison, Ralph, 137

Elsner, John, 30–31

empire: legacies of, 6, 16–17, 91–92, 167n47; looting practices of, 126–29, 131, 133–37, *134*, *136*, 142; military aggression of, 125–26; museums as archives/devices of, 13, 16, 30–31, 89–92, 103, 106–7, 116, 123–24, 151

Enxuto, João, 96

Ernst, Wolfgang, 149, 152, 163, 171n68

Ethiopia: 1974 revolution, 125; British expedition to Maqdala, 126, 142; foreign looting of, 123, 126–29, 131, 133–37, *134*, *136*, 142; Italian occupation of, 123, 125–34, 144; resistance to occupation, 125, 127, 132, 136–42, *139–40*. *See also Shadow King, The*

Etienne, Noémie, 118

Extinct (Penner et al.), 149

fabulography, 122

Falkoff, Rebecca R., 172n75

Farge, Arlette, 82, 84, 93, 100

Felski, Rita, 124

Fisher, Philip, 4

Fisk, Gloria, 71

Flaubert, Gustave, 6

Flights (Tokarczuk): constellation structure of, 12, 15, 105, 110–11, 114, 120–22; impermanence/decay in, 115–21, *119*, 135; relationality

Index

in, 105–6, 111–12, 119–22; relics/
specimens in, 104–6, 109–10, 112–14,
119–20
Fondazione Prada (Milan), 182n93
Fontana, Felice, 107
Forgacs, David, 130–31, 189n59
forgetting, 77, 100, 150, 155–61, 164
Forty, Adrian, 159
fragmentariness: of archive/
documentation, 85–87, 125, 137–
38, 151; as generative, 122, 159–63;
intertextual, 24–26, 25; of miniatures,
84–85; of stories told, 98–100, 131,
159; of traditional conservation/
collections, 118, 128–29, 135. *See
also* collage; salvage
Frammenti (Badagliacca), 91
Francis I, Emperor, 103, 113
Franz Ferdinand, Archduke, 26–27
Franz Joseph I, Emperor, 103
Freely, Maureen, 56
French, Jade, 175n68
Freud, Sigmund, 23, 83, 100
Fuentes, Marisa J., 80, 137–38, 182n91
Fuller, Mia, 126
Furlan, Stefano, 19

Gandolfo, Francesca, 128
Ganguly, Debjani, 38, 94, 98
Gardom, Tim, 46–47
Gee, Grant, 56
gender roles/restrictions, 60, 67, 125–26,
131–32, 138
Glasgow Museums, 178n1
Gold Museum (Bogotá), 161
Google Art, 96
Gopinath, Gayatri, 17
Graham, Beryl, 45
Gray, John Edward, 77
Grechi, Giulia, 133, 144, 189n50
Greenblatt, Stephen, 14–15, 144
Grey, Alison, 46–47
Grubišić, Dražen, 153
Grünfeld, Martin, 147, 149, 164
Gubbins, Sarah, 176n16
Guericke, Otto von, 163

Habta, Hailu, 125
Haile Selassie, Emperor, 125, 140–43

Haraway, Donna, 46, 119
Harman, Graham, 56, 58, 70
Harrison, Rodney, 151
Hartman, Saidiya, 174n54, 180n45
Hauptman, Jodi, 72
Hayes, Patricia, 131
Hemphill, Essex, 3
Henriquez, Diego de, 38–40, 43–44, 47–
50, 51. *See also Blameless*
Hepburn, Allan, 5, 8
Hetherington, Kevin, 147
Heti, Sheila, 148
Hicks, Dan, 40, 52
history: composed by collecting, 23,
28–34; counternarratives and, 131–
32, 135–38; destabilizing of, 34, 49;
museums of, 6–7; partial/unreliable
archives and, 80–83, 86, 125
Hitler, Adolf, 30
Holocaust, 7, 19–21, 24, 30–31, 140.
See also Nazism; Risiera di San Sabba
Holtorf, Cornelius, 160
Holubar, Karl, 107
Hooper-Greenhill, Eilean, 149
human-animal-object divide, 103–5,
107, 112–14, 117–21, 135, 152, 156,
163
human-object bonds, 86–90, 101, 128–
29, 132–33

ICOM (International Council of
Museums), 8–9
ICOMOS (International Council on
Monuments and Sites), 185n54
*Important Artifacts and Personal
Property* (Shapton), 145–50, 146,
152, 157, 161
Iñárritu, Alejandro G., 182n93
In Memory of Memory (Stepanova), 12,
150, 155–61, 164
Innocence of Memories (Gee), 56
Innocence of Objects, The (Pamuk,
museum catalogue), 56, 59, 64–66,
68–71, 176n18
International Red Cross, 29
interpretation: absented from museum
stores, 77, 81; archival meaning and,
82–83, 87–88; curation as, 17, 42–45,
49, 96–97, 133; gaps in, 129, 131,

216 Index

interpretation (*continued*)
135, 158–59; of multimedia narrative,
145–46, 149, 152–55; primacy in,
59, 64–69, 145, 161–62; retelling
of stories and, 80, 98–100. *See also*
visitor-reader
interpretive grids, 7, 55, 70, 112, 135
intertextuality: of *Lost Children
Archive*, 78, 80, 82, 84–88, 93–95,
100, 182n81; in *The Museum of
Innocence*, 56, 61, 68, 72–73; in
Trieste, 24–26, *25*
Inventory of Losses, An (Schalansky),
150, 163–64
Ireland, Tracy, 59
I Remember (Brainard), 158
Italian CIE (Center for Identification
and Expulsion), 142
Italian occupation of Ethiopia. *See*
Ethiopia
Izmir (ship), 66

Jahingir, Emperor, 73
Jakubowski, Zuzanna, 68, 72
James, David, 100
Jay-Z, 3–4, *4*
Jetñil-Kijiner, Kathy, 163
Jevons, W. Stanley, 4
Jewish Book Week, 21
Jewish Museum (Berlin), 6
Jones, Mark, 158
Jones, Mike, 88, 92
Jørgensen, Jørgen, 44
Joseph II, Emperor, 106–7, 113
Josephinum Medical Museum (Vienna):
history/site/layout of, 104–9, *108*;
wax model collections of, 104–5,
107–10, *109*, 113–14, *114*, 119, 158.
See also Flights
Joseph Wenzel von Lichtenstein, Prince,
113
Julien, Isaac, 3

Kairos, 121
Kavanagh, Gaynor, 11, 32, 42–43
Keene, Suzanne, 117
Ketelaar, Eric, 81
Kiefer, Tom, 91
Kill Your Darlings (Schrag), 101–2, *101*
Konso statues, 134–35, *136*, 143–44

Kopytoff, Igor, 12
Kowalcze, Malgorzata, 120
Krauss, Rosalind E., 95–96
Kristeva, Julia, 175n73

Laika (Soviet astronaut dog), 66
Lake, Crystal B., 15, 17, 124, 128,
169n15
Larkin, Jamie, 166n22
La Specola (Florence), 107, 109
Latour, Bruno, 56, 69–70, 112, 169n15,
184n4
La ville Louvre (Philibert), 3
Lebensborn program, 24, 28, 31
Léger, Nathalie, 80, 85–88
Lehrer, Erica, 45
Libeskind, Daniel, 6
Linnaean system, 13
L'Italia Coloniale, 138, 140
literature: archival novel, 78–81, 88,
93–94, 96; encyclopedic novel, 80,
110, 119–21; memory mediated in, 7,
87; museum practices as devices in,
10–14, 17–18; networked novel, 81,
94–95, 98; postfictional writing, 148–
50, 152–53, 155–58, 161–64; readers'
role in, 9–10, 17, 67, 94–95, 145–46,
152–53; temporal/spatial borders
and, 17, 28–29, 41, 98; world, 15–
17, 38, 40–45. *See also* narrative/
narrativization; *individual novels*
living history, 7, 98
Loden, Barbara, 85–88
Longair, Sarah, 13, 45
Looking for Langston (Julien), 3
Lorimer, Hayden, 86, 183n119
Lost Children Archive (Luiselli):
archival structure of, 78–81, *79*,
88, 93–94, 96, 100, 111; archiving/
collecting practices in, 83–86, 88, 129;
documentation/inventory practices
in, 78, 92–95, 97; human-object
bonds in, 88–92; intertexts in, 78,
80, 82, 84–88, 93–95, 100, 182n81;
photographs in, *79*, 79, 86–87, 91;
reenactment/play in, 93–94, 98–100,
102; sounds centered in, 78, 83–84,
86–87, 96, 100
Louvre, 3–4, *4*, 13
Love, Erica, 96

Index

Lowenthal, David, 116
Lubar, Steven, 77
Luiselli, Valeria, 80, 98–99. *See also*
  Lost Children Archive

MacKenzie, John M., 17
Mackenzie Owen, John, 92, 179n2
Magris, Claudio, 27, 43–44. *See also*
  Blameless
Malaquais, Dominique, 91
Maleuvre, Didier, 29, 91
Manovich, Lev, 94–95, 98
maps/mapping, 38, 41–42, 46–47, 55–
  56, 72, 78, 94, 127
Maria Theresa, Empress, 44, 103, 106
Marie Antoinette, Queen, 106
Mascagni, Paolo, 107
Mattern, Shannon, 144
Mbembe, Achille, 83 (qtd.)
McGurl, Mark, 94, 97
McSherry, Siofra, 71
Medici Venus (wax model), 109–10,
  109, 113–14
memory: affective engagement with,
  6–7, 63–64, 67, 70; ethics of, 151,
  158; held in objects, 21–22, 58, 60–
  64, 70, 72, 137–38, 155–63; limits
  of, 100–101; vs. photographs, 131,
  135–37, 159; post-, 6, 40; prosthetic,
  87; sites of, 6–7, 156–58, 161–62; vs.
  waste, 152–53
Mendel, Gideon, 91
Mengiste, Maaza, 125, 131, 144. *See
  also Shadow King, The*
Merleau-Ponty, Maurice, 70
Meszaros, Cheryl, 49
Michelstaedter, Carlo, 27
migrants/refugees/asylum seekers, 20,
  78, 80–81, 85–87, 97–98, 100, 142;
  documentation and, 89–92, 94. *See
  also Lost Children Archive*
Milton, Cynthia E., 45
Mir Ali, 63, 73–74, *73*
modernity, 58, 64, 85, 106–7, 115–16
monstrousness, 109–14
Montemaggi, Martina, 128
Montero Román, Valentina, 80
Monterroso, Augusto, 87
monuments, 8, 20, 33, 40, 45, 134–35,
  136, 156

Moradi, Fazil, 144
more-than-human subjectivities, 103–6,
  111–14, 120–22, 135, 163
Moretti, Franco, 38, 41
Morrison, Heather, 113
Mostra coloniale italiana (Genoa), 128
Mullins, Matthew, 5, 8
muraqqa' (Imperial Mughal albums),
  63, 73–74, *73*
Murawski, Mike, 9
Museo coloniale (Rome), 128, 133
Museo delle Civiltà (Rome), 124, 128–
  29, 133–35, *134*, *136*, 143–44, *143*
Museo Henriquez della Guerra per la
  Pace (Trieste): author's visit to, 49–52,
  51; in Magris's *Blameless*, 38–40, 43,
  47–49
Museum of Broken Relationships
  (Zagreb), 150, 153–55, *153–54*, 157,
  161
Museum of Fine Arts (Vienna), 103, *104*
Museum of Innocence (Istanbul
  museum): assemblage in, 55, 58, 60–
  74; audio guide for, 56, 59, 64, 70;
  author's visit to, 56–57, *57*; catalogue
  (*The Innocence of Objects*), 56, 59,
  64–66, 68–71, 176n18; chronology
  disrupted in, 57, 61–63, 66, 68;
  Kemal's story in, 58–59, 61–64, 66–
  69, 74; Mughal border used in, 63,
  73–74, *73*
Museum of Innocence, The (Pamuk):
  book/museum interplay, 72–73, 148,
  150; deictic storytelling in, 55, 57–64;
  Kemal's story in, 58–63, 67–69, 74;
  Pamuk as writer-character, 59–61, 67
Museum of Jurassic Technology (Los
  Angeles), 150
museums: vs. archives, 16, 42–43, 77–
  78, 82; culture/nature divide, 103,
  104, 113–14; vs. databases, 77–78,
  89, 94–96, 152, 154; future-facing,
  112, 117–22, 148–50, 152, 161–64;
  vs. mausoleum, 52, 88; narrative
  design of, 4–5, 9, 32, 37–38, 52–
  53; new museology, 5, 162–64;
  overcrowding of, 70, 76–77, 151–52,
  155; packaging of stories/history in,
  29, 32, 34, 42–43, 49–52, *51*, 97, 101;
  post-, 149–50, 155, 157–58, 162, 164;

museums (*continued*)
postcolonial, 124; public trust in, 11–12, 97, 105, 151–52; relational/ active, 13–14, 88–89, 96, 106; as site of memory, 6–7, 156–58, 161–62; as space of collecting, 8–9, 13, 22–23, 32, 76–77, 156; spatial design of, 38, 46–47, 55, 61–65, 68, 72; statis/ immobility of, 118–21, 162, 164; temporal/spatial borders and, 17, 28–29, 32, 41, 64, 72; violence enacted by, 91–92, 101, 124, 133, 144; "worlding" potential of, 40–41, 46, 144. *See also individual museums*
Museums (Weems), 3
Museums Are Not Neutral (global initiative), 9
Museums Association, 151–52
MuseumsQuartier (Vienna), 103–4, *104*, 107
Mussolini, Benito, 126–28, 140–42
My Cocaine Museum (Taussig), 161

Naimou, Angela, 14
Napoleon, Emperor, 30
Narkiss, Irit, 115
narrative/narrativization: of absence, 39–40, 48, 50, 52–53, 69, 74, 96, 99, 122; archival, 78–81, 88, 93–94, 96, 100, 111; of collection vs. history, 9, 21–23, 28–34; counter-, 131–32, 135–38; created by archivist/novelist/ curator, 82–88; curatorial strategies and, 37–39, 49–53, 77; vs. databases, 94–95, 98, 152; desire as driving force in, 23–24, 28, 58; human need for, 6, 11, 26, 52–53, 81, 99, 120–22, 123, 164, 173n10; invention/reality in, 59–62, 71; of loss, 92–94, 119–22, 125, 127, 150, 155–56, 163–64; memory/ photos and, 131, 135–37, 159; multimedia, 6–7, 72, 81, 145–46, 149, 152; postfictional, 148–50, 152–53, 155–58, 161–64; produced by visitors' imaginative work, 67, 69, 71–72; spatialization of, 4–5, 37–38, 41–42, 46–47, 55, 57, 61–68; storytelling and, 13, 55, 57–64, 80, 98–100, 120–22; "worlding" potential of, 15–17, 38, 40–42. *See also* literature

National Gallery (London), 13
National Museum Directors' Conference (NMDC), 151
National Museum of African American History and Culture (Washington, DC), 7
National Museum of Modern and Contemporary Art (Cheongju, Korea), 178n1
National Museum of Prehistory and Ethnography (Rome), 133
Natural History Museum (Vienna), 103
Navarrete, Trilce, 92, 179n2
Nazism, 19–22, 24, 28–31, 128; collaborators with, 27–29, 39, 50. *See also* Holocaust
necrography, 40, 52
Nerval, Gérard de, 61, 72
Newell, Jennifer, 105
new museology, 5, 162–64
New Yorker, 12, 98
Nicholas, Lynn H., 30 (qtd.)
Nixon, Rob, 122
Nobel Prize, 120
nonrepresentational theory, 184n4
Nora, Pierre, 156
Norme e consigli per chi va in A. O. Italiana 1 (pamphlet), 138, *139*
nostalgia, 16, 72, 106, 116, 159
Nuremberg trials, 24

Object Lessons series (Bloomsbury), 150
object-oriented philosophy, 55–56, 58, 68–70
objects: autonomy of, 62–63, 67–70, 95–97, 129; books of literature as, 21, 24–25, *25*, 42, 56, 72–74, 155; broken, 123–25, 127, 132–33, 135, 157–58; consolatory power of, 63–64, 70, 74, 162, 177n47; destruction/ death of, 102, 127, 138, 140, *140*, 147, 158; disrupting presence of, 29, 68, 124–25, 128–29, 137, 156; as "documents" of people, 89–93, 101, 127, 132–33; emotions evoked by, 63–67, 69–71, 157; human bodies as, 70, 106, 110, 112–14, 120, 131; as in/authentic, 59–64, 71–72, 80, 97, 148, 163; junk shop finds, 56–57, *58*, 144, 157–58; life cycles of, 114–15,

Index

119, 156–58, 162–63; memory held in, 21–22, 58, 60–64, 70, 72, 137–38, 155–63; necrographies/biographies of, 12, 40, 52; obsolete/extinct/failed, 149–50, 160–64; "orphaned"/decontextualized, 89, 91–94, 115, 121, 124, 128–29, 132–33; quasi/hybrid, 112–14, 119–21, 155; quotidian, 91, 95, 116, 127, 129–30, 144, 155, 158, 162; repatriation of, 142, 147–48, 151; as reticent, 32–33, 87–88, 116–17; sequencing/spatialization and, 4–5, 55, 61–63, 68, 72, 135; souvenirs/trophies, 26, 32, 58, 113, 131, 177n47; stolen, 20–21, 29–31, 89–92, 101, 123–24, 126–29, 132–35, *136*; storied/storying of, 17–18, 21–22, 25–26, 55, 82–83, 123; thingness/thing power, 60–64, 72–73, 105, 111–13, 117–18, 161, 169n15; wax/taxidermic specimens, 104–7, 113–15, *114*, 119, 158; as witness, 142–44, *143*; worn/annotated by reader, 138–41, *139–40. See also* collage; photographs

object valuations: collection's effect on, 23, 157; determinations of, 31, 49, 102, 145, 151, 164; of low/counterfeit items, 60–61, 63, 71, 157; monetary vs. symbolic/cultural, 8–9, 129–30, 132; of stolen/expropriated goods, 29, 89–91; use as factor in, 14–15, 147

Obrist, Hans Ulrich, 38, 49

O'Neill, Paul, 38, 49

Orcutt, Kimberly, 81

orientation devices: audio guides, 56, 59, 64, 70; catalogues, 8, 77, 89, 100; conceptualized, 4, 10; diagrams/illustrations, 108; guidebooks, 117; labels/captions, 41, 46, 133–34, 136, 138, 145–46, 153, *153. See also Innocence of Objects, The*

originality, 58–59, 62–63, 72, 97, 115

Osborne, Dora, 172n69

Ovenden, Richard, 111

overaccumulation: collecting mania and, 8, 31, 44, 48, 61–62, 128–29; in museum storage, 50, 89, 147–49, 151–52, 155–56, 162, 191n36

Paine, Crispin, 11

Pamuk, Orhan: collage methodology of, 71–74; on museum vs. novel, 59, 64–68, 71–72; Turkish "authenticity" and, 60–61, 67–68, 71. *See also* Museum of Innocence; *Museum of Innocence, The*

Pankhurst, Richard, 126, 142

Paolos, Medhin, 190n86

Parry, Ross, 96–97

Parthenon, 151

Pearce, Susan, 26, 32

Pepi, Mike, 94–96

Performed Furniture (Barrett), 167n47

Perth Museum and Art Gallery (Scotland), 101–2, *101*

Peter I, Czar, 119

Peter Leopold, Grand Duke, 107

Philibert, Nicolas, 3

photographs: as documentation, 126, 130–31, 135–37, 148; in *Flights*, 110, 116; in *Important Artifacts*, 145–46, *146*, 148–49, 152, 157; junk shop finds, 56–57, *58*, 144; in *Lost Children Archive*, 79, *79*, 86–87, 91; vs. memory, 131, 135–37, 159; in museum catalogues, 70; in museum collections, 49–50, 65–66, 129; in *Museum of Innocence*, 64; in *The Shadow King*, 125–26, 130–31, 135–36, 138; in *Trieste*, 24, *25*, 31

Piazzai, Michele, 157

Pigorini, Luigi, 133

Pilegaard, Ane, 69 (qtd.), 70

Pizzi, Katia, 169n2

police brutality, 16, 169n1

Poliquin, Rachel, 104, 113

Pollack, Martin, 52

Pomerantsev, Peter, 12

Pomian, Krzysztof, 181n78

postfictional writings, 148–50, 152–53, 155–58, 161–64

posthuman, 104–5, 119. *See also* human-animal-object divide

postmemory, 6, 40

postmodernism, 8, 88, 105, 152

postmuseum, 149–50, 155, 157–58, 162, 164

postobject futures, 148–50, 152, 161–64

Pound, Ezra, 87

220 Index

Prado, 13
preservation. *See* conservation
Project 3541 (online archive), 144
Puloy, Monika Ginzkey, 30

Ransmayr, Christoph, 52
Rauschenberg, Robert, 96
reader-response theory, 49
Reborn (Sontag), 85–86
reenactment, 7, 15, 93–94, 98–100
Reilly, Maura, 175n73
relationality: in display, 72, 74; of Konso
monuments, 134–35, *136*, 143–44;
in museum design, 13–14, 88–89, 96,
106; in storage, 85, 88–89, 92–93, 96;
in Tokarczuk's *Flights*, 105–6, 111–
12, 119–22
repair. *See* care; restitution
reparation. *See* conservation; restitution
residual unculture, 147, 149–50, 164
restitution: object repatriation, 142,
147–48, 151; repair/reparation
as, 116, 120, 124, 140, 144; as
restoration of order, 123–24, 142. *See
also* care; conservation
Rhodes Must Fall, 8
Risiera di San Sabba (Trieste): author's
visit to, 19–21, *20*, 33; in *Blameless*,
39–40, 43, 48, 50; in *The Shadow
King*, 140; in *Trieste*, 21, *25*, 27, 29–
30, 39, 43
Ruspoli, Marescotti, 134

Salvadori, Diego, 42
salvage: of absent/destroyed materials,
39–40, 48, 50, 52, 120; aesthetics of,
14–15, 64–65, 71; conservation and,
105, 119; of decay/rot, 20–21, *20*;
museum/literature's work of, 5, 34,
158, 164. *See also* fragmentariness
Sarr, Felwine, 124, 126, 142
Savoy, Bénédicte, 124, 126, 142
Scego, Igiaba, 142
Schaberg, Christopher, 150
Schalansky, Judith, 150, 163–64
Schimek, Otto, 43, 52, 123
Schrag, Anthony, 101–2, *101*
Schwenger, Peter, 7
Schwob, Marcel, 84
Sebald, W. G., 6–7

Sedgwick, Eve Kosofsky, 124
Serota, Nicholas, 49
Shadow King, The (Mengiste):
decolonial praxis and, 116, 123–24,
140–44; historical context of, 125–29;
kinetic force of, 123, 127, 135–37;
negotiation of history in, 131–32,
135–37; rifle/objects in, 123–25, 127,
129–30, 132, 135–38, 142
Shah Jahan, Emperor, 73
Shapton, Leanne, 159. *See also
Important Artifacts and Personal
Property*
slavery, 6–7, 17, 91, 113, 137–38, 161,
167n47
Smith, Terry, 45
Smithsonian, 7, 152
Soliman, Angelo, 113
Soliman, Josefine, 113
Sontag, Susan, 85–86
soundscapes, 47, 65, 67, 78, 83, 90, 96,
100, 141–42
Srivastana, Neelam, 126
Station Eleven (St. John Mandel), 150,
162–64
Steedman, Carolyn, 100
Stepanova, Maria, 12, 150, 155–61, 164
Stewart, Susan, 23, 28, 71–72, 170n28
Stille, Alexander, 118
stitching/tailoring metaphors, 93–94,
111, 113, 116
St. John Mandel, Emily, 150, 162–64
Stoler, Ann Laura, 16
storage: closed/private, 76–77, 101–2,
101, 128, 133–35, *134*, *136*, 154;
"cold," 94; of confiscated/stolen
property, 20–21, 29–31, 89–92,
101, 128–29, 133–35, *136*, 142;
databases, 77–78, 81, 89, 94–98, 152,
154; dead spaces of, 48, 112, 115,
118, 147; object deterioration due
to, 114–15, 119; open/visible, 75–
76, 81, 96, 133–35, *134*, *136*, 150;
"orphaned objects" in, 89, 91–94,
115, 133–35, *136*; overburdened, 50,
89, 147–49, 151–52, 155–56, 162,
191n36; relational approach to, 85,
88–89, 92–93, 96. *See also* archive;
documentation
Storr, Robert, 49

Index   221

Strathern, Marilyn, 32–33
structuralism, 96
Stuelke, Patricia, 93–94, 97, 100
Suite for Barbara Loden (Léger), 85–88
Sully, Dean, 121
supermodernity, 173n10
Susini, Clemente, 107
sustainability/climate action, 104–5,
    112, 116–20, 122, 148, 162–63
Szczepanowska, Hanna M., 117
Szeemann, Harald, 49

Taussig, Michael, 160–61
technology: in display, 40, 47–49, 56,
    65–67, 70, 72; multimedia narratives,
    6–7, 72, 81, 145–46, 149, 152; in
    storage, 75–76, 85, 88–89. *See also*
    digitization/digital realms
Tell Me How It Ends (Luiselli), 80, 99
temporality: of archive/collection, 23–
    24, 34, 83–84, 86; conservation and,
    115–16, 118, 121; of databases vs.
    novels, 94–95, 98; decolonial, 141–
    42; of desiring narrative, 28–29;
    disrupted chronologies, 57, 61–63, 66,
    68, 72, 105, 125, 183n119; of objects,
    135–37, 147, 149, 156–58
thingness, 64, 73, 105, 161
thing power, 60–63, 72, 111–13, 117–
    18, 161, 169n15
Tilden, Freeman, 175n72
Tokarczuk, Olga, 15, 111, 120. *See also
    Flights*
Tombstone (Arizona), 98
Too Much Stuff (NMDC), 151
translation: of *Blameless*, 38, 43, 173n5;
    curation as, 41, 43, 46, 48–49; of
    Flights, 118, 183n1; of *In Memory of
    Memory*, 155; Luiselli's work of, 80,
    99; of *The Museum of Innocence*, 56,
    70–71; objects and, 24, 70, 160; of
    Trieste, 21
Trieste (Drndić): author's own travels
    and, 19–21, *20*, 33–34, *35*; collecting
    as plot device in, 21–22, 24–28,
    31–32, 43, 58, 125; intertextual
    fragments in, 24–26, *25*; list of
    Jewish names in, 21, 24, 27–28;
    Risiera di San Sabba and, 21, 27,
    29–30, 39, 43

Ugresić, Dubravka, 80
Un altro mare (Magris), 27
Underground Railroad, The
    (Whitehead), 7
unlearning, 16
US ICE (Immigration and Customs
    Enforcement), 97
Utz (Chatwin), 7–8

Van de Wetering, Ernst, 138
Vannini, Phillip, 184n4
Vecco, Marilena, 157
Verheyen, Filip, 112
Victoria and Albert Museum (London),
    37–38, 178n1
Vila-Matas, Enrique, 84–85
"Visiting Hours" (Hemphill), 3
visitor-reader: active role in
    interpretation, 13–14, 41–42, 63–64,
    97, 102, 152–54; archive/repository
    accessed by, 43–44, 75–77, 82, 85,
    96; as collector, 25–26; curational
    work and, 9–10, 45–49; expectation/
    imagination and, 17, 67–73; material
    presence of, 70, 115; of networked/
    hyperlinked narratives, 94–95;
    supplementary annotations by, 138–
    41, *139–40*
Vištica, Olinka, 153
Vrolik Museum (Amsterdam), 111

Wachsberger, Haimi, 21
Walkowitz, Rebecca L., 38, 41–42, 45,
    49
Walsh, Kevin, 164
War Museum for Peace. *See* Museo
    Henriquez della Guerra per la Pace
Warwick Research Collective, 15
Washburn, Wilcomb, 152
Wasserman, Sarah, 15, 147, 156, 159
Watkins, C., 118
Weems, Carrie Mae, 3
Whitehead, Colson, 7
Whittle, Alberta, 174n54
Wikipedia, 117
Willman, Kate, 148
Winged Victory of Samothrace, 3
witnessing, 11–12, 142–44, *143*
Wolfson, Mitchell "Micky," Jr.,
    128–29

Wolfsonian–Florida International University (Miami), 124, 128–29, 137–40, *139–40*

Wood, James, 12, 111

world literature, 15–17, 38, 40–45. *See also* literature

World War I, 6, 26–27, 49–50

World War II, 6, 19–21, 24, 26–31, 39, 49–50. *See also* Holocaust; Nazism

Wright, Elaine, 74

Wu Ming, 148

Yohannes, Emperor, 142